Liberal Peace, Liberal War

A volume in the series

CORNELL STUDIES IN SECURITY AFFAIRS

edited by Robert J. Art, Robert Jervis, *and* Stephen M. Walt

A full list of titles in the series appears at the end of the book.

Liberal Peace, Liberal War

AMERICAN POLITICS
AND INTERNATIONAL SECURITY

John M. Owen IV

Cornell University Press

ITHACA AND LONDON

First published 1997 by Cornell University Press
First printing, Cornell Paperbacks, 2000

Printed in the United States of America

Library of Congress Cataloging-in-Publication Data

Owen, John M. (John Malloy) IV, 1962–
    Liberal peace, liberal war : American politics and international security
/ John M. Owen IV.
        p. cm. — (Cornell studies in security affairs)
    Includes bibliographical references (p.   ) and index.
    ISBN 0-8014-3319-3 (cloth : alk. paper)
    ISBN 0-8014-8690-4 (pbk. : alk. paper)
    1. United States—Foreign relations—1783–1865—Case studies.
    2. United States—Foreign relations—1865–1898—Case studies.
    3. Crisis management in government—United States—History—19th
century—Case studies. 4. Liberalism—United States—History—19th
century. I. Title. II. Series.
E183.7.094   1997
327.73'009'034—dc21   97-29419

Cornell University Press strives to use environmentally responsible
suppliers and materials to the fullest extent possible in the publishing
of its books. Such materials include vegetable-based, low-VOC inks
and acid-free papers that are recycled, totally chlorine-free, or
partly composed of nonwood fibers. Books that bear the logo
of the FSC (Forest Stewardship Council) use paper taken
from forests that have been inspected and certified as
meeting the highest standards for environmental and
social responsibility. For further information, visit our
website at www.cornellpress.cornell.edu.

1 2 3 4 5 6 7 8 9 10   Cloth printing
1 2 3 4 5 6 7 8 9 10   Paperback printing

To my mother and the memory of my father

Contents

Preface

The proposition that democracies, or what I call liberal states, seldom if ever wage war against one another is one of the most debated and studied in the social sciences. The debates are generally over two questions: Is it true? If so, why? Much progress has been made toward answering the first question. This book offers an answer to the second. I hope that the book will enhance understanding of liberal peace. I also hope it will both affirm what is good about liberal democracy and temper the post-millenialism into which we Americans in particular are prone to fall.

The debts I incurred in writing this book are enormous. I owe Stanley Hoffmann, Robert Keohane, and Ernest May thanks for their guidance. The Center for International Affairs at Harvard University provided crucial intellectual and financial support; I thank Joseph Nye and the John D. and Catherine T. MacArthur Foundation and the Andrew W. Mellon Foundation. I also thank many people who helped me think through the early stages, including James Alt, Peter Berkowitz, Houchang Chehabi, Michael Doyle, Michael Gilligan, Jay Greene, Mark Henrie, Kevin Hula, Marci Kanstoroom, Harvey Mansfield, Katharine Moon, Bruce Morrison, the late Judith Shklar, Daniel Stid, Patrick Wolf, and Stewart Wood.

The work matured under the kind and rigorous guidance of the Olin Institute for Strategic Studies at Harvard. Samuel Huntington was more than generous in allowing me time to rethink the project radically. Thomas Christensen, Andrew Cortell, Michael Desch, John Mearsheimer, Bruce Porter, Gideon Rose, Stephen Rosen, Byron Winn,

[ix]

Erik Yesson, Fareed Zakaria, and especially Randall Schweller were generous with their time and advice.

A year at Stanford's Center for International Security and Arms Control ripened the project into the current book. I thank Victor Cha, David Dessler, Lynn Eden, Sanjeev Khagram, Jonathan Mercer, and Scott Sagan for reading an earlier version and offering helpful criticism. I also owe Alexander George and the late Richard Smoke gratitude for their keen interest and encouragement. I thank the Carnegie Foundation for funding.

Along the way I have benefited from critiques from Yaacov Bar-Siman-Tov, Neta Crawford, Miriam Fendius Elman, Joanne Gowa, Joseph Grieco, Joe Hagan, Arie Kacowicz, Elizabeth Kier, David Lumsdaine, Judd Owen, James Lee Ray, Bruce Russett, David Spiro, and Spencer Weart. At Bowdoin College I thank Charles Beitz and Christian Potholm for reading portions of the manuscript, Paul Franco, Brooke Lea, and Scott Sehon for fruitful conversations, and Jean Yarbrough, the entire Government and Legal Studies Department, and the College as a whole for maintaining a congenial atmosphere for scholarship. For help in compiling the index, I thank Bradley Nelson and the Rowland Egger Small Grants Program at the Department of Government and Foreign Affairs, University of Virginia.

I join the dozens of authors who are indebted to Robert Art, Robert Jervis, and Stephen Walt, co-editors of Cornell Studies in Security Affairs, for their copious constructive criticism. (As it happens, it was Stephen Walt who first got me interested in liberal peace in a seminar at Princeton's Woodrow Wilson School in 1987.) And I join the even greater number of authors who appreciate Roger Haydon's skillful guidance.

My biggest intellectual debts are to Daniel Philpott and Sean Lynn-Jones, two colleagues who have been interested in the project nearly since I began it. They were as unsparing in their rigorous criticism as they were unyielding in their confidence that it would someday be a book.

The biggest debts I owe to any human beings for this book, however, are to my own family. My wife, Trish, has been a listener, a proofreader, an encourager, and a comfort for better for worse, for richer for poorer—a gracious woman graciously brought into my life. Her parents, Phil and Marguerite Hill, have provided support and a fine occasional working space. My sister Tricia and brother Judd and their families too have been gracious and patient. My father passed away as I was revising the manuscript at Stanford, and it is to him and my mother, to Malloy and Pat Owen, that I dedicate this book. Their love has been undying, their support unshakable; and their influence will be everlasting.

JOHN M. OWEN IV

Brunswick, Maine

[x]

PART I

Why Liberal Peace
and Liberal War

[1]

The Puzzle of Liberal Peace

"[World] peace must be planted upon the tested foundations of political liberty." The speaker might have been almost any American president, in almost any year. In fact, it was Woodrow Wilson in April 1917. Although a scholar, Wilson was not merely offering a discourse on international relations. He was asking Congress to declare war on Germany.[1] Seventy-seven years later, in January 1994, another president, Bill Clinton, announced to the nation, "Democracies don't attack each other."[2] Within a year he was readying an invasion to depose a military dictatorship in Haiti.

There is no necessary contradiction between the words and actions of these American presidents. In fact, their speeches and actions exemplify two sides of a single phenomenon. Bill Clinton, most scholars agree, was right: it is difficult to find a case of two democracies, or what I shall call liberal states,[3] going to war with one another. A liberal state I define as having two domestic institutions: freedom of discussion and regular competitive elections of those empowered to make war.[4] Such states have virtually formed a separate peace, and statistical tests indicate that the peace cannot be attributed solely to wealth, alliances, geography, or

---

1. Speech of Woodrow Wilson. *Congressional Record*, 65th Cong., 1st sess., 2 April 1917, 55, pt. 1:104.

2. "Excerpts from President Clinton's State of the Union Message," *New York Times*, 26 January 1994.

3. Claiming that there are probably no exceptions to the proposition are Bruce Russett, *Grasping the Democratic Peace: Principles for a Post–Cold War World* (Princeton: Princeton University Press, 1992), chap. 1; James Lee Ray, *Democracy and International Conflict: An Evaluation of the Democratic Peace Proposition* (Columbia: University of South Carolina Press, 1995), chap. 3.

4. As explained in Chapter 2, I actually place states along a liberal-illiberal continuum, classifying them as liberal, semiliberal, or illiberal. I also use the term *liberal* to describe persons and groups that want liberal institutions in their own state.

any other confounding variable.[5] At the same time, liberal states do fight wars against illiberal states, and often with the express purpose of making them liberal.[6] This book is an attempt to explain these twin tendencies, these two sides of one coin: liberal peace and liberal war.

The discovery of liberal peace has been greeted eagerly by statesmen in search of foreign policy principles and by scholars in search of regularities and theoretical puzzles. Clinton and George Bush before him made the peace among liberal democracies an axiom of foreign policy, with the corollary that the United States should therefore promote democracy—free and fair elections—in countries such as Panama, Haiti, and Cambodia. Such policies have a certain prima facie popularity because they confirm what Americans believe about their political system: it is not only the most just and the most conducive to prosperity, it is the most peaceful as well.

For scholars, liberal peace is especially compelling for two reasons. In one of the most quoted sentences in the discipline, Jack Levy noted that liberal peace is "the closest thing we have to an empirical law in the study of international relations."[7] No other system of government can claim such a record. Communist states, authoritarian states, and monarchies have all fought one another.[8] The only zone of peace grounded in a shared political system is, evidently, the liberal one. Liberal peace also poses a formidable challenge to realism, the dominant school of thought in politico-military affairs. Realism posits that power is the most important factor in international relations, and it expects that when it comes to war, liberal states will be no different from any other type of state.

It is no surprise, then, that liberal peace has spawned a lively research program that has generated many novel and useful findings.[9]

5. Stuart Bremer, "Democracy and Militarized Interstate Conflict, 1816–1965," *International Interactions* 18 (Spring 1993), 231–49; Zeev Maoz and Bruce Russett, "Alliances, Contiguity, Wealth, and Political Stability: Is the Lack of Conflict between Democracies a Statistical Artifact?" *International Interactions* 17 (Spring 1992), 245–67.

6. For a provocative argument that the desire to spread liberal democracy has been a crucial impetus behind U.S. foreign policy in the twentieth century, see Tony Smith, *America's Mission: The United States and the Worldwide Struggle for Democracy in the Twentieth Century* (Princeton: Princeton University Press, 1994).

7. Jack S. Levy, "Domestic Politics and War," in Robert I. Rotberg and Theodore K. Rabb, eds., *The Origin and Prevention of Major Wars* (New York: Cambridge University Press, 1989), 88.

8. Zeev Maoz and Nasrin Abdolali, "Regime Types and International Conflict," *Journal of Conflict Resolution* 33 (March 1989), 3–35.

9. Some of the main recent sources include Michael E. Brown, Sean M. Lynn-Jones, and Steven E. Miller, eds., *Debating the Democratic Peace* (Cambridge: MIT Press, 1996); Miriam Fendius Elman, ed., *Paths to Peace: Is Democracy the Answer?* (Cambridge: MIT

Still lacking, however, is a satisfactory account of how and why liberal states avoid war with one another but not with illiberal states—i.e., a causal story linking the alleged cause, liberalism, to the effect, liberal peace. This book provides such a story by observing closely the foreign policy processes of liberal states. I examine ten war-threatening crises involving the United States between the 1790s and the close of the nineteenth century to see precisely what keeps liberal states at peace with one another and what leads them into war with illiberal states. I present the perceptions of actors and the decision processes of statesmen in the United States and in Great Britain, France, Mexico, Spain, and Chile—countries against which America went, or almost went, to war. I pay particular attention to the development and effects of the perceptions that elites in each state held of the other state.

I argue that liberal states tend to remain at peace with one another, and to fight illiberal states, because they believe it is in their interests to have good relations with fellow liberal states and to oppose illiberal states. More precisely, liberal states contain elites who believe that peace is intrinsically good, that liberal states are more pacific and trustworthy, and that close relations with fellow liberal states strengthen liberal institutions in their own state. Conversely, they believe that illiberal states are belligerent and that close ties with them may corrupt their own state. They judge states based on their domestic political institutions and maintain those judgments through smooth or rocky relations with those states. These beliefs shape foreign policy because liberal states are also constituted by governmental institutions—namely, free discussion of public issues and regular elections of officials empowered to declare war—that constrain foreign policy decision making, especially during crises.

I do not claim that these beliefs and institutions are the only factors contributing to liberal peace and war. Liberal states tend to be economically interdependent and to form multilateral institutions to foster conflict resolution.[10] In any given case of war or war avoidance, moreover, a number of factors may be causal. Military power, geography, and other forces certainly do not drop out. The core of liberal peace, however, is liberalism itself.

Press, 1997); Russett, *Grasping the Democratic Peace*; Ray, *Democracy and International Conflict*. The first chapters in Elman and in Ray present excellent literature reviews.

10. Arguably, robustness in both of these pacifying factors presupposes domestic institutional similarity such as that which liberal states have. Immanuel Kant cites international commerce and international law as contributing to "perpetual peace" but holds republican government as a necessary condition. Kant, "To Perpetual Peace, a Philosophical Sketch," in *Perpetual Peace and Other Essays*, trans. Ted Humphrey (Indianapolis: Hackett, 1983), 112–15.

This book thus stresses several factors that the literature has tended to neglect. First, I emphasize *liberalism*, as distinguished from democracy.[11] Second, I emphasize that liberal states must perceive one another to be liberal. I show that elites classify as liberal those foreign states that have the institutions they want in their own state. Third, I bring history into the study of liberal peace, particularly the evolution over time and space of notions of liberalism and democracy and the effect of this evolution on international security. Fourth, I use both norms or ideas and institutions to explain liberal peace, rather than treating them as separate and competing explanations. Fifth, I answer skeptics who assert that if there really were a liberal peace then liberal states would never threaten to use force against one another. I show how in many cases their domestic institutions may fully constrain the leaders of liberal states only when war is at issue and public attention engaged. Finally, I argue that, unpleasant though it may be to contemplate, liberal peace always exists in the shadow of its twin, liberal war.[12]

Since the 1980s, the liberal peace proposition has excited both scholars and foreign policy makers.[13] For scholars, it proposes a regularity of a strength rarely seen in social phenomena. Political scientists despairing of being able to predict the future take heart at the prospect of saying with confidence that no two liberal states will wage war against

11. Of course, several writers, including most prominently Michael Doyle (under the influence of Kant) and, in a different sense, R. J. Rummel, have stressed liberalism over democracy. Doyle also emphasizes liberal war along with liberal peace; in general, the influence of his articles will be clear throughout this book. See Michael Doyle, "Kant, Liberal Legacies, and Foreign Affairs," pt. 1, *Philosophy and Public Affairs* 12 (Summer 1983), 205–35, and pt. 2, ibid. 12 (Fall 1983), pp. 323–53; Doyle, "Liberalism and World Politics," *American Political Science Review* 80 (December 1986), 1151–69; R. J. Rummel, *Understanding Conflict and War*, vol. 4 (Beverly Hills: Sage, 1974).

12. Spencer R. Weart has used methods, and produced findings, similar to mine. Among these are the importance of perceptions; the synergy of ideology (or political culture) and political institutions; and the centrality of internal threats in determining external enemies. Unlike Weart, however, I do not support the notion that there has never been a war between liberal states. Weart, *Never at War: Why Democracies Will Not Fight One Another* (forthcoming).

13. Besides works already cited, see Bruce Bueno de Mesquita and David Lalman, *War and Reason: Domestic and International Imperatives* (New Haven: Yale University Press, 1992), chap. 5; David A. Lake, "Powerful Pacifists: Democratic States and War," *American Political Science Review* 86 (March 1992), 24–37; Randall L. Schweller, "Domestic Structure and Preventive War: Are Democracies More Pacific?" *World Politics* 44 (January 1992), 235–69; T. Clifton Morgan and Sally Howard Campbell, "Domestic Structure, Decisional Constraints, and War: So Why Kant Democracies Fight?" *Journal of Conflict Resolution* 35 (June 1991), 187–211; T. Clifton Morgan and Valerie Schwebach, "Take Two Democracies and Call Me in the Morning: A Prescription for Peace?" *International Interactions* 17 (1992), 305–20; William J. Dixon, "Democracy and the Peaceful Settlement of Conflict," *American Political Science Review* 88 (March 1994), 14–32.

one another. The proposition has also generated attention as a potent challenge to realism, the dominant school of international relations in North America. Realism holds that power, rather than ideas, institutions, or processes, is ultimately most important in relations among nations. If realism is right, however, there should be no liberal peace: liberal states should wage war against one another as often as they do against other types of states.[14] what if it's in their interests?

Outside the academy, liberal peace has rekindled flickering hopes that perpetual peace is within humankind's grasp. The remarkable spread of political liberalism since the 1970s, most spectacularly in Central and Eastern Europe but also in Southern Europe, Latin America, Asia, and Africa, combines with the proposition to suggest that there will be fewer wars in the coming years—or at least that fewer pairs of states or dyads will make war on each other.[15] In Washington both Democrats and Republicans profess to believe in liberal peace. Two years before Clinton affirmed that "democracies don't attack each other," a Republican Secretary of State had announced:

> The Cold War has ended, and we now have a chance to forge a democratic peace, an enduring peace built on shared values—democracy and political and economic freedom. The strength of these values in Russia and the other new independent states will be the surest foundation for peace—and the strongest guarantee of our national security—for decades to come.[16]

Liberal peace has provided a ready-made principle for foreign policy makers in a time when, with no more Soviet threat, principles are difficult to come by.

The liberal peace proposition also has inherent appeal to people who strongly value self-government and peace and badly want these two things to go together. There was a time when, under the influence of the Enlightenment, Europeans and Americans tended to believe that if they were rational they could have all the things they valued at once: scientific progress would bring a better material existence for all; personal freedom would bring happiness; and, what is our concern here,

14. This is at least true of Kenneth Waltz's neorealism, which places any explanation that looks to individual characteristics of states outside the purview of international relations theory. See Kenneth N. Waltz, *Theory of International Politics* (New York: McGraw-Hill, 1979). This is not necessarily true of earlier realists, such as Hans Morgenthau and E. H. Carr, who do concede that liberal democracies are in some sense distinctive (see Chapter 2).

15. Francis Fukuyama, *The End of History and the Last Man* (New York: Free Press, 1992). On the spread of liberal democracy beginning in the 1970s, see Samuel P. Huntington, *The Third Wave* (Norman: University of Oklahoma Press, 1991).

16. James Baker, quoted in Russett, *Grasping the Democratic Peace*, 128–29.

self-government would bring peace. The eighteenth- and nineteenth-century revolutions that overthrew the old regime were supposed to bring freedom not only from coercion, poverty, and superstition but also from war. Self-government would take power from those who benefited from violence and conquest—princes, aristocracies, the church—and hand it to those who did not—the people. When those who fought and paid for war were granted the right to decide on war, the world would finally have peace.

Liberal government came, but war did not leave. Liberals have hardly been unique in arguing that if only nations would set up the right institutions, peace and security would reign: communists, monarchists, and fascists have all made similar claims about their own systems. All have been mistaken. Most studies show that no type of regime, liberal included, is more or less prone to war than any other.[17] The general disposition to peace is evidently only a story that ideologues tell to claim legitimacy for their preferred systems. Modern governments dress in the garb of peace but inevitably join the grim march of war. In recent American history, the Vietnam War, with its sometimes wanton televised destructiveness, was particularly damaging to the image liberals had of their countries. The liberal peace proposition partially vindicates liberalism.

This first chapter sets up the argument presented in Chapter 2 by staking out positions. First come some criticisms of the liberal peace thesis; second, existing explanations for liberal peace; third, the need for case studies such as those in this book; fourth, the importance of perceptions; fifth, the distinction between liberalism and democracy; and finally, the epistemological issue of ideas as explanations, especially the question of how ideas relate to "structures."

CRITIQUES OF THE LIBERAL PEACE THESIS

The liberal peace proposition is by no means universally accepted. It has been argued that random chance could account for the lack of war among liberal states—that since historically both liberal states and war have been relatively rare, the absence of wars among these states is no more significant than would be the absence of wars among states

17. Maoz and Abdolali, "Regime Type and International Conflict"; Melvin Small and J. David Singer, "The War-Proneness of Liberal Regimes," *Jerusalem Journal of International Relations* 1 (Summer 1976), 50–69. Some do argue that liberal states are somewhat less likely to go to war, or at least to initiate war, against even illiberal states. See R. J. Rummel, "Democracies Are More Peaceful Than Other Countries," *European Journal of International Relations* 1 (1995), 457–79; and David L. Rousseau, Christopher Gelpi, Dan Reiter, and Paul K. Huth, "Assessing the Dyadic Nature of the Democratic Peace, 1918–88," *American Political Science Review* 90 (1996), 512–33.

whose names begin with the letter K.[18] Moreover, like any statement whose terms—"liberal state," "democracy," "war"—are controversial, it tempts its proponents to tautology. One who wanted to confirm that no two liberal states have ever been at war with each other could carefully define liberal state in such a way as to safeguard the proposition.[19] Finally, some argue that there is no direct evidence of a causal link between liberalism and the alleged liberal peace.[20] Even if a strong correlation exists between liberal states and peace, it does not necessarily follow that it is liberalism causing these states to forgo war with one another. What looks like liberal peace may be spurious correlation. It may be that some other factor is at work, such as power or wealth, producing both liberal regimes and peace.

Unlike other works, this book is not a defense of the strong form of the liberal peace proposition, that "no liberal states have ever been at war with one another." As I explain below, the possible exceptions to the rule are too many. Thus I neither rebut the thesis that random chance could account for the finding,[21] nor attempt to answer the charge of tautology. Logically, critics of the proposition are just as vulnerable as supporters to the tautological temptation. One could define "liberal state" so as to demonstrate that liberal states have in fact fought one another. As it happens, most participants in the debate are careful and explicit in defining their terms. It is the third criticism, the lack of a causal link, that I address in this book. But there has been much work on the causes of liberal peace. Why is it inadequate?

EXPLANATIONS OF LIBERAL PEACE

Most of the liberal peace literature has used quantitative methods. This book is meant to complement rather than compete with that literature. Indeed, without quantitative methods, we could not be nearly so confident that liberal peace is genuine rather than spurious, because the possibility

18. David Spiro, "The Insignificance of Liberal Peace," in Brown, Lynn-Jones, and Miller, *Debating the Democratic Peace*, 202–38.

19. Kenneth N. Waltz, "The Emerging Structure of International Politics," *International Security* 18 (Fall 1993), 78; Jack Vincent, "Freedom and International Conflict: Another Look," *International Studies Quarterly* 31 (March 1987), 102–12; Henry S. Farber and Joanne Gowa, "Polities and Peace," in Brown, Lynn-Jones, and Miller, *Debating the Democratic Peace*, 239–62.

20. John J. Mearsheimer, "Back to the Future: Instability in Europe after the Cold War," *International Security* 15 (Summer 1990), 5–56; Christopher Layne, "Kant or Cant: The Myth of the Liberal Peace," in Brown, Lynn-Jones, and Miller, *Debating the Democratic Peace*, 157–201.

21. But see the exchange between Bruce Russett, Christopher Layne, David Spiro, and Michael Doyle in Brown, Lynn-Jones, and Miller, *Debating the Democratic Peace*, 337–73.

of a variable other than liberalism accounting for the peace would be too high.[22] The literature has been hampered by two features, however: commitment to a dubious typology and a paucity of case studies.[23]

A typology of explanations has taken hold that sets up liberal norms or culture or ideas as competing with liberal institutions or structures. Normative explanations look to the ideas and practices of liberal states. Perhaps these states believe it would be unjust to fight one another or are simply accustomed to compromise in settling disputes with parties they trust.[24] An early version of this view was stated by Voltaire, who argued that "growing enlightenment, rather than . . . international institutions" would end war. "The only perpetual peace which can be established among men is tolerance."[25] Institutional explanations, by contrast, hold that domestic liberal structures do the work. Liberal states are constrained from war by internal checks and balances and (in some accounts) know each other to be similarly constrained.[26]

Elsewhere I have challenged this typology for imposing a false dichotomy on research. There is no a priori basis for supposing that either norms or institutions alone are responsible for liberal peace. Just as gasoline and an engine are both necessary to make an automobile run, it could be that norms and institutions work in tandem.[27] In fact, I argue that the norms-institutions typology commits an endogeneity error, wherein the two supposedly independent variables are actually both intervening variables produced by the true independent variable, liberalism. Arriving at that conclusion, however, required a different methodology than has been used by most of the literature.

Joseph Nye writes that liberal peace "need[s] exploration via detailed case studies to look at what actually happened in particular instances."[28] The need for "small-n" studies, i.e., studies that look at a small number of cases, stems from the requirements of establishing causality. The first step in causal analysis is to use quantitative methods to establish a cor-

22. Here I should note that Immanuel Kant brilliantly foresaw a liberal peace in 1795 based purely on his theory of republican government. Kant's liberal peace, unlike ours, is purely deductive.

23. Two new books address this latter shortcoming: Elman, *Paths to Peace*, and Weart, *Never at War*.

24. Doyle, "Liberalism and World Politics"; Russett, *Grasping the Democratic Peace*; Dixon, "Democracy and Peaceful Settlement."

25. Voltaire, "De la paix perpétuelle" (1769), quoted in Patrick Riley, *Kant's Political Philosophy* (Totowa, N.J.: Rowman & Littlefield, 1983), 129.

26. Lake, "Powerful Pacifists"; Bueno de Mesquita and Lalman, *War and Reason*; Morgan and Campbell, "So Why Kant Democracies Fight?"

27. John M. Owen, "How Liberalism Produces Democratic Peace," in Brown, Lynn-Jones, and Miller, *Debating the Democratic Peace*, 116–54.

28. Joseph S. Nye, Jr., *Understanding International Conflicts* (New York: Harper Collins, 1993), 40.

relation, whereby one type of event (effect) regularly follows another (alleged cause). Second, one controls for other variables to see whether other possible causes can wholly account for the effect. But even if the alleged cause survives these tests, there remains a black box between cause and effect. A full scientific explanation opens the box.[29] David Dessler writes that studies of the causes of war need to go "beyond correlations" and generate the presence or absence of alleged "*generative* connection[s] between observed phenomena."[30] Quantitative studies shake the black box but by their very nature cannot open it. First, they infer processes from statistical relationships but do not observe those processes directly. Second, they use proxy variables that are often crude indicators of the factors being tested. In the case of liberal peace, one pair of scholars argues that liberal norms of compromise keep liberal states from fighting one another. Their metric for liberal norms are regime stability and levels of internal social and political violence. But totalitarian regimes such as the Soviet Union would rate high on such a scale—higher than, for example, the United States—yet have not adhered to liberal norms.[31] The case study method has limitations of its own, but because it is a sharp instrument it avoids distorting comparisons.[32]

The absence of detailed case studies has contributed to a recent tendency to treat as sufficient those explanations that use a rational choice framework. Such explanations endeavor to show why egoistic democratic governments with transitive preferences should avoid war with one another's states. Bruce Bueno de Mesquita and David Lalman assume that democracies are internally restrained from war and know their fellow democracies to be similarly constrained; thus, no war among democracies.[33] James Fearon hypothesizes that a democratic government, out of fear of electoral punishment, will carry out threats made to foreign states; since democratic governments know

29. Jon Elster, *Explaining Technical Change* (Cambridge: Cambridge University Press, 1983), 28–29.

30. David Dessler, "Beyond Correlations: Toward a Causal Theory of War," *International Studies Quarterly* 35 (September 1991), 337–45.

31. Zeev Maoz and Bruce Russett, "Normative and Structural Causes of Liberal Peace, 1946–1986," *American Political Science Review* 87 (September 1993), 624–38.

32. For an explanation of case study methods in political science, see Alexander George and Timothy J. McKeown, "Case Studies and Theories of Organizational Decision Making," in *Advances in Information Processing in Organizations*, vol. 2 (Greenwich, Conn.: JAI, 1985). A full exploration of the virtues and vices of quantitative and qualitative approaches to liberal peace research is found in Ray, *Democracy and International Conflict*, chap. 4.

33. Bueno de Mesquita and Lalman, *War and Reason*, chap. 5. Michael J. Gilligan argues that Bueno de Mesquita and Lalman's account is incomplete without assumptions about liberal ideology; see his review of *War and Reason* in *Journal of International Affairs* 48 (Winter 1995), esp. 651.

about these "domestic audience costs," they will take care not to push one another to the point of threatening force, and will thus not go to war against one another.[34] Kenneth A. Schultz argues that foreign states can see how willing and able a democracy truly is to go to war. Assuming that war occurs when one or more states misjudge their power and will, relative to the potential enemy, two democracies in a dispute would then be unlikely to go to war because each knows its relative power and the weaker democracy will back down.[35] These explanations are logically sound, but they omit and at times misrepresent some of the real processes of liberal foreign policy making. For example, rational choice explanations elide the issue of how liberal states identify one another, which as I explain below is crucial. These accounts also leave out the affinities that develop among liberal states. Liberal elites identify their state's interests with those of foreign states they consider liberal, and against those of states they consider illiberal.

THE IMPORTANCE OF PERCEPTIONS

The neglect of perceptions may not seem a deficiency, since logically it is not necessary that liberal states identify one another for liberal peace to happen. It could be, for example, that liberal states are generally dovish or inclined toward cooperation—that is, employ strategies that do not punish the other state the first time it "defects"[36]—whereas at least some illiberal states are not; when two liberal states enter a dispute, a pacific solution would then automatically emerge, but when a liberal and an illiberal state enter a dispute, the outcome would possibly be violent. There are three reasons, however, why perceptions matter, and two additional reasons why this book pays such close attention to them.

First, as Bueno de Mesquita and Lalman argue, if liberal states are known to be dovish and illiberal states may not be, a prudent liberal state will distinguish liberal from illiberal neighbors. Knowing that they are liable to exploitation by hawkish states, liberal states will be hawkish toward such states.[37] Second, the evidence in Part II shows that liberals do indeed want to cooperate with states they perceive to be liberal, and to be suspicious of those they regard as illiberal. For ex-

34. James D. Fearon, "Domestic Political Audiences and the Escalation of International Disputes," *American Political Science Review* 88 (1994), 577–82.

35. Kenneth A. Schultz, "Domestic Political Competition and Bargaining in International Crises" (Ph.D. diss., Stanford University, 1996).

36. For an exploration of "nice" and "forgiving" strategies in game theory, see Robert Axelrod, *The Evolution of Cooperation* (New York: Basic Books, 1984), chap. 2.

37. Bueno de Mesquita and Lalman, *War and Reason.*

ample, American Federalists in the 1790–1812 period considered England a free country and France (after 1792) a despotism. They were much more forgiving of British abuses than of French. Third, most published works on liberal peace assume that perceptions matter, that in fact a necessary condition for liberal peace is that liberal states identify one another as liberal.[38] Bueno de Mesquita and Lalman assert: "The presence of the [domestic institutional] constraint is not alone sufficient to ensure cooperation or harmony. However, it is common knowledge whether a given state is a liberal democracy."[39] *perceptions*

Scholars concede, then, that liberal peace should be studied as a phenomenon in which subjects' perceptions matter. Most of these same scholars, however, ignore perceptions by assuming that they are uniform. Such a move would seem to be justified by the strength of the liberal peace finding: if there really are no wars among liberal states, then these states must be perceiving one another uniformly (and correctly.) In fact, however, liberal peace is not the iron law that some suppose. The statement that liberal states have never fought one another places far too much confidence in today's scholarly definitions of "liberal state." The statement itself rests on the perceptions of a group of today's scholars as to which states qualify as liberal, perceptions that are themselves open to question. For example, David Lake labels Spain in 1898 a democracy and thus calls the Spanish-American War an exception to liberal peace.[40] In fact, a number of wars may plausibly be said to have been between liberal states, including three in this book: the War of 1812, the Spanish-American War, and even the U.S. Civil War.[41] By the criteria used in this book, the first two are only partial exceptions, since Britain in 1812 and Spain in 1898 were not fully liberal. The Civil War is a more serious exception. The Confederacy had free discussion and elections, making it (by my limited criteria) as liberal as the Union. Its constitution was very similar to that of the United States.[42] James Lee Ray and Bruce Russett

exceptions to lib. peace

38. A partial exception is T. Clifton Morgan and his associates, who attribute liberal peace to domestic constraints that some illiberal states also have. See Morgan and Campbell, "So Why Kant Democracies Fight?" and Morgan and Schwebach, "Take Two Democracies." It is significant, however, that these authors conclude that the term *liberal* or *democratic peace* is inappropriate. For the peace to be called liberal, it should be produced by liberal intentions.

39. Bueno de Mesquita and Lalman, *War and Reason*, 156. Michael Doyle, Bruce Russett, David Lake, R. J. Rummel, and Randall Schweller also treat liberal peace as conditional on perceptions (see note 13 above).

40. Lake, "Powerful Pacifists."

41. The War of 1812 and the Spanish-American War are treated in Chapters 3 and 5, respectively.

42. The main difference was that the Confederate Constitution more strictly guarded states' rights against the national government. E. Merton Coulter, *The Confederate States of America 1861–1865* (Baton Rouge: Louisiana State University Press, 1950), 28–32.

both offer refutations of these and other plausible exceptions,[43] but that they must offer refutations at all is the problem. There is no a priori reason to think that liberals in 1812, 1861, or 1898 would fully agree with these two particular American political scientists writing in the 1990s.

What is clear is that elites in the Union and the Confederacy did *not* perceive one another's polity as liberal. As I explain in Chapter 4, Northern abolitionists from the 1820s did not consider the South liberal, and in return many Southerners considered the North intolerant of their freedom. By 1855 the *New York Tribune* could write: "We are not one people. We are two peoples. We are a people for Freedom and a people for Slavery. Between the two, conflict is inevitable."[44] More generally, the scholarly assumption that perceptions of liberalism are uniform is false. In case after case the "knowledge" of which states are liberal is often far from common.

Margaret G. Hermann and Charles W. Kegley, Jr., call for case studies to explore the processes by which subjects come to perceive foreign states as liberal or illiberal.[45] The need is especially acute because subjective disagreements must raise suspicions that perceptions are epiphenomenal, that is, that subjects perceive a foreign state as liberal or not based on something other than its political system, such as power or wealth. If perceptions are epiphenomenal, then liberal peace itself is spurious.[46] I thus devote much attention to the question of the origins of perceptions. I argue that rather than being epiphenomenal, perceptions are usually tied to subjects' visions for their own state.[47] These visions are economic, social, and moral, but integral to them are always particular political institutions. They are also always formulated in contrast to an opposite; every utopia has a dystopia. These political visions profoundly shape foreign policy beliefs by telling liberals which foreign states are friends and which are foes. Jeffersonians hated

---

43. Ray, *Democracy and International Conflict,* chap. 3; Russett, *Grasping the Democratic Peace,* 16–23. Russett disqualifies the Civil War by categorizing it outside the set of interstate wars; Ray argues that the Confederacy did not have time to prove itself to be liberal.

44. Eric Foner, *Politics and Ideology in the Age of the Civil War* (New York: Oxford University Press, 1980), esp. 52–53.

45. Margaret G. Hermann and Charles W. Kegley, Jr., "Rethinking Democracy and International Peace: Perspectives from Political Psychology," *International Studies Quarterly* 39 (December 1995), esp. 520.

46. For a provocative argument of this type see Ido Oren, "The Subjectivity of the 'Democratic' Peace: Changing U.S. Perceptions of Imperial Germany," in Brown, Lynn-Jones, and Miller, *Debating the Democratic Peace,* 263–300.

47. Cf. David Halloran Lumsdaine, *Moral Vision in International Politics: The Foreign Aid Regime, 1949–1989* (Princeton: Princeton University Press, 1993). Lumsdaine shows that people who favored redistribution of wealth in their own states tended to favor international redistributive policies. People (and thus governments) thus see their political and social visions for their own countries as of a piece with conditions within foreign countries.

England and favored France in the 1790–1812 period because they did not want England's political system in their own country. The best alternative, they thought, was closer ties with republican (and even Napoleonic) France. The resulting foreign policy strategy—tilting toward France and away from England—was a major cause of the War of 1812.

In sum, then, logic and evidence strongly suggest that perceptions matter, but actual perceptions vary and often differ from those of today's scholars; thus, if liberal peace is real, a theory is needed to account for these perceptions. Such a theory is presented in Chapter 2.

LIBERALISM, NOT DEMOCRACY

Most scholars refer to *democratic* rather than *liberal* peace. Their definitions of democracy vary, but they generally mean a state with popular leverage over government. In holding the public will or particular institutional mechanisms responsible for the peace, however, they are invoking factors that are more properly subsumed by the term *liberalism.*

Democracy literally means the rule of the *demos,* originally the many, the common people, in classical Greek city-states. There is no necessary content to such a democracy, no particular worldview, anthropology, or vision of what the laws should look like. There is only the directive that the people ought to get what they want. In fact, many Enlightenment thinkers worried openly about the illiberal aspects of the rule of the *demos.* James Madison defines a democracy as a small society in which citizens "assemble and administer the government in person," and goes on to warn against the factions it would always produce and its "sacrifice" of "the weaker party or an obnoxious individual."[48] Kant's requirement that the executive and legislative powers be separate stems from a similar fear. A democracy "establishes an executive power through which all the citizens may make decisions about (and indeed against) the single individual without his consent, so that decisions are made by all the people and yet not by all the people; and this means that the general will is in contradiction with itself, and thus also with freedom."[49]Alexis de Tocqueville points out that the United States in the 1830s was often afflicted by a "tyranny of the majority," as when white Pennsylvanians disenfranchised blacks in spite of the law:

48. Madison, *Federalist 10,* in Clinton Rossiter, ed., *The Federalist Papers* (New York: New American Library, 1961), 81–83.
49. Kant, "Perpetual Peace," 101.

[15]

[Pennsylvanian:] "Oh! It is not that [Negroes] are reluctant to go [to the polls], but they are afraid they may be maltreated. With us it sometimes happens that the law lacks force when the majority does not support it. Now the majority is filled with the strongest prejudices against Negroes, and the magistrates do not feel strong enough to guarantee the rights granted to them by the lawmakers."

[Tocqueville:] "What! The majority, privileged to make the law, wishes also to have the privilege of disobeying the law?"[50]

J. S. Mill, greatly affected by Tocqueville's writings, favors a complicated voting scheme that would guard the individual from the oppression of the many.[51]

Majority rule begs the question of *what the majority wants*. The majority must seek the ends and means prescribed by liberalism in order to bring about the selective war and peace in question. The salient liberal end is individual autonomy or self-government. But for all individuals to be self-governing, each must tolerate all others. Thus liberal autonomy is a circumscribed autonomy: there are some actions an enlightened person will not choose. Liberals square the circle by positing that all rational, uncoerced persons will choose lives of toleration rather than violence, of quiet productivity rather than military glory or martyrdom.

Classical Greece illustrates why liberalism rather than democracy is the key. It has been considered a puzzle in the liberal peace literature that Greek democratic city-states fought one another frequently.[52] The brief answer to the puzzle is that ancient Greeks were not liberals. Thucydides shows that they believed neither in the superiority of ordinary life nor in the equality of all persons. An Athenian democrat felt little compulsion to spread freedom throughout the known world, or Greece, or even Athens. The Athenian liberal state is not the pacific system of government imagined by the Enlightenment. It is rather an unabashedly restive, adventurous, conquering regime.

According to Thucydides, the Corinthians told the oligarchical Spartans that they were sluggish compared to their rivals, the democratic Athenians, who "are adventurous beyond their power, and daring beyond their judgment, and in danger they are sanguine. . . . Their bodies they spend ungrudgingly in their country's cause . . . and to them laborious occupation is less of a misfortune than the peace of a quiet life."[53]

50. Alexis de Tocqueville, *Democracy in America*, ed. J. P. Mayer, trans. George Lawrence (New York: Harper and Row, 1969), 250–56.

51. Jon Roper, *Democracy and Its Critics* (London: Unwin Hyman, 1989), 145–50.

52. Bruce Russett and William Antholis, "The Imperfect Democratic Peace of Ancient Athens," in Russett, *Grasping the Democratic Peace*, 43–71.

53. Thucydides, *The Peloponnesian War* 1.70, ed. T. E. Wick, trans. Richard Crawley (New York: Random House, 1982), 40.

Later, Pericles celebrated Athenian democracy for its energy and bold-ness: "We have forced every sea and land to be the high-way of our daring, and everywhere, whether for evil or for good, have left imper-ishable monuments behind us."[54] No mention was made of commonal-ities with other Greek democracies, or all persons deserving self-rule. Rather, we see that the good life consisted in martial feats, or what Charles Taylor calls the warrior ethic. The Athenian view is coherent: if being democratic means being warlike, then there is less reason for democracies to trust one another or try to spread democracy.[55]

Athens is intolerant, warlike

A similar illiberalism is evident in many other "democracies." In the 1990s, Balkan peoples live in popularly governed polities; yet many define themselves primarily not as abstract individuals with the same interests but according to religious categories: Serbs are Orthodox Christian, Croats are Roman Catholic, and Bosnian Muslims are Mus-lim. The lack of commonality means no liberal peace among these peo-ples. Iranians live in a state with universal suffrage and vigorous par-liamentary debate, yet many do not view the world through a liberal lens. For them, people might not pursue the good life without a min-istry of culture to censor erroneous ideas. Other new democracies, such as those arising from the ruins of the Soviet Union, may be illib-eral as well. In Chapter 2 I link liberal values and institutions: if citi-zens value individual liberty and prosperity, and believe that all per-sons potentially value these as well, liberal government is likely to be present.

*Balkans
Iran*

IDEAS AND STRUCTURES

My argument, then, begins with ideas, specifically liberal ideas. After a long period of dormancy, ideas have recently regained some prestige as a category of explanation in international relations.[56] Many scholars remain convinced, however, that any explanation that invokes

---

54. Ibid., 2.41.

55. As Russett and Antholis write, "The citizens of most democratic cities probably did not think of democracy as a trans-Hellenic project, at least at the outset of the Pelo-ponnesian War. The individual liberties central to liberal democracy were not so univer-salized in the ancient world" ("Imperfect Democratic Peace," 45).

56. Two recent compilations are Judith Goldstein and Robert O. Keohane, eds., *Ideas and Foreign Policy: Beliefs, Institutions, and Political Change* (Ithaca: Cornell University Press, 1993), which is an attempt to incorporate ideas into a rationalist framework; and Peter Katzenstein, ed., *The Culture of National Security: Norms and Identity in World Politics* (New York: Columbia University Press, 1996), which explicitly poses a sociologically ori-ented alternative.

a causal role for ideas is probably tautological. The difficulty lies in inferring the ideas that subjects hold independent of the behavior to be explained. If I argue that a group of states refrain from war with one another because they hold liberal ideas and then I demonstrate those ideas through their pacific behavior, I have a circular explanation. This difficulty makes the "rationalist" approach, which de-emphasizes ideas, appealing. Rationalists take subjects' ends as given and explain behavior via the external incentives they face, incentives that can supposedly be measured objectively. These incentives are conceived as structures, virtually material constraints whose meanings are self-evident.

As mentioned above, I do not demonstrate the causal force of liberal ideology through outcomes, but rather examine the presence and strength of the ideas prior to the outcome. But I do not argue thereby that ideas overcome structures or that norms supersede interests. Rather, I argue against those who would pit these factors against one another. I begin with the premise that people perceive their material environment through "lenses," formed by the ideas they hold, that give that environment meaning. The lenses, and thus the meaning assigned to the material environment, vary according to the ideas held by the subject. To a gambler, a thousand dollars won in an evening in Las Vegas may be especially valued for the way in which it was acquired. To a devout Christian, it might be ill-gotten gains, and that at least partly because the Christian believes that gambling is bad for society and thus for him personally. The Christian is no more or less rational or self-interested than the gambler; the two simply have different beliefs and attach different meanings to that particular thousand dollars. For American Federalists in the 1790s, economic growth that resulted from trade with England was healthful for the nation; for Republicans, it was a source of corruption (see Chapter 3).

The liberal imperative I describe is not a radical idealism, a triumph of ideology over reality. Objective reality is much more than the sum of material factors such as power or wealth. It also comprises the attitudes and beliefs of actors and the interaction of those attitudes and beliefs. Material factors alone often explain very little. Consider two states, A and B, each materially capable of hurting the other. A realist may believe these states threaten each other. Yet if the two do not believe each other to be threatening, then the objective reality is that they do not threaten each other.[57] (They may come to do so at some point, for a variety of reasons, but that is not the issue.) Such has been true of Russia and the United States since the downfall of the Soviet Union. Nor do

*norms
interests,
ideas,
structures
work together
to create
liberal
peace*

*materials
AND
ideas are
important*

57. For an application of this notion to international relations, see Alexander Wendt, "Anarchy Is What States Make of It: The Social Construction of Power Politics," *International Organization* 46 (Spring 1992), 391–426.

liberal peace and liberal war result from altruism triumphing over selfishness. Liberals believe it is entirely in their own interests to respect the rights of others, as long as those others will respect their rights in turn. Stemming from that belief is the corollary that it is in their interests to support liberalism in foreign countries.

Rather than treat ideas and structures as mutually exclusive analytic categories, I assume that ideas are inescapable filters through which actors read the world. In fact, what social scientists call structures are nearly always partly constituted by ideas.[58] A warship is more than simply a material object: it gets its power from the understandings people have of it. In the 1790–1812 period Federalist Americans perceived British warships as benign protectors of international commerce, while Republicans perceived them as a threat to U.S. sovereignty. In a sense, this book is an attempt to expand the range of ideas that are admitted to constitute structures. *perceiving w/ a liberal lens*

Liberals perceive their situation and the correct course of action through a liberal lens. Liberalism is first a worldview, a set of fundamental categories through which individuals understand themselves and the world. It thus shapes individuals' conceptions of their identities and interests by telling them of what human nature and the good life consist. In giving an account of how the world works, particularly what causes people to act as they do, liberalism acts not only as a road map, illumining and obscuring various options for actions,[59] but also as a travel guide that helps them to choose the right destination and to know which people (states) are helpful and which to avoid.

This worldview has implications for politics. First, it generates a political ideology, "a belief system that explains and justifies a preferred political order for society . . . and offers at least a sketchy notion of strategy for its maintenance or attainment."[60] Liberal ideology posits that liberal states should not wage war against one another, but sometimes must fight illiberal states. People holding this ideology tend to read the balance of power and their own economic interest so as to conform with these prescriptions.[61] Second, the liberal worldview leads those who accept it to set up governmental structures that make individual autonomy more likely. The institutions of free discussion and regular competitive

58. For a philosophical treatment of this issue, see John R. Searle, *The Construction of Social Reality* (New York: Free Press, 1995).

59. The "roadmap" metaphor is used by Goldstein and Keohane, *Ideas and Foreign Policy*, 13–17.

60. Alexander L. George, "Ideology and International Relations: A Conceptual Analysis," *Jerusalem Journal of International Relations* 9, no. 1 (1987), 1–21.

61. One valuable effort to separate ideology from interest is Bruce M. Russett and Elizabeth C. Hanson, *Interest and Ideology: The Foreign Policy Beliefs of American Businessmen* (San Francisco: W. H. Freeman, 1975).

elections instantiate liberal ideas.[62] Liberalism insists that laws be rational, and that rationality emerges from full discussion and due process rather than arbitrary decisions. Liberals thus set up institutions that give the governed leverage over the governors. Liberal ideology and institutions work synergistically to prod liberal states toward war and peace.

Part II shows liberalism at work in a number of cases, most dramatically in three types of cases. First, liberals in state A sometimes shifted from a belligerent to a cooperative attitude with State B when B liberalized internally. In the U.S. Civil War, British Liberals and Radicals began pushing for a pro-Union policy after Abraham Lincoln issued the preliminary Emancipation Proclamation in the fall of 1862. Americans stopped threatening intervention in Cuba when the Spanish monarchy was replaced by a republic in February 1873. Americans granted the Spanish government a brief respite from criticism when a Liberal government took office from a Conservative one in October 1897.

Second, in some cases subjects in state A advocated policies toward B in violation of their immediate material interest. In 1795–96 Americans in Virginia and elsewhere refused to support a treaty with Britain even though it provided for assumption of their debts by the federal government, because they considered England the greatest enemy of political liberty. For the same reason, in 1845–46 Congressmen representing western U.S. farmers refused to support compromise with England over the Oregon territory even when London lowered tariffs that had kept American grain out of England.

Third are those cases in which subjects in state A disagreed over whether B was a threat, and their disagreement correlates with their judgments of whether B is liberal. The debates between Federalists and Republicans between 1790 and 1812, between Democrats and Whigs in the 1840s, and between Democrats and Republicans in the 1860s over whether Britain should be conciliated or confronted reduce for many to different positions on the question of whether America's political system should imitate Britain's. British, Mexican, and Spanish disagreements over policy toward the United States reduce to analogous debates in those countries.

In all three types of cases, one cannot understand perceptions and strategies, and thus crisis outcomes, without understanding ideology.

THE PLAN OF THE BOOK

I begin in Chapter 2 by discussing liberalism as a worldview. I then explicate my argument of how liberalism gives rise to both a foreign

62. For the notion that ideas may be consequential by being instantiated in institutions, see Goldstein and Keohane, *Ideas and Foreign Policy*, 20–24.

policy ideology and political institutions that translate that ideology into policy. I consider alternative explanations and derive testable hypotheses that could falsify the argument.

In Chapters 3 through 5 I illustrate the validity of the argument via ten historical case studies. In each case, a liberal state, the United States, was in immediate danger of war. Sometimes the war would be with a state its citizens considered a fellow liberal state, sometimes with a state its citizens thought despotic, and sometimes with a state on which opinion was deeply divided. I look at the public debate and official decision making in each case, both in the United States and in the foreign state. In Chapter 6 I look back briefly at each case to test two crucial sets of hypotheses, one having to do with the origins of perceptions, the other with the effects of liberal institutions. In Chapter 7 I apply the argument to current Japanese–South Korean and Indo-Pakistani relations. I close with a discussion of implications for policy makers and scholars.

[2]

Identity, Ideology, and Institutions

*The British Government cannot undertake to declare war, for any pur-
pose, unless it is a purpose of which the electors of this country would approve. If the Government promised to declare war for any object which
did not commend itself to public opinion, the promise would be repudiated, and the Government would be turned out.*

Lord Salisbury, 1901

This chapter explains how liberalism pulls liberal states away from war
with some states and sometimes pushes them toward war with others.
I open by discussing the general tendency of proponents of a given set
of domestic political institutions (particularly elites) to favor foreign
states that have those institutions, and to be suspicious of states having
institutions they would oppose in their own state. I then explain why
liberal states are peculiarly adept at remaining at peace with their own
kind. I pay particular attention to the high value liberalism places on
individual autonomy, the foreign policy ideology to which this attachment gives rise, and how liberal governmental institutions translate
this ideology into policy during crises. I adduce hypotheses that, if my
argument is correct, should be borne out in the case studies in Part II.
Finally I consider alternative hypotheses that could account for the
same phenomena I attribute to liberalism.

FAVORITISM IN FOREIGN POLICY

As Chapters 3–5 will make clear, people strongly tend to favor a foreign state if it has their preferred system of government. A corresponding tendency also exists to discriminate against a foreign state that has
a system of government they would regard as dangerous in their own

state. That is, a fair predictor of someone's attitude toward a foreign country is whether that country matches the person's political vision for his or her own country. Monarchists favor monarchies, republicans favor republics, communists favor communist states, Islamicists favor Islamic states.[1] This favoritism certainly does not explain all of international politics, and similar regimes may at times even become bitter enemies. But the explanation of liberal peace and liberal war begins with this discrimination, for it means that people identify their own (and their state's) interests with the interests of like states, and against those of unlike states.[2] As Michael Doyle writes, "fellow liberals benefit from a presumption of amity; nonliberals suffer from a presumption of enmity."[3]

The tendency to categorize foreign states according to internal characteristics is ubiquitous. Ancient Greeks divided the world into Greek and barbarian; orthodox Islam, into believers and infidels.[4] Even realist writers make such distinctions. E. H. Carr argued for a *Pax Anglosaxonica* over German-Japanese hegemony, evidently believing that cooperation would be easier between Britain and the United States because both held that political legitimacy is based on the consent of the governed.[5] Hans Morgenthau wrote that absolutist states are quicker than constitutional states to go to war because leaders of the former are less hampered by political constraints.[6] In all of these views, cooperation within one's own type of state is easier than with other types of state.

Why this favoritism? Stephen Walt lists four reasons why similar states might ally with one another: defense of their own political principles; trust in one another's inherent goodness; enhanced domestic legitimacy;

1. See Spencer Weart, "Peace among Democratic and Oligarchic Republics," *Journal of Peace Research* 31 (August 1994), 299–316.

2. Margaret G. Hermann and Charles W. Kegley, Jr., have called for an exploration of the perceptual-psychological side of liberal peace and suggest that social identity theory may be especially helpful. Hermann and Kegley, "Rethinking Democracy and International Peace: Perspectives from Political Psychology," *International Studies Quarterly* 39 (December 1995), 511–34. David E. Spiro is skeptical of liberal peace but does argue that liberal states are unusually likely to align with one another because they perceive common interests. Spiro, "The Insignificance of the Liberal Peace," in Michael E. Brown, Sean M. Lynn-Jones, and Steven E. Miller, eds., *Debating the Democratic Peace* (Cambridge: MIT Press, 1996), 231–33.

3. Michael W. Doyle, "Liberalism and World Politics," *American Political Science Review* 80 (December 1986), 1161.

4. See Sohail H. Hashmi, "Islamic Ethics in International Society," in Terry Nardin and David Mapel, eds., *The Constitution of International Society* (Princeton: Princeton University Press, 1997).

5. Edward Hallett Carr, *The Twenty Years' Crisis*, 2d ed. (London: Macmillan, 1946), 235–36.

6. Hans J. Morgenthau, *Politics among Nations*, 3d ed. (New York: Alfred A. Knopf, 1965), 131.

and ideological imperatives (epitomized by communist states).[7] Walt's reasons are suggestive but leave us with important questions. Most important, people and groups exhibit a *general* tendency to favor their own type, be that type racial, ethnic, religious, or something else. Discrimination is not limited to international relations. Although the reasons Walt lists are probably causal in many cases, they themselves may have deeper causes. The foreign policy discrimination that Doyle, Walt, and others identify should be subsumed under the more general phenomenon of favoritism.

The question should thus be broken into two parts. First, why *favoritism*? Why the propensity to identify one's interests with those of some and against those of others? Second, why *this* favoritism? Why use what I shall call *institutional identity*, that is, why identify with states based on their domestic political institutions rather than ethnicity, religion, history, language, degree of modernization, or some other criterion?

In answering these questions we must move from the state level to the levels of individuals and groups within states. The favoritism discussed below is primarily a phenomenon among elites within states. Institutional identity vis-à-vis foreign states is latent among the general population, who know and care little about foreign countries most of the time. Favoritism is alive among a highly motivated liberal elite, whose members are what James Rosenau calls *opinion leaders*: people "who occupy positions which enable them to regularly to transmit, either locally or nationally, opinions about any issue." They may include "government officials, prominent businessmen, civil servants, journalists, scholars, heads of professional associations, and interest groups."[8] In a later section I explain how and when liberal elites activate institutional identity among the general population and thus affect foreign policy. It is important to note here that not all elites in a liberal country hold a strong institutional identity. Many, for example, perceive that their interests depend more on the health of their employer than on particular political institutions. Thus the "liberals" to whom I refer in this chapter are usually only a subset of a country's elites.

Favoritism in general. It is tempting to consider as an adequate explanation for favoritism that it serves actors' interests. Such an explanation, however, begs the question of how actors arrive at a given conception of self-interest.[9] Sociology provides the useful insight that one's

7. Stephen M. Walt, *The Origins of Alliances* (Ithaca: Cornell University Press, 1987), 34–35.

8. James Rosenau, *Public Opinion and Foreign Policy: An Operational Formulation* (New York: Random House, 1961), 35–39.

9. "All the activities and situations constituting an historically given culture affect the formation of material wants." Max Weber, "'Objectivity' in Social Science and Social Policy," in Weber, *The Methodology of the Social Sciences* (Glencoe, Ill.: Free Press, 1949), 66.

conception of self-interest is related to one's identity, and one's identity derives from social interaction.[10] At bottom, social interaction is necessary because identities are formed in a dialectic of negation described well (if abstrusely) by G. W. F. Hegel. For Hegel, determination *is* negation, because one can have no self without other selves with which to compare oneself. A thing does not exist without having a determinate quality—animal, vegetable, or mineral; pure being is really nothingness. Yet a quality can only be determinate by being contrasted with another quality. We cannot know what the property "animal" is without contrasting it to "vegetable" or "mineral." Hegel thus reasoned that a thing is defined by what it is not.[11] The inference for identity formation is that for a person to have a determinate self, he or she must have qualities, and thus must have (or find, or create) an "other" against which to contrast those qualities. *the "other"*

Of course, people identify *with* as well as *against* others, else no human cooperation would occur. In identifying with others, one conceives of one's interests as congruent with theirs. Yet, positive identification is never divorced from its negative counterpart. Comparison and opposition are always present. There can be no "in-group" without an "out-group," no "we" without a "they." A group identity may originate in either of two ways. First, it may be created by one or more innovators or entrepreneurs who formulate the idea that disparate individuals have a common interest. The innovators then persuade the disparate individuals that they should identify with one another and form a group.[12] In the very act of forming, this group creates an opponent against which to define itself. The opponent will not necessarily be other people (mountain climbers may identify with one another against a mountain; a society may declare a common interest in eradicating poverty).[13] In politics, however, the adversary will usually be

10. The point that part of what makes human beings *human* is life with others is made early by Aristotle: "He who is without a city through nature rather than chance is either a mean sort or superior to man; he is 'without clan, without law, without hearth.'" *The Politics* I.2.ix–xi, trans. Carnes Lord (Chicago: University of Chicago Press, 1984), 37. More recently the point is made by Peter L. Berger and Thomas Luckmann: "Man's self-production is always, and of necessity, a social enterprise. . . . *Homo sapiens* is always, and in the same measure, *homo socius*." Berger and Luckmann, *The Social Construction of Reality: A Treatise on the Sociology of Knowledge* (New York: Doubleday, 1966), 51. For a helpful review of social identity theory and an application to international relations, see Jonathan Mercer, "Anarchy and Identity," *International Organization* 49 (Spring 1995), 229–52.

11. The argument is spelled out in Hegel, *The Science of Logic*, pt. 1, chap. 1–2. For an accessible explanation see Charles Taylor, *Hegel* (Cambridge: Cambridge University Press, 1975), chap. 10–11, esp. 232–39, 260–62.

12. I borrow the notion of an "entrepreneur of ideas" from Daniel Philpott, "Two Roles of Ideas," typescript, Princeton University, 1996.

13. Interestingly, however, mountain climbers and societies against poverty will tend to anthropomorphize their opponent, as when Lyndon Johnson declared a "war on poverty."

other people, and that is the second route by which disparate individuals become a group: the common identity may be forced on them by an opposing group. When disparate individuals notice a common opponent that identifies *them* as a group, and this opponent has the ability to hurt their (perceived) interests, they will take on this new identity and envisage their self-interests as congruent.

In the modern world the strongest political identifications are typically with the nation-state. Persons and groups come to identify themselves positively as a nation, a people with a common culture that has or deserves statehood. At the same time they define their nation-state negatively, against the rest of the world, against other nation-states.[14] Jean-Jacques Rousseau recognizes that negative identification inheres in the modern state: "the size of the body politic being purely relative, it is forced to compare itself in order to know itself."[15] Kenneth Boulding, who places enormous emphasis on states' self-images in explaining stable peace, likewise acknowledges this negative type of identification among states.[16] But positive identification also takes place among states. Boulding writes that states identify with one another for reasons of enlightened self-interest. They can get more of what they want if they cooperate with at least some others, and they thus identify their interests with those others' interests.[17] Hegel combines the two forms of identification in critiquing Kant's plan for perpetual peace. Republics may form a league—identify with one another—but that league would be an "individual," necessarily defining itself against its opposite, a supposed league of despotisms with which it would be in perpetual struggle.[18]

Just as individuals identify with one another to form groups, and groups do the same to form nation-states (typically imposed by force), then, nation-states identify with one another to form leagues. They do not thereby necessarily sacrifice their perceived personal, group, or national interests to those of the other nation-states in their league, or the league as a whole. Rather, they conceive of their interests as ultimately congruent with those of the league. There may come a point at which the league's interests clearly conflict with those of their own nation-state, at which time they must make a choice. But what is crucial is that

14. For a good compendium of theories of nationalism, see John Hutchinson and Anthony D. Smith, *Nationalism* (New York: Oxford University Press, 1994), 47–131.

15. Jean-Jacques Rousseau, "The State of War," in *Rousseau on International Relations*, ed. Stanley Hoffmann and David C. Fidler (New York: Oxford University Press, 1991), 38.

16. Kenneth Boulding, *Stable Peace* (Austin: University of Texas Press, 1977), 15–19.

17. Ibid., 19, 47–62.

18. G. W. F. Hegel, *The Philosophy of Right*, trans. T. M. Knox (New York: Oxford University Press, 1967), 295. I take up this argument further in Chapter 7.

they will resist recognizing such conflicts. The next question is, how do persons and groups come to identify their state's interests with and against other states based on common domestic political institutions (republicanism, federalism, laissez-faire, social democracy, etc.)?

When institutional identity is central. A person takes on an institutional identity when he or she perceives it to be more adequate than his or her status quo identity. According to the reasoning above, this will happen either when innovators persuade the person of the adequacy of an institutional identity or when an opposing group identifies the person according to institutional criteria. In either case, one will identify with the institution that is the opposite of the institution perceived to be the greatest threat to one's interests. If one is a slave, then one will identify with the abolition of slavery; if one is a business owner, with free-market capitalism; if one is a religious dissenter, with freedom of religion. A full account of why there have been certain times and places in which institutional identity is so compelling is beyond the scope of this book. Suffice it to say that there have been epochs in history in which loyalty to political systems has trumped loyalty to ethnic, religious, and other groups—when large numbers of elites have believed that their own and their nation's interests are tied up with those of nations with the same institutions. Arguably the last two hundred years of Western history has been such an epoch, and arguably it was the French Revolution that made it so.

The French Revolution began as the Third Estate (or commoners), encouraged by certain aristocrats influenced by Enlightenment thought, began defining their interests in stark opposition to the ancien régime of crown, church, and nobility. By 1791, two years into the revolution, radicals had become so hostile toward the aristocracy that they drove the "reactionaries" among them into exile in Austria and elsewhere. The so-called *émigrés* began to identify their interests not only *against* those of the revolutionaries back in Paris but also *with* the aristocrats and monarchs elsewhere in Europe. The émigrés worked to convince the emperor of Austria that even though he was a Habsburg who had struggled against his own nobles, and France was ruled by Bourbons, they were indeed part of the same group, whose deadly adversaries were the French revolutionaries.

In August of that year the Austrian Emperor announced that the European powers might collectively intervene against the revolution in France. Now more and more French revolutionaries declared that their enemies were monarchy and aristocracy throughout Europe rather than simply in France. In April 1792, as leading revolutionaries declared a crusade to free the common man throughout Europe, the French Assembly declared war on Austria; by the next year Prussia and

[27]

Great Britain were at war with France.[19] Intellectual underpinning for the monarchists was provided by Edmund Burke, who had been arguing in Britain that the French Revolution was an attack on the "European Commonwealth," the very social fabric of Christendom that stretched back to the Middle Ages.[20]

In this story, we see members of the Third Estate identifying with one another against France's aristocrats; the Austrian emperor identifying with the French aristocrats against the revolutionaries; the French revolutionaries identifying against the monarchs and with the commoners throughout Europe; and the European monarchs (and their supporters) identifying with one another against France. What began as a domestic French struggle over political institutions grew into a multistate war, because the struggle within France caused new identities and groups to form all over Europe. Prior to 1789, George III of England would have had little reason to identify his interests very strongly with those of the Leopold II of Austria or Frederick II of Prussia. George was king of England and a Hanover. The French Revolution made him one of Europe's monarchs.

Some realists would interpret this account of Europe in the 1790s as confirming the rationalist tenet that identities derive wholly from material interests and may thus be ignored by analysts. The monarchs banded together to balance against Republican France, on such an interpretation, to protect themselves from a material threat. But that interpretation ignores the socializing role of ideas. The monarchs were certainly self-interested, and their loyalties to one another weak, as seen by the periodic attempts by some to make a separate peace with France. It was the republican ideology of the French revolutionaries, however, that shaped the general configuration of the powers. The revolutionaries were suspicious even of those who wanted to appease them (see Chapter 3). Realism pictures a world where states are extremely sensitive to changes in material power, and perhaps to gestures of friendship and hostility. A state will identify with any country whose help it needs, and against any country with the power and apparent intentions to harm it. In my account, identities are less sensitive to material factors and more sensitive to changes in domestic political institutions.

In any case, institutional identity persisted into nineteenth-century Europe, as the Holy Alliance of Austria, Prussia, and Russia that

19. R. R. Palmer, *The Age of the Democratic Revolution: A Political History of Europe and America, 1760–1800*, vol. 2, *The Struggle* (Princeton: Princeton University Press, 1964), 3–15. Palmer argues that the French declared war on Austria more for domestic political reasons than out of ideology; nonetheless many elites in France, Austria, England, and elsewhere fought to vindicate their conceptions of legitimacy.

20. Jennifer M. Welsh, *Edmund Burke and International Relations: The Commonwealth of Europe and the Crusade against the French Revolution* (New York: St. Martin's, 1995), 93–114.

emerged after the defeat of Napoleon was constituted by opposition to revolution. As I recount in Chapter 4, many American and British liberals defined their countries in opposition to this league (Americans believed the struggle was between republicanism and monarchy). Twentieth-century international history has also been marked by institutional identity. The First World War was for the British, French, and Americans a war of democracy versus autocracy; the Second, democracy versus fascism; the Cold War, democracy versus communism. Western countries would make common cause with nondemocracies when it was useful, but those alignments were much more temporary because they were not based on institutional affinity.

Of central importance to these institutional identities is that they all were based on one or another central institutional criterion. Also crucial is that the institutional criterion is the opposite of that institution thought to pose the biggest threat to an individual liberal's own interests—and thus to the nation's interests as he or she conceives them. People typically see states as black or white rather than shades of gray. A state is either monarchical or republican, slave or free, federal or centralized, democratic or autocratic. In the case of liberals, while this tendency to dichotomize makes for intolerance of illiberal states, it makes for a high degree of toleration of those states that qualify as liberal.

Belligerent liberals. Many readers may doubt the applicability of the negative dialectic described above to liberals and liberal states. The suggestion that liberals can be belligerent, that they can and must in fact define themselves in opposition to and struggle with others, will dismay and perhaps offend many. Liberalism is surely a tolerant ideology, they will protest, one that strives to include rather than exclude. If the French revolutionaries were intolerant, it was because they were illiberal, as seen in the Reign of Terror that began in 1793. As I discuss below, liberalism is indeed tolerant relative to its alternatives and is in fact partly constituted by toleration. But whenever a group forms, liberal or not, it cannot escape the necessities of exclusion and opposition. The views on the wars of the French Revolution of Condorcet, Paine, and Kant, three liberal thinkers par excellence, will make the point clear.[21]

The Marquis de Condorcet was a Physiocrat who had helped lay the philosophical groundwork for the revolution. Condorcet argued that peace would arise from "new institutions and a sentiment of internationalism which would bind nations together. The idea must be spread

---

21. Michael Doyle has recognized this tendency for liberals to be intolerant of their illiberal opponents. See especially Doyle, "The Voice of the People: Political Theorists on the International Implications of Democracy," in Geir Lundestad, ed., *The Fall of Great Powers: Peace, Stability, and Legitimacy* (Oxford University Press, 1994), 284, 293–96.

that no one, except a few generals and ministers, gains anything as a result of even the most successful war." Yet, sitting in the French Assembly in 1792, faced with the possibility of war with Austria, Condorcet voted for war. He declared that Austria was protecting the French émigrés, and that war was preferable to a shameful peace.[22]

Thomas Paine, pamphleteer for the American and French revolutions, wrote that the cause of the world's wretchedness "lies not in any natural defect in the principles of civilisation but in preventing those principles having a universal operation; the consequence of which is, a perpetual system of war and expense that drains the country and defeats the general felicity of which civilisation is capable." For Paine, it was only the continued existence of some illiberal polities that kept war alive.[23] Paine was an active apologist for the France's anti-British policies, arguing that one could not reason with the unreasonable.

Immanuel Kant similarly set down as a necessary condition for perpetual peace that "the constitution of every state shall be republican."[24] Republics were in a state of law with one another and would not fight one another, but they remained in a savage state of nature with despotisms. They could not only expect attacks from despots but could even rightfully attack them with the purpose of making them into republics. Kant referred to "the original right of free states in the state of nature to make war upon one another (for example, in order to bring about a condition closer to that governed by right)." He wrote moreover that a vanquished despotism could "be made to accept a new constitution of a nature that is unlikely to encourage their warlike inclinations,"[25] that is, a republican constitution. Kant did not hesitate to apply his principles to events of his time. A staunch defender of the French Revolution even after the Terror, he wrote a "justification" of the French Directory's war on England, a country he regarded as despotic, in 1798.[26]

22. J. Salwyn Schapiro, *Condorcet and the Rise of Liberalism* (New York: Harcourt, Brace, 1934), 92, 144–47. Interestingly, Condorcet later added a clause in the first constitution of the French Republic that "the French Republic renounced annexation of territory except as a result of a free vote of the inhabitants, and only when such territory was under autocratic rule." I am grateful to Thomas Spragens for alerting me to Condorcet's views.

23. Paine, *The Rights of Man*, quoted in Michael Howard, *War and the Liberal Conscience* (New Brunswick, N.J.: Rutgers University Press), 29.

24. Immanuel Kant, "To Perpetual Peace, a Philosophical Sketch," in *Perpetual Peace and Other Essays*, trans. Ted Humphrey (Indianapolis: Hackett, 1983), 112.

25. Kant, "The Metaphysics of Morals," in *Kant's Political Writings*, trans. H. B. Nisbet, ed. Hans Reiss (New York: Cambridge University Press, 1970), 170, 166. The point is made more recently by Robert Conquest in a book significantly titled *We and They*: "The most useful distinction appears to be that between the 'civic' and the 'despotic' cultures." Conquest, *We and They* (London: Temple Smith, 1980), 12.

26. Kant, "Rechtfertigung des Direktoriums der französische Republik wegen seines angeblich ungereimten Planes, den Kreig mit England zu ihrem Vorteil zu beenden.

The tenacity of institutional identity. Liberal peace and liberal war happen because these institutional identifications are highly durable. They do not collapse at the first sign of a conflict of interest. More precisely, people do not see conflicts of interest with those with whom they identify as readily as do scholarly observers. Rather, people toil mightily to reconcile their perceptions of interests with those of the people with whom they identify. An example explored more fully in Chapter 3 is Americans' attitudes toward the wars of the French Revolution. Americans had strong opinions especially about the Anglo-French war, and in fact tended to identify with either the French or the British. Republicans, the nascent party of Thomas Jefferson and James Madison, saw the French struggle as a continuation of the American struggle against monarchy and privilege. Federalists, the anti-party of Alexander Hamilton, saw the British as fighting civilization's fight against lawless Jacobinism. Each faction clung to its favorite despite evidence that the rulers of its favorite did not identify with the United States. Federalists forgave England its treaty violations and abuses of U.S. commerce, and saw an anti-American plot behind every French move. Republicans forgave the French even for attempting extortion against U.S. diplomats (the XYZ Affair), and were convinced that Britain was trying to overthrow the American Republic.

Political elites generally strive to maintain their prejudices about foreign states out of a need for cognitive consistency. As Robert Jervis writes of all statesmen:

> [Fitting data to preexisting beliefs] means not only that when a statesman has developed a certain image of another country he will maintain that view in the face of large amounts of discrepant information, but also that the general expectations and rules entertained by the statesman about the links between other states' situations and characteristics on the one hand and their foreign policy intentions on the other hand influence the images of others that he will come to hold. Thus Western statesmen will be quicker to see another state as aggressive if a dictator has just come to power in it than if it is a stable democracy.[27]

These "motivated biases"—a product of identity formation—influence how domestic elites interpret the actions of foreign states and thus how their own state reacts.[28]

1798," in *Sämtliche Werke* (1867–1868), 8:644–45; cited in Palmer, *Age of the Democratic Revolution*, 329. Kant did not publish his essay.

27. Robert Jervis, *Perception and Misperception in International Politics* (Princeton: Princeton University Press, 1976), 146. See also Alexander George, *Presidential Decision-making in Foreign Policy: The Effective Use of Information and Advice* (Boulder: Westview, 1980), chap. 3.

28. In psychological terms, liberals commit "attribution errors." They find ways to avoid blaming those they are predisposed to like, and they attribute malicious intent to

But if social identity were the entire story, we would expect to see communist, fascistic, and other types of states forming zones of peace as well. In fact, liberal states—defined, as explained more fully below, as states with freedom of discussion and regular competitive elections of those empowered to declare war—show an especially strong tendency to stay at peace with one another. In the next two sections I argue that the content of liberalism gives liberal favoritism a peculiar durability. First, liberal persons highly value both peace and individual autonomy and believe that the two can ultimately be maximized simultaneously. Liberals believe that it is rational to choose peace as a means to the good life. Believing that all persons are at least capable of this rationality, liberals tend to trust properly informed, uncoerced people to be pacific. These beliefs produce a foreign policy ideology that insists on peaceful relations with rational ("liberal") states and is stubbornly suspicious of irrational states. Second, liberal political institutions allow ideological favoritism to shape foreign policy, especially during war-threatening crises. States lacking liberal institutions may be less internally constrained when making foreign policy.

LIBERALISM AS A SYSTEM OF THOUGHT

Here I do not assume the task of a political philosopher, seeking to enter the centuries-old and still flourishing normative debate over liberalism. Rather, I simply attempt to describe the liberal worldview by briefly tracing its origins and contrasting it to its alternatives. I define liberalism as a system of thought that seeks to uphold individual autonomy (i.e., self-legislation or self-government). Liberalism so defined may involve laissez-faire economics, including the doctrine of free international trade, or it may involve the New Deal and Great Society programs Americans today identify with the word. Whatever the particular strategy chosen to secure individual autonomy, liberals are strongly attached to peace and self-determination rather than violence and coercion. These attachments give rise to the foreign policy ideology and domestic political institutions that give liberal states their peculiar foreign policies.

---

those they are predisposed to dislike. For an application of this concept to foreign policy decision making, see George, *Presidential Decisionmaking*, 58–61. On motivated bias in international relations, see Chaim D. Kaufmann, "Out of the Lab and into the Archives: A Method for Testing Psychological Explanations of Political Decision Making," *International Studies Quarterly* 38 (December 1994), 557–86.

Autonomy and "Ordinary Life"

Liberalism is a set of ideas that refract the world for those holding them. Among the most basic ideas to any worldview are those concerning the nature of the person and, as a corollary, proper human ends.[29] Some liberal theorists argue that because liberalism seeks self-governing individuals, it is neutral on questions of ends—that, in fact, it is constituted by the notion that all persons should be permitted to select their own notions of the good life.[30] Individuals may choose lives of heroism or hedonism, charity or acquisitiveness, so long as they respect others' decisions. No institution or individual has the authority to impose a particular way of life on anyone. The neutrality thesis, however, implies that liberalism makes no normative judgments. In fact, liberalism does make such judgments, condemning, for example, intolerance and coercion. As Charles Taylor argues, any worldview that makes such judgments holds at least implicitly a vision of proper human ends, linked to a "human ontology" or an account of human nature. In judging the rightness of an action or a life one is holding it up to a higher standard embedded in a notion of the good life.[31] In condemning coercion, liberalism strongly values personal autonomy, but the sort of autonomy that respects others' autonomy.

The self-government that respects the self-government of others rules out a coercive or violent life. In theory, liberals can value lives of religious contemplation or self-sacrifice. In practice they have tended to value what Taylor calls the "ordinary life" of "production and the family." Taylor contrasts this modern Western value with the values held by other systems of thought. Many civilizations have seen labor, household management, and even commerce as necessary evils, to be endured or foisted on inferior persons for the sake of higher goods such as heroism or spirituality. But from the seventeenth century onward Westerners have tended to see these everyday activities as

29. See the discussion of ideas as worldviews in Judith Goldstein and Robert O. Keohane, *Ideas and Foreign Policy: Beliefs, Institutions, and Political Change* (Ithaca: Cornell University Press, 1993), 8–9.

30. See for example John Rawls, *A Theory of Justice* (Cambridge: Harvard University Press, 1970); Ronald Dworkin, *A Matter of Principle* (Cambridge: Harvard University Press, 1985), 181–204; John A. Hall, *Liberalism: Politics, Ideology and the Market* (London: Paladin, 1988).

31. Charles Taylor, *Sources of the Self: The Making of the Modern Identity* (Cambridge: Harvard University Press, 1987), 3–24. Taylor calls these judgments "strong evaluation." On the inseparability of basic worldviews from rationality in international politics, see David Halloran Lumsdaine, *Moral Vision in International Politics: The Foreign Aid Regime, 1949–1989* (Princeton: Princeton University Press, 1993), esp. 20–21.

intrinsically worthy.[32] The importance of this modern end is seen when it is contrasted with alternative notions of ends. In Homer's ancient Greece, for example, a "warrior ethic" dominated. There, "what is valued is strength, courage, and the ability to conceive and execute great deeds, and . . . life is aimed at fame and glory, and the immortality one enjoys when one's name lives for ever on men's lips."[33]

History shows that material prosperity is usually advocated by liberals and associated with political liberalization. Thomas Paine, agitator in the American and French revolutions, valued self-government at least in part because it would bring prosperity.[34] Richard Cobden, a leading British nineteenth-century liberal, integrally tied political liberty to commercial prosperity. Today, advocates of liberalism tirelessly proclaim that it will improve the material lot, or "standard of living," of those who live under it. The attachment to material goods derives from the notion held by many liberal thinkers, most prominently John Locke, that personal property is a necessary condition of personal autonomy.[35]

Other liberals de-emphasize material prosperity in favor of other goods—in Kant's case, morality. In any case, whether a liberal person chooses to acquire wealth or to serve God or other people, his or her life must avoid violence and other forms of coercion. For Kant, the purpose of government is to bring about "public right," which is "the limitation of each person's freedom so that it is compatible with the freedom of everyone."[36] The only occasion when coercion may be used is with people who are either irrational or already being coerced by someone else. Such people throw the delicate apparatus of public right

liberalism as non-violence [margin note, handwritten]

32. Taylor, *Sources of the Self*, 13–18, and pt. 3.

33. Ibid., 115–18. As we saw in Chapter 1, this Homeric warrior ethic was still alive in Periclean Athens.

34. David M. Fitzsimons, "Tom Paine's New World Order: Idealistic Internationalism in the Ideology of Early American Foreign Relations," *Diplomatic History* 19 (Fall 1995), 569–82.

35. For an argument that liberalism is fundamentally about protecting individual property as a necessary means to individual autonomy, see C. B. Macpherson, *The Political Theory of Possessive Individualism: Hobbes to Locke* (New York: Oxford University Press, 1962). John Locke, for example, writes, "The great and *chief end* therefore, of Mens uniting into Commonwealths, and putting themselves under Government, *is the Preservation of their Property.*" Property for Locke is one's "Life, Liberty, and Estate." Locke, *Second Treatise of Government*, in *Two Treatises of Government*, ed. Peter Laslett (New York: Cambridge University Press, 1988), chap. 9, para. 124. Thus, ironically, liberalism's commitment to a particular sort of autonomy actually brings a kind of conformity. Those who do not value autonomy may not fit in. Tocqueville spotted such pressure to conform in the United States of the 1830s. See his *Democracy in America*, ed. J. P. Mayer, trans. George Lawrence (New York: Harper and Row, 1969), chap. 7.

36. Kant, "On the Proverb: That May Be True in Theory, But Is of No Practical Use," in *Perpetual Peace*, 72.

out of balance by not understanding or respecting true autonomy. Thus liberals coerce their children because they are not yet fully rational (although even that exception has eroded in liberal societies in recent years). And, more to the point, liberals allow and may even support war against a state that coerces its own people. Force may be used against such a state because it may act in ways that are not compatible with the freedom of other states. *rationalizing liberal force*

Universal Rationality

The Enlightenment thinkers who produced the liberal tradition believed that all men (later, all persons) in society are potentially autonomous and are thus equal in a fundamental and significant sense. When social contract theorists such as Hobbes, Locke, and Kant begin with abstract man in a state of nature, they imply that there is some essential, significant trait that all men share. For Hume, this trait is "the characteristics of the passions"; for Kant, it is "the universal and categorical character of certain rules of reason."[37] Regardless, this anthropology is sharply different from that with which most illiberal views begin.[38] Ancient or medieval views see some persons—kings, heroes, clergy—as better or higher than others—peasants, laborers, laity.

If all persons have the same reason or passions, then they will all recognize the same good life. That is, if properly educated and uncoerced, they will all choose a life that respects the autonomy of all others. Liberalism values voluntarism, but it can do so because it assumes that free choice will yield not chaos or self-destruction but peace. Liberals are thus not (necessarily) altruistic. They are simply, on their own view, smarter than illiberals, who do not understand the value of ordinary life. Kant writes that a republic (liberal state) is possible "even for a people comprised of devils (if only they possess understanding)."[39] Liberals have transformed, rather than transcended, selfishness.

Still, their commitment to voluntarism makes liberals more tolerant of others than illiberals tend to be. As long as those others seem rational and uncoerced, liberals tend to allow them to make their own decisions. This tolerance is a salient difference between liberalism and

37. For Hume, reason discovers the means for reaching the ends set by passion. Yet, as Alasdair MacIntyre writes, "Underlying this view is an implicit, unacknowledged view of the state of the passions in a normal and what we might call, but for Hume's view of reason, reasonable man. . . . The normal passions are those of a complacent heir of the revolution of 1688." Alasdair MacIntyre, *After Virtue*, 2d ed. (Notre Dame: University of Notre Dame Press, 1984), 46–50.

38. Compare Aristotle's view that "man is by nature a political animal," i.e., not an isolated being. Aristotle, *Politics* 1.2.

39. Kant, "To Perpetual Peace," 124.

Marxism, another system of thought that professes to value ordinary life. Marxism rejects voluntarism as the means to its desired ends. Where liberalism attempts to wed reason and consent, Marxism (at least in its Leninist and Maoist manifestations) wants to keep them apart until a ripe old age. Communist doctrine postulated that leaving people alone to make their own private decisions will not enhance the material welfare of all, at least until the final stage of communism. Instead, the dictatorship of the communist party is needed.

This contrast between liberalism and Marxism reveals why Marxist states have had much less success in maintaining peace among themselves. Liberals apply the rule of tolerance not only to persons within their own country but to foreign states as well. Those states that respect their own citizens' autonomy will be trusted to be rational and pacific. Marxist states have been much quicker to declare one another heretical, as happened between the Soviet Union and China in the Khrushchev years, or North Korea and China, or Albania and the rest of the communist world. A similar tendency is seen in the First French Republic, which after losing its liberal character was quick to declare the United States a heterodox republic. Stephen Walt makes a similar point when he notes that the principles of legitimacy held by liberal states (and monarchies), unlike communist or Islamicist states, claim no right to meddle in one another's internal affairs.[40] Liberals are content to trust the reasonableness of those states that recognize their citizens' right to self-rule.

Here a crucial question arises: What is thought to make a state liberal? The question is especially acute because liberals are not tolerant of *every* country. Only those believed to be tolerant are tolerated.

In fact, as noted earlier, liberals disagree across time and space as to what constitutes a liberal state. So the question becomes: *How do liberals themselves identify liberal states?* The answer is that they do so via those states' domestic political institutions. Liberals' commitment to voluntarism causes them to judge states by the procedures through which their governments make decisions. Liberals devote much attention to due process in their own states to make sure that individual self-government is respected. Their belief in universal rationality implies a corollary that the same institutions will work in any country. Thus, the institutions they want in their own state, that make their state pacific, are the institutions all other states ought to have.

---

40. "Because the principles of monarchical or liberal rule grant legitimate authority over one's own domain but imply no such authority over the domain of others, alliances between monarchies or between liberal states are not torn by ideological conflicts." Walt, *Origins of Alliances*, 36–37.

But states have many domestic institutions. How do liberals decide which particular institution constitutes the liberal state? They derive the institutions they want for their own state from these institutions' opposites, that is, through the dialectic of negation. Liberals judge which institutions would most threaten their autonomy if implanted in their own country, and they define the right or rational institutions as the opposite of those wrong institutions. A person who saw limits on suffrage as the biggest threat to his or her autonomy would then favor universal suffrage in his or her own state, favor good relations with states having universal suffrage, and be suspicious of states that limit suffrage.

Liberals, then, have a central institutional criterion for judging foreign states, and that criterion is always defined in terms of its opposite. Liberals who believe in republican government are ipso facto anti-monarchists; federalists are anticentralists; laissez-faire liberals are antistatists. Like any group, liberals always see themselves in opposition to an "out-group." They cannot escape the negative dynamic of identity formation. To know who they are, liberals must define their states against illiberal states. The result is a foreign policy ideology of trust in liberal states and suspicion of illiberal states. This ideology produces the special crisis dynamics that produce liberal peace and liberal war.

LIBERAL FOREIGN POLICY IDEOLOGY

Picture person A, a liberal, walking alone and with no predatory intentions through what he takes to be a dangerous neighborhood. He encounters person B. If B appears benign, A will be disinclined to take precautions. If B appears menacing, A may take precautions, such as moving across the street or even touching a weapon he carries as a deterrent for such occasions. The latter gesture might arouse B's suspicion of A, exacerbating the problem and perhaps spiraling the encounter to violence. The question is: by what criteria does A decide whether B is dangerous? He will probably consider B's ability to hurt him, as evidenced through size and any sign of weapons. But he will probably also try to judge B's *intentions*. First, A will watch B's gestures and motions. But A will also (consciously or not) consult his own prejudices about race, age, class, sex, etc. Perhaps he thinks white persons are safer, or young males with baggy clothes are dangerous. The point is that, rightly or not, he looks to attributes other than sheer ability to hurt, and his prejudices can make violence more or less likely.

Similarly, liberals view foreign states with prejudice. Prima facie, they believe that, irrespective of physical capability, liberal states are

[37]

safe and illiberal states potentially dangerous. The ground of this belief is the premise that states whose governments respect their citizens' autonomy will behave rationally and responsibly, while coercive governments may not. Kant, for example, conceived of a rational state ("republic") as one where the government had to receive the citizenry's permission before going to war; a despotism was a state lacking such a requirement:

> If . . . the consent of the citizenry is required in order to determine whether or not there will be war, it is natural that they consider all its calamities before committing themselves to so risky a game. (Among these are doing the fighting themselves, paying the costs of war from their own resources, having to repair at great sacrifice the war's devastation, and, finally, the ultimate evil that would make peace itself better, never being able—because of new and constant wars—to expunge the burden of debt.) By contrast, under a nonrepublican constitution, where subjects are not citizens, the easiest thing in the world to do is to declare war. Here the ruler is not a fellow citizen, but the nation's owner, and war does not affect his table, his hunt, his places of pleasure, his court festivals, and so on. Thus, he can decide to go to war for the most meaningless of reasons, as if it were a kind of pleasure party, and he can blithely leave its justification (which decency requires) to his diplomatic corps, who are always prepared for such exercises.[41]

For Kant, government via rational institutions ensures that liberal states will be more inclined toward peace. Illiberal states, on the other hand, are believed to be ruled by despots who have little to lose from war and are unconstrained from initiating it. (Note that Kant must define republics in contrast to nonrepublics.)

Liberals, moreover, believe that despots are particularly hostile to liberal states. Despots, according to liberals, correctly believe that liberalism is contagious. When their own subjects observe liberal peoples flourishing through self-government and enjoying freedom and material prosperity, those subjects will demand liberalization in their own country. Liberals' mistrust of illiberals is especially acute when liberals are threatened by illiberals within their own country. Domestic illiberals, they contend, are helped materially and symbolically by foreign illiberal regimes.

The truth of these propositions is not at issue here. Liberals believe them to be true, and they therefore act as though they were true. Illiberalism's galvanizing effect on liberalism is seen not only in Kant's own support of France against England in the 1790s, but also in the American opposition to war with the Spanish Republic in 1873. As one

41. Kant, "To Perpetual Peace," 113.

prominent American then wrote, "A war with the Republic of Spain if successful for us would result I doubt not in ending the Spanish Republic, and would surely endanger our own not less by a victorious result which would come to us I believe, than if we should be defeated. How the Despots and monarchists of the world would rejoice at the spectacle."[42] Fourteen years later Andrew Carnegie, the Scottish-born steel magnate, declared in a treatise about the inevitable victory of republicanism over monarchism, "There is not a crowned head in the world, nor a member of a royal family who could refrain from secretly rejoicing at any disaster which fell a republic, and the joy would be in proportion to the magnitude of the disaster."[43]

The liberal suspicion and hostility toward illiberal states does not mean they will fight all illiberal states in an endless crusade of freedom, however. Keeping their ends in mind, they usually estimate that the costs of liberalizing another state are too high, often because the state is too powerful.[44] For Ronald Reagan, invading Grenada was something to do; bombing the Soviet Union was something to joke about. Liberals, being self-interested and wanting to survive, are still constrained by power politics. Liberalism is a lens, not a kaleidoscope. Still, as the Mexican-American and Spanish-American wars show, liberals can be extremely aggressive toward states they perceive to be illiberal.

Their intolerance of states in the "illiberal" category, however, coexists with a strong tolerance of states in the "liberal" category. The liberal emphasis on voluntarism or consent makes liberals slow to turn against liberal states for doctrinal reasons. As long as a liberal state does not violate their central institutional criterion (whatever it may be) and switch over to "illiberal" institutions, liberals will trust it and not insist that it conform precisely to their notions. Thus during the Cold War Americans tolerated a measure of social democracy in many West European states but actively worked against communist parties in France and Italy.

Previously I mentioned that early Americans disagreed vehemently as to which state, France or Great Britain, was liberal. Federalists classified Britain as liberal, while Republicans saw France as their sister republic. No one seems to have believed that both Britain and France

42. J. R. Doolittle to Charles Sumner, 20 November 1873, *Papers of Charles Sumner* (Alexandria, Va.: Chadwyck-Healey, 1988).

43. Andrew Carnegie, *Triumphant Democracy: Fifty Years' March of the Republic* (New York: Charles Scribner's Sons, 1887), 507.

44. For explanations of liberal peace that see prudence as more central, see Randall L. Schweller, "Domestic Structure and Preventive War: Are Democracies More Pacific?" *World Politics* 44 (January 1992), 235–69; David A. Lake, "Powerful Pacifists: Democratic States and War," *American Political Science Review* 86 (March 1992), 24–37.

[39]

were liberal. Such disagreements among liberals have been fairly common historically.

These empirical disagreements complicate the explanation. They will also rouse the suspicions of skeptical readers. If liberals can have such divergent perceptions of foreign states, then something other than liberalism may be producing those perceptions. But the differences in perceptions are typically produced by variation in the institutional identities liberals form. Liberals may have different visions for their own state—different strategies by which they believe individual autonomy is best secured. Two liberal parties in the same country may disagree as to whether a foreign state is liberal because they disagree as to what makes (or would make) their own state liberal. The American Federalists believed a liberal state would have government by the propertied rather than the poor and uneducated. England was just such a state. The early Republicans believed in more influence for the common man. Revolutionary France epitomized this egalitarian state, at least until the rise of Bonaparte. Each party viewed Britain and France through the prism it used for American politics.

How people sharing a basic worldview can have such divergent visions for their own polity is a puzzle that ultimately involves the dialectic of ideas and interests. Solving that puzzle is beyond the scope of this book. It is enough to note here the scholarly consensus that there have virtually always been different varieties of liberals. Michael Doyle argues that "the liberal tradition has evolved two high roads to individual freedom and social order; one is laissez-faire or 'conservative' liberalism and the other is social welfare, or social democratic, or 'liberal' liberalism."[45] Louis Hartz argues in great depth that from the time of its founding the United States has been a thoroughly liberal nation despite vehement disagreements over what sorts of institutions liberalism implies.[46] Federalists and Republicans, Democrats and Whigs, Progressives and conservatives, Roosevelt and Reagan, have all operated from Lockean premises. As Part II shows, other countries have had competing conceptions of liberalism as well. Britain had its Whig-Liberals and its Radicals; Mexico its moderate and radical liberals; Spain its constitutional and republican liberals; Chile its Presidentialists and Congressionalists.

The influence of domestic vision on foreign policy thinking may be seen in the attitudes of the American Left and Right during the Cold War. The Left generally pushed for more governmental intervention in

45. Doyle, "Kant, Liberal Legacies, and Foreign Affairs," pt. 1, *Philosophy and Public Affairs* 12 (Summer 1983), 207.

46. Louis Hartz, *The Liberal Tradition in America* (New York: Harcourt Brace Jovanovich, 1955).

the economy to bring about more equality of wealth. It thus generally perceived a relatively benign Soviet Union, Cuba, and other countries where the state was responsible for effecting economic equality, and took a harsh view of right-wing states such as South Korea and El Salvador. The Right generally pushed for private enterprise and law and order. It thus was fervently anticommunist and more sympathetic toward authoritarian states. Hartz tells us that both Left and Right in America are liberal, but clearly they have envisaged different Americas and thus perceived foreign states differently. Objectively it may appear that both Left and Right misperceived the true nature of certain states, but according to the dialectic of negation they had good reasons for seeing the world as they did.

In summary, liberalism's supreme commitment to individual autonomy makes liberals especially tolerant and prone to continue identifying with states they have previously regarded as liberal. It does not make them any more tolerant of states previously regarded as illiberal. Liberals may disagree as to which states are liberal, but those disagreements are produced by their competing institutional visions for their own state.

In the next section I shift from discussing subjective notions of liberal institutions to an "objective" notion.[47] Despite the enormous variation in how liberals across time and space have identified liberal states, we can attempt an institutional definition of our own that has some objective validity. The task is to find those institutions that instantiate the liberal doctrines of individualism and consent. Such institutions are those that constrain political leaders from going to war except when the autonomy of their citizens would most likely be greater than if the state were to remain at peace.

LIBERAL GOVERNMENTAL INSTITUTIONS

In the Great Britain of the 1790s, as we shall see in Chapter 3, many liberals or "Radicals" admired the United States and wanted their government to pursue a conciliatory policy toward it. Yet the British government was able to punish the United States with an unequal treaty because the government had a great deal of control over information and was responsible to neither Parliament nor the electorate. In later cases, when elections were fairer and information flowed more freely, the British government was more institutionally constrained by its pro-American constituents. Over the course of the nineteenth century,

---

47. By "objective," I do not mean that my definition of a liberal state is eternally valid. Rather, I mean that it is mine as analyst rather than that of the subjects of this study.

liberal ideas influenced the British to widen the electorate and grant it more control over foreign policy.

Over time, then, the British people gained more self-government, and thus a more liberal polity. At bottom what gave them these things were two institutions: freedom of discussion and regular competitive elections. Liberalism insists that these two institutions are needed to maximize the probability that rationality will prevail in foreign policy. As John Stuart Mill writes, "Since the general or prevailing opinion on any subject is rarely or never the whole truth, it is only by the collision of adverse opinions that the remainder of the truth has any chance of being supplied."[48] Any given person will probably not arrive at the right policy alone, so free and open deliberation is necessary. Moreover, to ensure that they are responsive to public debate, leaders must be accountable to the people. Liberalism weds reason and consent by means of free discussion and regular elections.

It is important to note that a liberal state need not turn over governmental decisions directly to the people. Historically, in fact, most liberal thinkers have considered direct democracy an invitation to irrationality. A duly elected representative is to decide questions based on what he or she believes constituents would wish if they knew all the facts and were perfectly reasonable. "If *only* it is *possible* that a people could agree to [a law]," Kant writes, "it is a duty to regard that law as just, even if the people [is] presently in such a position or disposition of mind that if asked it would probably withhold its consent."[49]

How do we as observers determine if a state has these two liberal institutions and is thus "objectively" liberal? Gauging whether elections are regular and competitive is in principle relatively easy. Gauging whether discussion is free is less so. We shall look for constitutional rights that protect citizens from persecution for their opinions. Such rights include freedoms of speech, the press, assembly, and religion, as well as equality before the law, no arrest without formal charges (habeas corpus), the right to a fair trial, prohibition of unreasonable search and seizure, and the right to petition the state for redress of grievances. Our measures of a state's liberalism are stylized; for reasons already discussed, liberals themselves will usually use different criteria such as republican government, federalism, or absence of slavery.

48. John Stuart Mill, *On Liberty,* in Mill, *Utilitarianism and Other Writings,* ed. Mary Warnock (New York: New American Library, 1974), 181. On the importance of free discussion to liberal peace, see Stephen Van Evera, "Primed for Peace: Europe after the Cold War," *International Security* 15 (Winter 1990/91), 27.

49. Kant, "Theory and Practice," in *Perpetual Peace,* 78–79. Significantly, Kant here gives a war tax as an example of a right policy that might not be supported by a majority of the people.

The Role of Liberal Institutions

Some may ask at this point why liberal institutions are needed for liberal peace and war if a populace comprises liberal citizens. I discussed in Chapter 1 how the liberal peace literature typically posits two competing causes, "norms" and "structures," and tests them against each other. Those arguing for a "normative" liberal peace downplay any role for domestic structure.

Institutions matter for three reasons.[50] First, liberals may disagree among themselves as to the liberal status of a given foreign state. In that case, they will disagree as to whether to accommodate or confront that state. To understand the outcome in such a case, we must study the processes by which one liberal faction triumphs over another. Second, in some cases a state with liberal institutions may elect leaders who are not liberal. Such leaders would have to be domestically constrained to pursue liberal foreign policy. Third, liberal states contain elites for whom institutional identity is trumped by other identities. These include economic and bureaucratic interests who will push for foreign policies irrespective of the domestic institutions of foreign countries. Under any of these three conditions, in fact, two objectively liberal states may fall into a war-threatening crisis. The leaders of one or both may not recognize the other state as liberal, or may not care, or may be influenced by actors who do not care.

Liberal institutions matter because they make it likely that during crises, robust deliberation will take place and thus that foreign policy will be liberal. Institutions work much best when the public's attention is engaged, for then liberal elites are most active and the leaders are more immediately accountable to electors. The public pays little attention to foreign affairs except during crises, when war is seriously considered by at least one side.[51] Thus we must briefly examine the differences between everyday and crisis foreign policy.

Everyday Foreign Policy Making

Quotidian relations with foreign states are typically handled by the executive branch, especially its bureaucratic side. Average citizens

50. See also Joe D. Hagan, "Domestic Political Systems and War Proneness," *Mershon International Studies Review* 38 (1994), 183–207. Hagan calls for a synthesis of the literatures on liberal peace and domestic constraints on foreign policy.

51. My definition of crisis is different from the two that have dominated the foreign policy literature. Those two are "a significant change in the quantity, quality, or intensity of interactions among nations" and "a situation characterized by *surprise*, a *high threat* to important values, and *short decision time*." Ole R. Holsti, "Theories of Crisis Decision Making," in Paul Gordon Lauren, ed., *Diplomacy: New Approaches in History, Theory, and Policy* (New York: Free Press, 1979), 101. My definition is a circumscribed version of the second.

allow this for what seem to them good reasons. Ordinary interactions with foreign states do not perceptibly affect their welfare, and keeping up with these interactions would cost them time. The rational citizen calculates that the expected payoff from following foreign affairs is not worth the time investment.[52] Instead, he or she delegates the authority to representatives. Foreign policy is then by default the province of governmental and special interest elites. In some cases the chief executive or his chief diplomats will not truly be liberals.[53] In some, liberal elites will differ on which states are liberal and must compete with others for influence. In all cases they must compete against economic and bureaucratic interests who push for foreign policies—for example, favoritism toward states that benefit a particular economic sector—that may contradict the policies liberals want.[54] In E. E. Schattschneider's terms, the *scope* of political conflict is limited.[55] In this way the liberal state may fall into a crisis with a state that its liberal elites (or some of them) regard as liberal.

Crisis Foreign Policy

During any war-threatening crisis, however, it becomes in each citizen's interests to pay attention. War has high costs, blood and treasure, and these costs are felt throughout society. Taxes may rise, debt may be incurred, lives may be lost.[56] If the adversary is powerful enough, the nation's future sovereignty may be at stake. The expected benefits of following foreign affairs become greater than the expected costs. The scope of the debate becomes much wider, and foreign policy making is quickly transformed from a relatively closed process to an open one. A debate ensues at several levels of society, as the executive, legislature, media, business leaders, intellectuals, clergy, and others discuss grounds for and against war. All wage a fierce battle to win over public opinion. Knowing that the potential costs to each citizen are so high, policy makers who

52. This reasoning follows that of Anthony Downs, *An Economic Theory of Democracy* (New York: Harper and Row, 1957), 207–76.

53. Partially or highly liberal states governed by illiberal leaders arguably include Britain under Pitt, Perceval, Peel, and Salisbury, and Spain under Canovás (see Chapters 3, 4, and 5).

54. For a theory of how special interests can "hijack" foreign policy, see Jack Snyder, *Myths of Empire: Domestic Politics and International Ambition* (Ithaca: Cornell University Press, 1992), 31–55.

55. E. E. Schattschneider, *The Semisovereign People: A Realist's View of Democracy in America* (Hinsdale, Ill.: Dryden, 1975), chap. 1.

56. David P. Forsythe shows that the United States has not been domestically constrained from covert action against elected governments. He argues that this is in part because when few American lives are apt to be lost, a president can bypass representative decision mechanisms. Forsythe, "Democracy, War, and Covert Action," *Journal of Peace Research* 29 (November 1992), 385–95.

want war realize they must mobilize public opinion. If they do not, the public may not fight the war wholeheartedly; and at the next election they may oust those officials who led them into a bad war.[57]

At this point, however, a realist theory of foreign policy says that if *Realpolitik* requires war, a smart statesman will jettison his own liberal views and be able to persuade his country to do the same. Since liberal publics generally are not convinced by appeals to balance-of-power politics, the statesman will be forced to resort to rhetoric. He might demonize the adversary with atrocity stories or otherwise portray the adversary as illiberal, remind the public of the nation's alliance and other international commitments, or conjure up stirring narratives of the nation's history and destiny. If the public perception of the adversary up to this time has been of a fellow liberal state, realism says, the clever statesman can convince the public that the adversary is no longer liberal. The public, wanting to be patriotic, gives the statesman the benefit of the doubt. In the United States, this is called the "rally round the flag" effect.[58] The president, general thinking goes, deserves public support in this crucial time.

Scholars have disagreed over how manipulable public opinion is in liberal states. One school has held that government can use a number of means, including control of information, to mobilize consent for any foreign policy. Another school has held that governments are constrained by various institutions, particularly in liberal democracies.[59] I argue that the second school is correct. Liberal elites who believe the foreign state to be liberal will make it very difficult for the government to persuade the public to go to war. If before the crisis liberals perceived

57. Kurt Taylor Gaubatz has demonstrated that democracies are less likely to become involved in wars during periods leading up to elections. See Gaubatz, "Election Cycles and War," *Journal of Conflict Resolution* 35 (June 1991), 212–44. Miroslav Nincic and Barbara Hinckley have shown that foreign policy plays a role in the American public's evaluation of presidential candidates. See Nincic and Hinckley, "Foreign Policy and the Evaluation of Presidential Candidates," ibid., 333–55.

58. See for example John E. Mueller, "Presidential Popularity from Truman to Johnson," *American Political Science Review* 64 (1970), 18–34; Charles W. Ostrom and Brian Job, "The President and the Political Use of Force," *American Political Science Review* 80 (1986), 541–66; Patrick James and John R. Oneal, "The Influence of Domestic and International Politics on the President's Use of Force," *Journal of Conflict Resolution* 35 (1991), 307–32. Studies finding a weak rallying effect include Brad Lian and John R. Oneal, "Presidents, the Use of Military Force, and Public Opinion," *Journal of Conflict Resolution* 37 (1993), 277–300; and John R. Oneal and Anna Lillian Bryan, "The Rally 'Round the Flag Effect in U.S. Foreign Policy Crises, 1950–1985," paper presented at the annual meeting of the American Political Science Association, Washington, D.C., September 1993.

59. For a literature review on this question, see Bruce Russett and Thomas W. Graham, "Public Opinion and National Security Policy: Relationships and Impacts," in Manus Midlarsky, ed., *Handbook of War Studies* (Boston: Unwin Hyman, 1989), 239–57; see also Michael Leigh, *Mobilizing Consent: Public Opinion and American Foreign Policy, 1937–1947* (Westport, Conn.: Greenwood, 1976), x–xvi.

the foreign state to be liberal, their government will face a domestic constraint against war as long as the foreign state keeps the same institutions. Statesmen will find it difficult to convince the public that war is in the national interest if that war is against a nation that liberal elites already consider liberal. Conversely, if liberal elites believe the state to be illiberal, their government will face domestic pressure to be hostile to that state.

A government's leverage will be limited because of free discussion and elections. The government of an objectively liberal state may exercise some dominance over public perceptions by controlling the flow of certain types of information to the news media. Yet, by its own laws it cannot control the expression of contrary opinions, withdraw information the public previously had about the other state, or prevent its citizens from receiving information from governments, media, and citizens of other states. The government of an objectively liberal state cannot wholly manipulate its public because it does not have a monopoly over the dissemination and discussion of information. The government's competition in the marketplace of ideas is the liberal elite. These are the opinion leaders who identify most strongly with those foreign states that have the domestic institutions they want for their own state and against those states that have "opposing" institutions. Liberals in the news media make their opposition to or support for war clear in the newspapers, magazines, and airwaves. Liberal academicians and clergy deliver pacific or belligerent addresses.[60] Liberal legislators make antiwar or prowar speeches.

Liberals have a good chance to win the minds of enough legislators and citizens because large sections of the general public share their institutional identity. They see themselves, if only latently, as people who value personal autonomy and the institutions that go with it. When war is at issue, they agree that the national interest is served by good relations with fellow liberal states, and perhaps by confrontation of illiberal states. In some cases, knowing of the power of liberal agitation in advance, a statesman will not even try to argue for war. In 1798 President John Adams, considering Britain to be a more liberal state than France, seriously contemplated war with the latter over a series

---

60. Deliberation, led by a liberal elite, is essential to Kant's account of liberal peace. A "secret article for perpetual peace" is that legislators consult philosophers on war questions. So as not to be humiliated by appearing "to seek advice from *subjects*," legislators receive this counsel through public comment by the philosophers, allowed by law. Philosophers, uncorrupted by power, are most likely to give statesmen rational advice. "That kings or sovereign peoples . . . should not allow the class of philosophers to disappear or to be silent, but should permit them to speak publicly is indispensable to the enlightenment of their affairs." Kant, "To Perpetual Peace," 125–26.

of French abuses. But knowing that the Republican opposition would never agree to hostilities with a nation they regarded as their sister republic, Adams never delivered his war message (see Chapter 3).[61]

Should the government be tempted even then to risk an unpopular war, it will be given pause by the promise of an eventual election. Liberal states have such elections in legally prescribed intervals, and a seriously unpopular war could result in the loss of office. Most elected officials want above all else that they and their party will continue in office. Defying the popular will, they calculate, is not worth the risk.[62] Thus, as Schattschneider argues, widening the scope of domestic political conflict—"socializing" it—can alter the policy outcomes.[63]

Recent research suggests a dialectic among elites, the public, and government in policy making similar to the one I describe. A number of studies indicate that opinion changes precede and cause policy changes rather than vice versa.[64] Moreover, a recent work finds that in the 1970s and 1980s the greatest influences on aggregate shifts in U.S. public opinion were television news commentators and experts. For example, pundits' statements on crises in Vietnam in 1969 and the Middle East in 1974–75 and 1977–78 evidently swayed public opinion.[65] Together, these findings suggest that at least in the United States, an opinion elite at times shapes public positions on issues, thus constraining foreign policy.

Strategic Interaction

The dynamics between the two states during a crisis will always be somewhat unpredictable, but the forces I have described will lead to

61. Experimental evidence that war decision makers have political incentives to follow liberal policy is presented in Nehemia Geva, Karl R. DeRouen, and Alex Mintz, "The Political Incentive Explanation of 'Democratic Peace': Evidence from Experimental Research," *International Interactions* 18, no. 3 (1993), 215–29. For a systematic treatment of political constraints on foreign policy decisions, see Barbara Farnham, "Satisfying the Acceptability Constraint: A Political Approach to Decision-Making," paper presented at the annual meeting of the American Political Science Association, Washington, D.C., September 1993.

62. Works that have used the assumption that elected officials value re-election above all else include Downs, *Economic Theory*, and David R. Mayhew, *Congress: The Electoral Connection* (New Haven: Yale University Press, 1974).

63. Schattschneider, *Semisovereign People.*

64. For a summary, see Lawrence R. Jacobs and Robert Y. Shapiro, "Studying Substantive Democracy," *PS* 27 (March 1994), 9–10.

65. Popular presidents had strong effects, while unpopular ones had little effect. Interestingly, special interest groups usually caused public opinion to move in a *contrary* direction. Benjamin I. Page, Robert Y. Shapiro, and Glenn R. Dempsey, "What Moves Public Opinion," *American Political Science Review* 81 (March 1987), 23–43.

certain regularities.[66] When state A makes a gesture toward state B (recalls its diplomats, sends a naval squadron, imposes economic sanctions, delivers an ultimatum, etc.), then if state B is liberal, B's response to A will be shaped by liberalism—both the ideology held by B's liberals and the institutions in B which translate the ideology into a policy response. Specifically, if liberal elites in B regard A as a fellow liberal state, they will agitate for accommodation; if these elites in B regard A as an illiberal state, they will agitate for confrontation; if liberals are divided over the status of A, each group will agitate for its preferred response. Since B is objectively liberal, B's government will have to tailor its response to the wishes of B's liberal elites. If B's elites are divided—as often happens—then B's government will lean toward accommodation particularly if the war is expected to be arduous, since strong public support is needed for a sustained war.[67]

How will state A respond to B's responding gesture? If A is illiberal—not responsible to an electorate—then my argument has nothing to say. If A is liberal, however, its response will be shaped by the same forces as those that shape B. If A's liberal elite perceives B to be liberal, then they will agitate for an accommodating response, *regardless of the character of B's gesture*. If A's liberal elite perceives B to be illiberal, they will push for confrontation. A divided elite will likely lead to a response more accommodating than confrontational.

Via this process of action, interpretation, and reaction, states resolve their crises either peacefully or not. Here is where liberalism inclines states that practice it away from war with one another: the more objectively liberal are two states, the more likely they will be to make accommodating gestures toward one another during a crisis.[68] They will certainly do so if liberal elites in both perceive the other to be liberal. They will probably do so even if some liberal elites in one or both perceive the other as illiberal. When they will not do so is when the liberal elites in one or both predominantly perceive the other as illiberal. In such cases, liberal institutions may make the crisis especially dangerous by forcing a government to go to war.[69]

66. The approach in this section has much in common with the interaction model used by Ole R. Holsti, Robert C. North, and Richard A. Brody to analyze the July 1914 crisis. See J. David Singer, ed., *Quantitative International Politics* (New York: Free Press, 1968), 132–58.

67. For a discussion of mechanisms working at cross purposes and yielding a weak aggregate outcome, see Jon Elster, *Political Psychology* (Cambridge: Cambridge University Press, 1993), 2–7.

68. For a similar conclusion derived differently, see William J. Dixon, "Democracy and the Peaceful Settlement of International Conflict," *American Political Science Review* 88 (March 1994), 14–32.

69. Partial exceptions to the liberal peace thesis, including the War of 1812 and the Spanish-American War, are cases of this type.

To sum up the argument thus far: (1) Liberals believe that their nation's interests depend on its having liberal institutions, which are necessarily defined against those institutions that liberals believe are the greatest threat to their own liberty. (2) The belief that rational, uncoerced people will choose peace inclines liberals to want good relations with foreign states having institutions they regard as liberal; they are suspicious of states having illiberal (coercive) institutions. (3) If their state is objectively liberal—has the institutions of free discussion and regular competitive elections—then during a war-threatening crisis, these beliefs will affect its policy toward the other state. (4) Interstate actions and reactions in a crisis, and thus the outcome of the crisis, will be shaped by the degree to which the involved states' institutions are liberal and by the perceptions that liberals in each state have of the other as liberal or not.

Many readers may be skeptical of this argument, in particular on two points. First, some readers will reasonably suspect that liberals' perceptions of whether a foreign state is liberal will be epiphenomenal, driven by something other than liberal ideology. It may be that liberals will want compromise or war for other reasons, and then they will categorize states as liberal or illiberal in order to make otherwise distasteful policies easier to swallow. Such a process seems to have happened in the United States during the Second World War, when America joined the Soviet Union in fighting Germany and the murderous communist Joseph Stalin suddenly became "Uncle Joe." The liberal and illiberal labels may simply be psychic devices trotted out to rescue cognitive consistency. Second, some readers will reasonably question whether these perceptions, even if produced by liberal ideology, truly affect foreign policy. Even in a liberal state, a prudent government will be able to manipulate or ignore these perceptions and pursue whatever policy it believes to be in the national interest.

Most such skeptics will be informed by a realist theory of international politics. Realism is, at least in the United States, the leading school of thought in international security. The essence of realism is a matter of some controversy, but in general realists hold that material power, not ideas or institutions, is what ultimately decides the quality of relations among nations. States seeking survival in an anarchic world give first attention to threats to their own survival and autonomy. This means they must respond to imbalances in material power, either by balancing against or "bandwagoning" with states or groups that have the power to hurt them. The international system, then, socializes states into a particular type of rationality called *Realpolitik*. If states are "irrational," neglecting to give power its due, they will bring on disaster; so most states are rational.

[49]

Especially since the late 1970s, realist scholars have tended to ignore domestic politics and foreign policy processes, concentrating instead on the effects of the international system on state behavior. Neorealism treats states as black boxes or, in Arnold Wolfers's words, billiard balls, pulled and pushed from the outside.[70] Thus, with a significant exception noted below, most realists of late have little to say that directly contradicts my hypotheses. Rather, realism (at least the late twentieth-century variety) is simply suspicious of any explanation that gives ideas and institutions independent causal effect. Ideas and perceptions are derivative and thus melt away as material conditions change. Still, realist writers have made statements implying that liberal ideas will have much less force in international security than what I have argued.

To strengthen my case I shall now compare my institutional identity theory with two specific realist challengers and, after that, contrast my theory of foreign policy processes to a more general realist challenge.

How Do Liberals Identify Liberal States?

I argue that variations in perceptions of foreign states are produced by variations in institutions. Suppose that liberals in state A regard state B as illiberal. They will reclassify B as liberal under either of two conditions: (1) state B's institutions change to match the a priori criteria of the liberals in state A; or (2) state A's liberals change their criteria—i.e., the institutions they want for their own state—such that B meets the new criteria. Conversely, liberals in state A who regard state B as liberal will reclassify B as illiberal if (3) B switches to institutions that A's liberals regard as illiberal or (4) A's liberals change the institutions they want for A such that they match B's institutions. Thus I argue that perceptions of a foreign state are insensitive to the changes to which realists and economic determinists would look. If A and B are in a military or economic confrontation, liberals in A will maintain their prior views of B. The causal chain producing liberals' perceptions is then:

vision for own state → favored domestic → foreign states judged
institutions via domestic institutions

---

70. Arnold Wolfers, *Discord and Collaboration: Essays on International Politics* (Baltimore: Johns Hopkins University Press, 1962), 19–20. Kenneth Waltz asserts that the billiard ball approach is the only that can truly be called a "theory of international politics"; all else falls under a theory of foreign policy. That assertion, of course, begs the question of whether we can understand all we want to about international politics—viz., more than the basic tendency of states to balance against one another's power—without considering foreign policy.

Alternative 1: Walt's Balance-of-Threat Theory

I argue that when liberals admire the internal regime of a state, they perceive that state to be benign; and when they detest its internal regime, they consider the state malign. What, precisely, would a realist's objection to this argument be? Probably the outstanding example of a realist explanation of threat perception is given in Stephen M. Walt's *The Origins of Alliances*.[71] Walt argues that states ally with one another in response to threats to their security. One state will judge the seriousness of another state's threat based on that state's aggregate power, geographic proximity, offensive capability, and aggressiveness of intentions. Walt's balance-of-threat theory is a modification of much of traditional balance-of-power theory, in that it includes a state's perception of its adversaries' intentions.[72] Walt claims his theory is superior to balance-of-power theory in that it subsumes that theory and explains more facts without losing parsimony.[73]

Walt also finds his theory superior to an idealist alternative positing that states with similar domestic ideologies are likely to ally with one another. Ideology possibly had a weak effect on alliance patterns in the Middle East between 1955 and 1979, he writes, but in the end "ideology may be more of a rationalization than a cause."[74] That is, external threats drive states to ally in particular ways, and states then invoke ideology to justify those alliances. Walt interprets the effects of ideology as weak, however, in part by invoking a "self-fulfilling prophecy" hypothesis. If state A believes that ideology breeds solidarity, it will be suspicious that states B and C holding a rival ideology are ipso facto hostile to it; A will then become hostile toward B and C, thus signaling

---

71. In fairness, Walt does allow for the possibility that liberal states are distinctive and may even have peculiarly pacific relations with one another because of liberal ideology (see note 40 above).

72. Of course, realism is by no means limited to Walt's theory. For example, traditional realists often emphasize that states respond to opportunities as well as threats (for a current exploration of opportunistic realism, see Fareed Zakaria, *The Rise of a Great Power* [Princeton: Princeton University Press, forthcoming]. I do not explicitly test this alternative version of realism, in part because identifying opportunities objectively is problematic. It will become clear from the case studies, however—particularly U.S. behavior in the Oregon and Mexican crises of 1845–46 and British behavior in the U.S. Civil War—that ideology affects perceptions of expansion opportunities just as it does perceptions of threat.

73. Walt, *Origins of Alliances*, 21–26, 263–65. Walt's move does in fact sacrifice parsimony, because he adds the independent variables of propinquity and intentions to that of power. He also abandons Waltzian neorealism by introducing the minds of subjects into his theory. A state's intentions are on Waltz's terms a "second-image" variable, arising from the level of the state rather than of the international system. See Kenneth Waltz, *Man, the State, and War* (New York: Columbia University Press, 1959). In my view a compelling explanation of alliance formation is worth a loss of parsimony.

74. Walt, *Origins of Alliances*, 214.

those states that it is a threat to them, causing them to become hostile in return and fulfilling A's prophecy. The question then becomes, when B and C become hostile toward A, are they driven by A's hostile actions or by their own ex ante ideological hostility toward A?

Walt concedes that both forces may be at work, as when American hostility toward the new leftist government of Syria in the middle 1950s coincided with Syria's moving closer to the Soviet Union and Egypt.[75] His argument is that the power of ideology is exaggerated in such cases, that pure "threat balancing" is going on as well. The rub is that Walt separates ideology from threat assessment, while I consider it integral to such assessment. I argue that states (or actors within states) view other states' actions through ideological prisms; in particular I argue that liberals are biased to interpret as friendly the actions of states they consider liberal, and unfriendly the actions of those they consider illiberal. For Walt, one state's gestures toward another are "brute data," self-evidently either hostile or friendly.[76] States radically update their assessments of each other's intentions with every interaction.

Since Walt explicitly detaches ideology from threat assessment, his balance-of-threat theory supplies a clear alternative to my hypothesis on perceptions. Walt's theory implies that the labels liberals give to foreign countries are consequences rather than causes of state behavior. Liberal perceptions are epiphenomena, caused by imbalances of threat. The causal chain is as follows:

threat assessment $\rightarrow$ benign states liberal,
(power, propinquity,   threatening states illiberal
intentions)

Alternative 2: Snyder's Domestic Politics Theory

Another argument that liberal perceptions are epiphenomenal is suggested in Jack Snyder's theory of imperial overexpansion.[77] Snyder's study, like this one, looks to domestic politics rather than international pressures to account for foreign policy. Like this book, it treats ideas as a causal variable: "Counterproductive aggressive policies are caused most directly by the idea that the state's security can be safe-

---

75. Ibid., 184–85.

76. At one point Walt does recognize the "close relationship between ideological factors and security considerations" and acknowledges that "the distinction between these hypotheses may not be as sharp as the realist perspective suggests" (ibid., 40). I borrow the term "brute data" from Charles Taylor, who uses it to mean data that empirical scientists claim are beyond interpretation. Taylor, "Interpretation and the Sciences of Man," in *Philosophy and the Human Sciences* (Cambridge: Cambridge University Press, 1985), 18–19.

77. Snyder, *Myths of Empire*. Snyder labels his theory realist (64), but it is obviously different enough from Walt's theory to warrant separate treatment.

guarded only through expansion."[78] But unlike this book, Snyder's treats such ideas as rationalizations, "myths of empire," created and propagated by coalitions of actors with material interests in territorial expansion, military growth, or international competition. The more fundamental cause, then, is material interest.

The powerful thesis that ideology is a mask for material interest is stated most famously by Karl Marx, who held that material conditions were the fundamental force in human history: "The class which is the ruling *material* force in society, is at the same time its ruling *intellectual* force."[79] Early theorists of the "new imperialism" of late-nineteenth-century Europe, such as J. A. Hobson and V. I. Lenin, attributed the scramble for Africa in the 1880s to capitalists' needs to invest abroad.[80] Like these writers, Snyder asks *cui bono?* and finds that the material beneficiaries of imperialism are able to manipulate the state into territorial expansion. The benefits of imperialism tend to be more concentrated than the costs, and so beneficiaries—industries wanting markets, bondholders, armies, navies, colonial bureaucrats, and others—are easier to organize than the taxpayers who lose from expansion. Beneficiaries also tend to have greater access to information about expansion and ties to the state than taxpayers.[81]

Snyder is most interested in *overexpansion*, however, which he defines as expansion leading either to encirclement by a coalition of hostile powers or to a point at which costs exceed benefits.[82] The state has no interest in such counterproductive imperialism, yet it sometimes occurs. Snyder writes that this could be because elites begin to believe their own imperial propaganda (ideological "blowback") or because elites believe overexpansion will sustain them in positions they are afraid of losing.[83] The dominant mechanism behind overexpansion, however, is "logrolling," or vote trading, among parochial interests. Groups that benefit in various ways from expansion form cartels in which they compromise to arrive at an expansionist policy that actually hurts the state as a whole. Logrolling works best in "cartelized" polities, those dominated by a number of interest groups. It tends to work worst in democratic polities, where parochial interests have more

78. Ibid., 1.

79. Karl Marx, *The German Ideology*, in Robert C. Tucker, ed., *The Marx–Engels Reader* (New York: W. W. Norton, 1972), 136–37.

80. See J. A. Hobson, *Imperialism: A Study* (1902), and V. I. Lenin, *Imperialism: The Highest Stage of Capitalism* (1916), reprinted in Harrison M. Wright, ed., *The "New Imperialism": Analysis of Late Nineteenth-Century Expansion*, 2d ed. (Lexington, Mass.: D. C. Heath, 1976), 5–58.

81. Snyder, *Myths of Empire*, 31–39.

82. Ibid., 6.

83. Ibid., 39–43.

trouble monopolizing information and controlling state policy. Its effects are unpredictable in "unitary" polities, those controlled by one party or individual, because the unitary leadership may or may not benefit from expansion.[84]

Snyder's argument about the difficulty parochial interests have in "hijacking" foreign policy in democracies is similar to this book's argument about the effects of liberal institutions on foreign policy. Yet we argue for different mechanisms.[85] For Snyder, self-interest is a "brute datum," just as threat is for Walt—a fact self-evident to both subjects and analysts independent of any interpretation. A manufacturer, merchant, or banker wants to maximize profits; a bureaucrat, power. There is little or no room for more ideologically shaped notions of self-interest such as that for which I argue. That an actor might see his or her interests as best served by living under a given set of institutions, and might formulate a foreign policy ideology based on that vision, is not entertained. Snyder's actors are strategic, but their strategies do not include political institutions. Thus, if we observe actors justifying accommodation of a foreign state by claiming that the state is liberal, it must be the sign of a ruse: either they are materially interested in good relations with that state and are trying to fool those who are not so interested into supporting such a policy, or they have themselves been fooled by others with that goal. It cannot be that they have a prior ideological motivation to favor good relations with that state.[86] Since ideology is a tool of parochial interests, the labels "liberal" and "illiberal" must be rationalizations and epiphenomena. Actors will proclaim a state to be liberal if it is useful to them, for example, as home to their customers or suppliers. They will declare a state illiberal if it is home to rival producers or potential victims. The causal chain is thus:

parochial interest → useful states (customers, suppliers, etc.) liberal, rivals or potential victims illiberal

84. Ibid., 43–55.

85. Strictly speaking, there is no *necessary* contradiction between my theory and Snyder's, because we are trying to explain different dependent variables: imperial overexpansion in his case, war and peace in mine. Moreover, Snyder accepts the notion that *mature* liberal democracies are pacific toward one another. See Edward D. Mansfield and Jack Snyder, "Democratization and the Danger of War," in Brown et al., *Debating the Democratic Peace*, esp. 301 and 334.

86. Here Snyder builds himself a way out with the concept of "blowback," where actors begin believing their own myths. For two reasons, however, I shall ignore blowback as not essential to Snyder's theory. First, he emphasizes logrolling over this mechanism. Second, he does not explain how blowback happens; more fundamentally, it is not at all clear how blowback jibes with the rest of his account, since allowing ideas a life of their own is a departure from the rational choice approach he uses throughout the rest of the book.

Of course, liberals themselves have tended to make similar arguments. Kant wrote that the *"spirit of trade* cannot coexist with war."[87] Richard Cobden and other advocates of laissez-faire in the nineteenth century were certain that free trade would engender peace by making nations economically interdependent. As we shall see in Chapter 4, in the 1840s citizens in the western United States called for war against England over the Oregon territory, insisting that monarchical Britain was endangering republicanism in that region. British liberals argued that republican ideology was a rationalization of western farmers' economic interests, and that if Britain repealed the Corn Laws, which kept U.S. grain out, the crisis would end. Thus, while Snyder's argument may thus be labeled liberal (despite his labeling it realist), its materialism clearly makes it distinct from the idealist argument of this book.

Do Liberal Institutions Constrain Foreign Policy?

Even if liberals do categorize foreign states based on a priori criteria, realists would say that a competent government will not be constrained by these liberal categories. A government that wants war but faces liberal dissent among its citizens will be able to manipulate liberals' perceptions. It will discover or fabricate information making the state look illiberal. Even if the government does not win unanimous public support for war, citizens will rally behind the government once hostilities have commenced.[88] Conversely, if liberals favor a war the government opposes, government will be able to manipulate public opinion into opposing the war. It will portray the foreign state as progressive and enlightened, on the way to liberalism if not there yet. If such propaganda fails, the government can count on eventual public support once voters see the benefits of maintaining the peace.

The claim behind this skeptical hypothesis is summed up by Kenneth Waltz, writing on U.S. foreign policy in the 1950s and 1960s: "The chances that a President will be unable to carry out a controversial policy are slight, nor is it at all likely that he will be dissuaded from pursuing a difficult and possibly unpopular line of policy by the fear that he and his party will thereby be electorally punished."[89] Theodore Lowi in fact argues that ordinary and crisis foreign policy are precisely the opposite of what I claim: viz., that everyday foreign policy is subject to the

87. Kant, "To Perpetual Peace," 125.
88. For the "rally 'round the flag" literature see note 60 above.
89. Kenneth N. Waltz, *Foreign Policy and Democratic Politics: The American and British Experience* (Boston: Little, Brown, 1967), 286.

vagaries of democratic politics, but that crisis policy is the exclusive province of a small elite.[90]

Each of these alternative accounts contradicts my claim that liberalism, as defined in this book, is a truly *causal*. Instead, the cause is power politics or some other source of physical threat, or material interest, and liberalism is a garland covering the true causal chain. These alternative propositions suggest the competing hypotheses adduced below. The temporal ordering of perceptions and interests will help us adjudicate between explanations. If I can establish that images of a foreign country as liberal or not preceded purely military or economic reasons to perceive that country as such, then my argument is strengthened and competing explanations are undermined.

I turn now to the search for clues that the causal pathways I describe really exist. If my argument is valid, what can we expect to observe in the foreign policy processes in liberal states?[91] I check these expectations or hypotheses against ten historical cases. Each case involves both *process tracing* and *structured, focused comparison*.[92] I do not pretend to give the definitive description or causal analysis in any particular case, and I leave out many factors that others will deem important. My object is to see if the cases unfold as my argument anticipates.

I begin by reiterating a few definitions which, for the purposes of this book, will be taken as objective. *Liberal institutions* are free discussion of foreign policy (implying freedoms of speech, the press, assembly, freedom from arbitrary arrest and punishment) and regular competitive elections of those empowered to make war or of those to whom they are responsible (e.g., a legislature). Together these institutions give electors leverage over their government. Objectively, a *liberal state* is constituted by these liberal institutions. Such a state must have these institutions codified into a constitution or common law, and must uphold them in practice as well. I categorize states as liberal, semiliberal, or illiberal. Subjectively, a *liberal state* is one perceived to be liberal by its contemporaries. A subjectively liberal state will not necessarily be objectively liberal. *Liberals* are those persons who favor objective liberal institutions within their own country. I identify liberals through their own writings and through secondary historical literature.

90. Theodore Lowi, "Making Democracy Safe for the World," in James N. Rosenau, ed., *Domestic Sources of Foreign Policy* (New York: Free Press, 1967), 301.

91. For a recent explanation of hypothesis derivation and examples from political science, see Gary King, Robert O. Keohane, and Sidney Verba, *Designing Social Inquiry: Scientific Inference in Qualitative Research* (Princeton: Princeton University Press, 1994).

92. Alexander L. George and Timothy J. McKeown, "Case Studies and Theories of Organizational Decision Making," in *Advances in Information Processing in Organizations* (Greenwich, Conn.: JAI, 1985), 2:21–58.

In Part II (Chapters 3–5) I engage in process tracing by giving an account of the objective degree of liberalism in each state; the processes by which actors in one state came to perceive a given foreign state as liberal or illiberal; how the crisis arose; how prior perceptions affected crisis interactions; and how the crisis ended. For example, in the first case, relations between the United States and Great Britain from 1794 to 1796, I (1) rate each state objectively as liberal, semiliberal, or illiberal according to the institutional criteria defended above; (2) describe and account for American perceptions of Britain, and British perceptions of America, prior to the crisis; (3) describe an action by Britain toward America, the interpretations of that action by Americans, the agitation by Americans for a response, and the effect of that agitation, as transmitted through American political institutions, on the American response; (4) do the same with the British reaction, then again with the British reaction to the American reaction, etc., until the crisis is peacefully resolved.

In so doing, I show how perceptions of a foreign state before the crisis shape interpretations of that state's actions during the crisis. That is, I show the degree to which the crisis itself changes liberals' perceptions of the foreign state (i.e., whether liberals "update"). I also show how liberal institutions allow those perceptions to affect the outcome of the crisis.

In Part III (Chapter 6) I engage in structured, focused comparison of the cases to test two particularly crucial components of my explanation: that liberals' pre-crisis perceptions of foreign states as liberal or illiberal hold during crises (i.e., are not epiphenomenal) and that liberal political institutions allow those perceptions to affect crisis outcomes.

The hypotheses fall into two sets: those pertaining to the perceptions liberals will display of foreign states and those pertaining to the constraining force of liberal institutions on war decisions. For the first set, what is to be explained—the dependent variable—is the variation in how liberals perceive foreign states. For the second, the dependent variable is the degree to which the government is constrained in deciding for war or peace.

LIBERAL IDEOLOGY HYPOTHESIS

I argue that institutional identity motivates liberals to favor fellow liberal states and be hostile to illiberal states—that is, that ideology is the independent variable. If that is true, what should we observe in the foreign policy process? I have argued that we must take subjective perceptions into account, that for liberal peace and war to happen, subjects must see themselves as remaining at peace with certain states *because* those states are (subjectively) liberal. Thus, for example, liberals should argue that a war would be wrong or imprudent because the potential enemy is liberal and thus an ally in the struggle against illiberalism. They need not explicate the tenets of liberalism in every argument, but should cite the foreign state's regime type as a reason for or against war.

Yet, realists and others have good reason to be skeptical of subjects' stated rationales for foreign policy. Effective advocates will marshal every argument they can find, whether or not they personally find them persuasive. Even in private communications, people may lie about their true motives in hopes of persuading their audience or justifying themselves. Furthermore, as Hans Morgenthau argues, actors may not truly know their own motives.[93] Psychologists have demonstrated that when choosing an action people tend to avoid trading off values against one another. They want to believe the action they have chosen is the best from all angles, that they are not sacrificing one good for another. They therefore persuade themselves that the world is constructed in such a way that all good things go together.[94] What enhances national power is also seen as good for wealth and personal freedom. It is difficult for individuals, and more so for those studying their statements, to know which motive or combination thereof is doing the work.

Thus I must look for other evidence. My argument also implies that a given group of liberals in state A will apply consistent criteria in judging whether states B, C, D, etc. are liberal. For example, if A's liberals oppose hierarchy and privilege in their own state as threats to personal liberty, they should also be consistently hostile to B if it is an aristocracy. Perceptions of a foreign state as liberal or illiberal should not vary with power factors, economic interest, or quality of interactions among states, but only with the perceivers' vision for his or her own state. Thus the ideological hypothesis is:

1.a. *Liberals will perceive a foreign state as liberal if it matches their criteria for liberalism within their own state; conversely, they will perceive a foreign state as illiberal if it violates those criteria.*

LIBERAL INSTITUTIONS HYPOTHESIS

I also argue that governments of objectively liberal states will tend to be constrained by liberals within their own state. If liberal institutions

93. Morgenthau, *Politics among Nations*, 5–6.
94. Jervis, *Perception and Misperception*, 128–42.

truly constrain foreign policy, what should we observe? A government pursuing a policy that violates the wishes of liberal citizens will have to modify its preferred policy to conform with that of the liberals. That is, if government wants war but liberal citizens want peace, government will find it difficult to go to war. If government wants peace but liberals want war, government will find peace difficult. If liberals are split, as explained above, government will tend to avoid war. Evidence of this constraint may be found in statements, diaries, writings, and legislative votes.

> 2.a. *During crises, the stronger liberal institutions are within a state, the more constrained its decision makers will be to follow policies advocated by its liberal elites.*

Note that these hypotheses do not state categorically that objectively liberal states will always forgo war with one another, much less never threaten one another. They simply adduce two key observable manifestations of the force that I argue liberalism exerts on foreign policy and international relations.

REALIST HYPOTHESES

Some would argue that threat assessment drives liberal perceptions. As discussed above, Walt's theory of alliance formation says that states react primarily to threats, and that threat is a function of power, geographical proximity, and intention—i.e., that threats are the independent variable. Balance-of-threat theory would interpret a finding that actors label some states liberal and some illiberal as a liberal justification of a policy dictated by threat imbalances. Liberals will view a state as threatening if its aggregate and offensive power are great enough, it is physically near enough, and its intentions are hostile enough; they will then classify it as illiberal to make defensive or hostile policies toward the state palatable to themselves and the public. At the same time, actors will label a foreign state liberal if it poses no threat to them, or if they want it to help their own state oppose a threat, or if it is already doing so.

Formulating a testable hypothesis from this theory requires measuring power, propinquity, and intentions independent of the outcome they are supposed to explain. Yet measurements of the first and third factors are very difficult to carry out. Realists have long acknowledged how ambiguous power levels can be.[95] More recently, a realist scholar

95. See Morgenthau, *Politics among Nations*, 101–63.

has convincingly shown that statesmen's power perceptions do not always vary with "objective" measures.[96] In some of the cases examined below, moreover, figures on economic and military strength are sketchy at best. Still, I use the extant data on armies, navies, industrial production, and population, as well as alliances if relevant.

Assessing intention is if anything more difficult; indeed, it is my argument that such assessments are inseparable from ideology. Yet since Walt treats intentions as self-evident, I shall describe the gestures states make to one another before and during crises, and offer a judgment as to how hostile the gesture should have been taken as by a neutral observer. Thus balance-of-threat theory yields the following hypothesis:

1.b. *Liberals will perceive a foreign state as liberal if that state poses no threat to them, or may help or is helping them oppose a state or states that threaten their own state; they will perceive a foreign state as illiberal if it poses a threat to them. The more powerful, the closer, and the more hostile a foreign state is, the more threatening it is.*

Some would argue that parochial interest drives liberal perceptions. As explained above, the notion that economic ties can give states a vested interest in peace is compatible with an explanation of liberal peace. Nonetheless, a theory that reduces liberal peace to economic interest is very different from the explanation presented in this book, which recognizes a causal role for liberal ideas and perceptions. Snyder's theory of imperial overexpansion grants a role to ideas, but it treats those ideas primarily as rationalizations of material interests and thus as "intervening" variables. The independent variable is the economic or power interest of a given actor. Industrialists, bankers, or militaries will bargain with one another for a foreign policy, then propagate an ideology to fool the public into believing the policy is in the national interest. As with power resources, economic and bureaucratic interests are not always clear to the analyst, and data from historical cases are sometimes difficult to come by. Still, in each case I shall present the material interests of relevant parties as far as possible. If a case shows that the owner of a factory in state A dependent on raw materials from state B declares B liberal, the parochial interest theory will be supported. The hypothesis is:

1.c. *Liberals will perceive a foreign state as liberal if their immediate material well-being depends on good relations with that state, and illiberal if their*

96. William Curti Wohlforth, *The Elusive Balance: Power and Perceptions in the Cold War* (Ithaca: Cornell University Press, 1992).

immediate material well-being would be served by hostile relations with that state.

Some would argue that government can ignore or override liberal agitation. Realism also would also argue that domestic politics is so much sound and fury, signifying nothing—that whatever liberal perceptions and their origins, governments will be able to ignore or manipulate them and act instead on the imperatives of power. Thus a skeptical realist hypothesis on liberal institutions would be:

2.b. *Decision makers will not be constrained to follow liberal elites in making foreign policy.*

In Part II, I use ten historical case studies to illustrate the validity of the hypotheses. The cases are all war-threatening crises that occurred between 1794 and 1898 and involved the United States and the following foreign countries (an asterisk indicates that the crisis ended in war): Britain, 1794–96; France, 1796–98*; Britain, 1803–12*; Britain, 1845–46; Mexico, 1845–46*; Britain, 1861–63; Spain, 1873; Chile, 1891–92; Britain, 1895–96; Spain, 1896–98*. Crises should be particularly difficult tests for liberal solidarity. In each case I examine evidence in both the United States and the foreign state. I chose these particular crises for five reasons. First, they control for the effects of two variables that (according to realism) pacified relations among liberal states after 1945, namely, bipolarity and nuclear weapons.[97] Second, they hold constant the identity of one state, the United States. Throughout its history America has had liberal factions—indeed, as discussed in the next chapter, has been thoroughly dominated by Lockean liberalism—and featured free discussion and regular competitive elections (although as with every country its franchise was limited in the eighteenth and nineteenth centuries).[98] Third, the cases allow the perceptions of the governmental systems of the other state, threat factors, and parochial interests to vary.

97. According to realism: (1) bipolarity, or the concentration of military power into two "poles" (the United States and Soviet Union), would tend to cause states to coalesce with one or the other pole and not to fight states in their own coalition; and (2) the United States could coerce its allies into remaining at peace with one another by implicitly threatening to withdraw its nuclear protection. These propositions may or may not be valid, but I chose to control for the two variables in question.

98. Joe D. Hagan counsels scholars of foreign policy not to assume that legal accountability implies actual effective government opposition. See Hagan, "Regimes, Political Oppositions, and the Comparative Analysis of Foreign Policy," in Charles F. Hermann, Charles W. Kegley, Jr., and James N. Rosenau, eds., *New Directions in the Study of Foreign Policy* (Boston: Allen & Unwin, 1987), 309–38. In each case I examine whether actual opposition existed.

In some crises, liberal Americans had previously considered the foreign state liberal; in others they had not; in still others opinion was divided. Fourth, the objective liberal status of the foreign states varies across the cases. Fifth, among liberals in those states perception varies as to how liberal the United States was.

There are disadvantages in using these cases. First, in selecting crises—discrete periods of time—I am biasing the sample. I handle this by examining liberal perceptions of the foreign state *before* the crisis, and also discussing how the crisis arose. Thus the most important inferences I draw from the cases—that liberals are ideologically motivated to bring about certain foreign policies and that the liberal political system allows them to succeed—are not hampered by this selection bias. Second, in looking only at crises involving the United States, I risk missing the possibility that some sort of American exceptionalism is at work. I handle this in two ways. First, I look at foreign policy processes on the other side in each case to see if they conform to the argument.[99] Second, in Chapter 6 I briefly examine recent relations between Japan and South Korea and between India and Pakistan to see if the processes obtain in cases not directly involving the United States at all.

A third problem is that the cases took place before the twentieth century, raising the question of relevance to today's world. It is arguable that the liberalism of the late twentieth century is essentially different from that of the eighteenth and nineteenth centuries. In the nineteenth century, for example, women and some racial minorities were not granted full (or any, in some cases) political rights in polities I label liberal. Yet, both the liberal emphasis on personal autonomy and the liberal foreign policy ideology I described above have endured into the twentieth century.[100] When Woodrow Wilson asked Congress to declare war on Germany in 1917, he used appeals straight out of Kant and Paine:

> [The Great War] was a war determined upon as wars used to be determined upon in the old, unhappy days when peoples were nowhere consulted by their rulers and wars were provoked and waged in the interest of dynasties or of little groups of ambitious men who were accustomed to use their fellow men as pawns or tools. Self-governed nations do not fill their neighbour states with spies or set the course of intrigue to bring about some critical posture of affairs which will give them an opportunity to strike and make conquest.[101]

99. As noted below, in some cases, particularly Chile in 1891–92, information on the non-U.S. side is scant.

100. See Tony Smith, *America's Mission: The United States and the Worldwide Struggle for Democracy in the Twentieth Century* (Princeton: Princeton University Press, 1994).

101. Woodrow Wilson, address to a joint session of Congress. *Congressional Record*, 65th Cong., 1st sess., 2 April 1917, 55, pt. 1:103.

In 1943, when the Allies were considering how to treat Germany after its hoped-for defeat, Sumner Welles noted in a meeting with Anthony Eden and Lord Halifax:

> I felt a more practical solution [for the pacification of Germany] would be the agreement that any nation which became a member of the international organization which I hoped would be created must automatically in order to achieve membership provide in its constitution for the granting to its individual nationals the right of free speech, of free press, of free information, and of freedom of worship, et cetera, and that in this manner I believed the kind of education which we believed would make the Germans safer members of the family of nations would be attained.[102]

Finally, as noted in Chapter 1, American presidents in the 1980s and 1990s have based foreign policy on the belief that democracies do not fight one another.

Part II will make clear that while liberalism often operates as I predict, the other theories provide plausible explanations in many cases as well, sometimes pointing in the same direction as liberalism. For example, economic interest often covaries with ideological proclivity: a nation on which actors depended economically was often the same nation whose system of government they admired. It is difficult if not impossible to adjudicate between these two competing sources of perceptions in many cases. Institutional identity often has the advantage of explaining more facts over the set of ten cases than the other theories, however. That finding implies that subjects do indeed perceive their self-interests through ideological lenses and that liberal peace and liberal war are therefore genuine.

102. Sumner Welles, "Memorandum of Conversation," Washington, 16 March 1943, in *Foreign Relations of the United States, 1943*, vol. 3 (Washington: Government Printing Office, 1963), 21. It must also be noted, however, that Welles was speaking of a divided Germany; he did not think a united Germany in any form, communist, socialist, or liberal democratic, would be safe. I thank Gideon Rose for bringing this source to my attention.

PART II

*American Diplomatic
Crises, 1794–1898*

[3]

*From the Jay Treaty
to the War of 1812*

*America has accustomed herself to perceive in France only the Ally & the
friend. Consulting the feelings of her own bosom, she has believed that between Republics an elevated and refined friendship could exist, & that
free nations were capable of maintaining for each other real & permanent
affection. If this pleasing theory, erected with so much care and viewed
with so much delight, has been impaired by experience, yet the hope continues to be cherished, that this circumstance does not necessarily involve
the opposite extreme.*

John Marshall to Talleyrand,
17 January 1798

The liberal revolution that founded the United States in 1776 was contagious. It erupted in France in 1789 and wracked most of Europe for
two and a half decades thereafter. But the French Revolution abandoned liberalism for radicalism in 1793. The execution of Louis XVI
and the inauguration of the Reign of Terror constituted a brutal departure from toleration. The Jacobins turned against all foreign "cosmopolitan" revolutionaries, declaring "revolution in one country first."[1]
The French Republic declared war on Great Britain on 1 February 1793,
eleven days after the regicide. For most of the next twenty-two years
these two nations and the other great powers of Europe were at war.
First under various republican factions, then under Napoleon Bonaparte, the French tried to remake the European order. While certain
powers aligned with France temporarily in the struggle, in the end the
monarchical powers combined to oppose it. The great conflict ended in

1. R. R. Palmer, *The Age of the Democratic Revolution: A Political History of Europe and
America, 1760–1800*, vol. 2, *The Struggle* (Princeton: Princeton University Press, 1964),
116–23.

1815 with Napoleon's final defeat at Waterloo, the restoration of the French monarchy under Louis XVIII, and the Concert of Europe.

Despite its geographical distance from Europe and its official neutrality, the young United States was caught in the middle of the struggle it helped inspire. In 1793 the British and French began seizing each other's cargoes from the West Indies on the high seas. The American merchant marine rushed in to fill the void, carrying goods from the New World to both belligerents in the Old. In turn, the British and French navies began seizing American cargoes, each hoping to deny its enemy any commerce. American ideological sympathies were also engaged in the war. Federalists wanted their country to be like, and to draw closer to, Great Britain; Republicans wanted the same vis-à-vis France.

The maritime troubles and ideological conflicts brought the United States to the brink of war three times. In 1794 the British were confiscating U.S. cargoes at such a rate that President George Washington was compelled to send a special envoy, John Jay, to London to negotiate a solution. The resulting Jay Treaty appeared so one-sided that many Americans demanded war, but peace was maintained as Congress approved the pact. In response to this tilt toward England the French began seizing U.S. cargoes, leading President John Adams in 1797 to send three special envoys to Paris. Rather than negotiate a treaty, however, the French government tried to extort millions of dollars from the Americans, and simultaneously redoubled its punishment of the U.S. merchant marine. War was never declared, but the United States initiated a "quasi-war" against France, a series of naval battles between 1798 and 1800. Finally, the Anglo-French-American triangle led to a third crisis beginning in 1803. Two U.S. presidents, Thomas Jefferson and James Madison, tried various embargoes against the British and French. The utter failure of these economic sanctions to modify the behavior of the belligerents led Congress to declare war on Britain in 1812.

THE ANGLO-AMERICAN CRISIS OF 1794–96

How Liberal Was the United States?

Measured by the criteria of freedom of discussion and elections, the United States qualifies as a highly liberal state in the 1790s. The first ten amendments to its constitution, while not yet applicable to the states, guaranteed to citizens freedoms of religion, speech, the press, and assembly against federal encroachment.[2] Only Congress could declare

2. The institution of slavery flourished, especially in the South, which means that individual rights were not recognized for all residents. The pared-down institutional

war, and its lower house (the House of Representatives) was elected directly by the people every two years. Members of its upper house (the Senate) were chosen every six years by state legislatures, which in turn were usually popularly elected. The President was selected every four years by the Electoral College, whose members were chosen either by the people or the state legislators, depending on the state.[3] Electors were not bound by law to follow voters' or legislators' instructions, but in both 1789 and 1792 (as in most elections since) they all did so. The Bill of Rights allowed highly competitive elections, and the Republican opposition was vibrant.[4]

How Did Americans Perceive Great Britain?

Between 1790 and approximately 1820, Americans were politically divided into Federalists and Republicans. Both parties should be seen as liberal, but the two disagreed vehemently about the form liberal government should take. Federalists, whose numbers included Alexander Hamilton of New York, the treasury secretary, and John Adams of Massachusetts, the vice president, cared more for energy in the executive than limits on it. They envisaged a hierarchical society, where the propertied had the greatest control over government. The Hamiltonians sought to use national debt and protective tariffs to build an empire to rival that of ancient Rome. Hamilton had resisted inclusion of the Bill of Rights in the Constitution and wanted the President to have quasi-monarchical status. Still, as Louis Hartz writes, Federalists were committed to government by law and to material prosperity, tenets held dear by liberals. Federalists were more pessimistic about human nature than Republicans, but unlike European reactionaries

---

definition of a liberal state used in this study, however, does not touch on the question of slavery. *Subjectively*, as we shall see especially in Chapter 4, slavery mattered a great deal to many liberals in the United States and abroad.

3. In 1792, electors were chosen by popular vote in Maryland, Pennsylvania, Virginia, and Kentucky; by state legislature in Connecticut, Delaware, Georgia, New Jersey, New York, North Carolina, Rhode Island, South Carolina, and Vermont; and by a combination in Massachusetts and New Hampshire. Congressional Quarterly, *Guide to U.S. Elections*, 2d ed. (Washington: Congressional Quarterly, 1985), 254.

4. As for the voters themselves, the franchise was relatively limited in 1794. Voting restrictions varied by state, but only Vermont had universal adult male suffrage. All other states had various taxation and property requirements. Slaves and women, of course, could not vote. Indians living in tribal nations were not considered citizens; subject to separate laws and governance, they could not vote either. Chilton Williamson, *American Suffrage: From Property to Democracy 1760–1860* (Princeton: Princeton University Press, 1960), 150, 156, 208–9; Robert Weil, *The Legal Status of the Indian* (1888; reprint, New York: AMS, 1975), 70–73.

they believed in scientific constitution making and the commercial way of life.[5]

The Republicans, the party of Virginians Thomas Jefferson and James Madison, were highly concerned with individual liberty and limited government. It was they who had pushed through the Bill of Rights, and they opposed governmental debt and any other instrument that would build up the central government at the expense of the states. Their very use of the name "Republican" implied that their rivals in Hamilton's party were not committed to elective government. They had a moral vision of an America that prospered not from state power but from small-scale commerce and agriculture. They believed in and cheered the possibility of liberal revolution throughout Europe.[6]

Integral to the visions that Federalists and Republicans had for America were their respective evaluations of England and France. In fact, the schism that produced the two factions was partly a product of a vehement disagreement between Hamilton and Madison over policy toward Britain. The two men had cooperated in 1787 in writing the Federalist, the series of newspaper articles arguing for ratification of the U.S. Constitution. They split in 1789–90 over commercial ties to England. Hamilton's plan was for the young United States to enrich itself by trading with and indeed imitating Britain, the wealthiest and most financially sophisticated nation in the world. Madison, by contrast, wanted his country to reject the British model of political economy, especially the use of debt, which he and most of his fellow Virginians regarded as immoral. Hamilton wrote in 1792 that the foreign policy views of Jefferson and Madison were "unsound and dangerous. They have a womanish attachment to France and a womanish resentment against Great Britain."[7] Hamilton admired Britain's economic dependence on trade, credit, and banks. He praised its government's powerful executive and ability to maintain public order. "The English model [is] the only good one on this subject," he declared, the only one "which unites public strength with individual security."[8] John Adams, although no friend of

5. "There is a feudal bleakness about man which sees him fit only for external domination, and there is a liberal bleakness about man which sees him working autonomously on the basis of his own self-interest; Maistre believed in the one, Adams believed in the other." Louis Hartz, *The Liberal Tradition in America* (New York: Harcourt Brace Jovanovich, 1955), 79–80.

6. Paul A. Varg, *Foreign Policies of the Founding Fathers* (East Lansing: Michigan State University Press, 1963), 70–71. On the moral component of Republican political economy, see Drew R. McCoy, *The Elusive Republic: Political Economy in Jeffersonian America* (Chapel Hill: University of North Carolina Press, 1980).

7. Ralph Ketcham, *James Madison: A Biography* (New York: Macmillan, 1970), 337.

8. Stanley Elkins and Eric McKitrick, *The Age of Federalism: The Early American Republic, 1788–1800* (New York: Oxford University Press, 1993), 129.

Hamilton, held a similar view of the British political system. One historian writes that Adams "approached the English constitution with reverence not to be outdone by any eighteenth-century Whig" because of the "liberty and prosperity" he believed it engendered.[9]

Madison and Jefferson took the opposite view of England. The Virginians' repulsion from the English model had been shaped by the high dependence on British credit that had contributed to the economic crises in Virginia of the 1760s and 1770s. Debt and England were inextricably linked in their minds, and both were hated and feared. It was well known that Britain had for a century financed its wars through debt, in which the Bank of England played a major role.[10] Jefferson, Madison, and other Republicans saw the English financial system as a source of corruption. It allowed unnatural power to be amassed in the central government, far from the people, and enriched the moneyed interests at the expense of the independent farmer-owners.[11] The United Kingdom was the font of such vicious political economy, and commercial intercourse with that country would corrode American virtue.[12]

As a member of the House of Representatives, Madison thus strove from 1789 onward to place discriminatory tariffs on England. Madison claimed to want reciprocity in trade, the end being a Smithian vision of global laissez-faire. Yet, it is clear that what he really wanted was to wean the United States from its mother country. The Republicans saw politics and economics as linked: political independence from England required economic independence, and national virtue required both. As Madison wrote, the greatest problem with close ties to London was "the influence that may be conveyed into the public councils by a nation directing the course of our trade by her capital, and holding so great a share in our pecuniary institutions, and the effect that may finally ensue on our taste, our manners, and our form of Government itself."[13] Madison's brand of liberalism, shaped by past economic hardship and his own position as a Virginia planter, thus gave rise to his anglophobic strategy.

The other side of Republican loathing of England was admiration and even affection for France. This francophilia is at first puzzling in

9. Edward Handler, *America and Europe in the Political Thought of John Adams* (Cambridge: Harvard University Press, 1964), 98, 166, 49.

10. See Paul Kennedy, *The Rise and Fall of the Great Powers* (New York: Random House, 1987), 79–82.

11. Lance Banning, "Republicanism," in Robert A. Rutland, ed., *James Madison and the American Nation, 1751–1836: An Encyclopedia* (New York: Simon & Schuster, 1994), 358. See also Banning, *The Jeffersonian Persuasion: Evolution of a Party Ideology* (Ithaca: Cornell University Press, 1978).

12. Elkins and McKitrick, *Age of Federalism*, 92.

13. Ibid., 384.

light of the fact that by any reasonable liberal measure, France at least prior to 1789 was politically a more repressive country than England. If Republicans wanted to shun despotisms, the France of Louis XVI would seem a better candidate than the England of George III. Evidently gratitude for French aid in the War of Independence is partly responsible for Republican affinity for France. It is clear, however, that Jefferson, Madison, and their allies saw in France not a corrupting influence but a partner in liberty. Jefferson's time as envoy in Paris convinced him that France was moving inexorably toward American-style liberalization. Jefferson had befriended such liberals as Lafayette, Condorcet, La Rochefoucauld, and DuPont de Nemours, all pro-American would-be reformers of the Bourbon monarchy. Jefferson found no such men on his several visits to London. Thus he could write to James Monroe in 1788, "I think it probable [France] will within two or three years be in enjoiment of a tolerably free constitution, and that without it's having cost them a drop of blood."[14]

When the French Revolution did come, it confirmed and strengthened the Jeffersonian bias toward France. Most applauded the events of July 1789. Jefferson, Madison, and their allies went further and began identifying the cause of the French revolutionaries with their own. Thus the Republicans interpreted the more disturbing news from France that followed over the next decade in the best possible light. As secretary of state, Jefferson castigated those Americans who criticized the excesses of the Jacobins: "There are in the U.S. some characters of opposite principles; . . . all of them hostile to France and looking to England as the staff of their hope." Such men saw the U.S. constitution "only as a stepping stone to monarchy"; the "successes of republicanism in France have given the coup de grace to their prospects, and I hope to their projects."[15] Public enthusiasm at the news of the establishment of the French Republic in late 1792 supported Jefferson's contention that his views were popularly shared. Massive public demonstrations and feasts were held in Boston, New York, Philadelphia, Baltimore, Charleston, and Savannah.[16]

Those men later to be identified as Federalists were cheered but not intoxicated by events in Paris in 1789. Hamilton wrote to Lafayette in the fall that he felt both "pleasure and apprehension." The apprehension had its source in signs of "excess," which he attributed to factionalism, the "vehement character" of the French, insubordination by the

14. Ibid., 210.

15. Ibid., 317. Jefferson wrote to George Mason: "I look with great anxiety for the firm establishment of the new government in France. . . . I consider the establishment and success of their government as necessary to stay up our own and to prevent it from falling back to that kind of Half-way-house, the English constitution" (315–16).

16. Ibid., 310.

nobles, the extreme abstraction of the *philosophes*, and the destructive potential of the people. Still, Hamilton was encouraged at the prospects of increased Franco-American trade.[17]

Hamilton turned decisively against the French Revolution two years later with the deposition and subsequent execution of Louis XVI. Republican papers cheered that the nation that had helped them gain independence from England had overthrown its own king and was now fighting monarchists throughout Europe. Donald Stewart writes that after the regicide "democratic papers commenced a calculated program of justifying those in power in Paris. This practice was consciously pursued throughout the remainder of the decade and must be acknowledged in order to assess the part of foreign relations in the political propaganda of the period. A defense was found for every French action, from Robespierre's Feast of the Supreme Being to the seizures of American ships."[18]

Federalists were not so generous to the French revolutionaries. They began to see France in the same way that Republicans had long seen England: as a threat by example and direct influence on American institutions and society. Hamilton advised Washington to withhold payments on debts to France, since that nation's republican government had been illegally established. The execution of Louis drew Hamilton's staunch condemnation, especially since the evidence on which he was convicted was not made public.[19] In short, the Federalists feared a contagion effect from France similar to that which Republicans feared from England. The "murderous orgies of Paris" could spread to America via a French alliance.[20] The virtues of drawing closer to Britain were as obvious to Federalists as those of drawing closer to France were to Republicans.

John Adams, meanwhile, was perhaps the only American statesman to have been hostile to the French Revolution from the start, viewing it "not as a 'minister of grace' but as a 'goblin damned.'"[21] Having served twice as a diplomat in France prior to the revolution, Adams was familiar with the attachment of the philosophes to the notion that France needed a unicameral legislature to destroy the power of the monarchy. For a staunch advocate of checks and balances such as Adams, such thinking was heretical. When the revolutionaries set up just such a unicameral system in 1790, Adams was appalled. This "must involve

17. Gilbert L. Lycan, *Alexander Hamilton and American Foreign Policy: A Design for Greatness* (Norman: University of Oklahoma Press, 1970), 134.

18. Donald H. Stewart, *The Opposition Press of the Federalist Period* (Albany: State University of New York Press, 1969), 120.

19. Lycan, *Hamilton and Foreign Policy,* 139–43.

20. Ibid., 156–57.

21. Handler, *Political Thought of Adams,* 98.

France in great and lasting calamities," he wrote.[22] Adams was a prolific political theorist, and his suspicion of France stemmed primarily from his conviction, so carefully laid out in his *Thoughts on Government* and his three-volume *Defence of the American Constitutions*, that balance among various entities—such as England had had prior to the usurpations of George III—was necessary for good government.[23]

How Liberal Was Great Britain?

Britain may fairly be called the birthplace of modern liberal rights. Yet measuring how liberal Britain is at any given moment is difficult, both because the country lacks a written constitution, and because many of the individual rights upheld in practice have been spelled out in the common law made by judges rather than Parliament.[24] Still, we can say with some confidence that Britain in 1794 only qualifies as semiliberal.

Favoring liberalism in Britain was the fact that by 1794 Parliament had triumphed in its struggle to limit the monarchy. The king could not refuse assent to laws passed by the legislature. The individual rights of trial by jury and freedom of speech, religion, assembly, and the press were upheld more faithfully than in most countries. The practice of reporting parliamentary debates in the press was well entrenched, as the House of Commons had stopped interfering in political reporting in 1771. Members of the Commons were elected, and Whig opposition to the Tory government was active.

Full individual rights, however, were not extended to those outside the Church of England, especially Catholics. Fears of a revolutionary contagion led the government of William Pitt the Younger to suspend habeas corpus in 1790, and arrests and suppression of lower-class Radical leaders became common. A harsh Treason and Sedition Act was passed in 1795.[25] War decisions, then as now, rested with the executive rather than the legislature. Most important, the government was dismissed by the Crown rather than the legislature or people. Furthermore, the unelected House of Lords could veto laws passed by the Commons. And Commons elections themselves were corrupt. Counties were represented by seats controlled by the propertied families; in

22. Elkins and McKitrick, *Age of Federalism*, 312–13.

23. Ibid., 529–37.

24. As one scholar writes, "His Majesty's subjects possess no guarantees of freedom. The 'rights of man' are not guaranteed, nor even mentioned anywhere in English constitutional law.'" S. B. Chrimes, *English Constitutional History*, 3d ed. (London: Oxford University Press, 1965), 63.

25. Sir David Lindsay Keir, *The Constitutional History of Modern Britain*, 8th ed. (Princeton: D. Van Nostrand, 1966), 319, 342–43, 398, 429; J. H. Plumb, *England in the Eighteenth Century (1714–1815)* (Harmondsworth, England: Penguin, 1950), 157–58.

small boroughs, a patron could determine who would hold the parliamentary seat. Because electoral districts had not changed for decades, some populous industrial areas were virtually disenfranchised. Votes in the Commons were effectively bought and sold in an open market, as men or parties could buy boroughs for representation.[26] All in all, the executive was not nearly as institutionally constrained from declaring war or maintaining peace as that of the United States.

How Did the British Perceive the United States?

Strongly favoring the United States were British Radicals, whose movement was born during the American Revolution. Radicalism was a movement that sought to strengthen the political standing of the common people and weaken the Crown and aristocracy. In 1785 one Radical writer called the United States "the fairest experiment ever tried in human affairs." Radicals agreed with Thomas Paine that "the system of Government purely representative, unmixed with anything of hereditary nonsense, began in America."[27]

Most Radicals lacked the franchise, but they had their sympathizers among the ruling class. Charles James Fox praised the French Revolution and sought to bring British institutions more in line with Enlightenment principles, which for him meant parliamentary reform and a widened franchise. A decade later the British minister to the United States said of Fox, "I know that he has a strong prejudice in favor of this country, but I should like to know whether it is not confined merely to the theory of the Constitution which they profess."[28] The Marquess of Lansdowne was a liberal Whig who shared many of Fox's goals as well as his predilection toward America. It was Lansdowne who, as the Earl of Shelburne, had favored generous terms of Anglo-American separation as head of the government in 1783. Richard Brinsley Sheridan, the politician and playwright, was a reformer who admired the French Revolution and pointed out to his countrymen the benefits of enlightened American government: "America remains neutral, prosperous, and at peace. . . . Observe her name and government rising above the nations of Europe with a simple but commanding dignity which wins at once the respect, the confidence, and the affection of the world."[29]

26. E. L. Woodward, *The Age of Reform 1815–1870* (Oxford: Clarendon, 1938), 18–28.

27. Henry Pelling, *America and the British Left: From Bright to Bevan* (New York: New York University Press, 1957), 1.

28. Augustus J. Foster to Lady Foster (30 June 1805), quoted in Bradford Perkins, *The First Rapprochement: England and the United States 1795–1805* (Philadelphia: University of Pennsylvania Press, 1955), 21.

29. Ibid. See also Madeleine Bingham, *Sheridan: The Track of a Comet* (New York: St. Martin's, 1972), chap. 10.

Yet, Britain was ruled in 1794 by the Tory government of Pitt, and the Fox faction had little effect on foreign policy between 1795 and 1800. Once an economic liberal and disciple of Adam Smith, Pitt by now had been led into reaction by the French Revolution and the sympathy it engendered in Britain.[30] Pitt held no visible affinity for the United States.[31] In fact, the attitude of his government toward America is best described as indifferent except as it had to do with the war with France. France was the military and ideological threat to Britain. The United States was simply, in the eyes of Pitt and Grenville, a tool, to be used either by England or by France.

Actions, Interpretations, Reactions

The Anglo-French war presented Americans with an opportunity to make money, and they leapt at it. The U.S. merchant marine eagerly took up the carrying trade that Britain and France had denied it in peacetime. Yet the war also affected domestic U.S. politics, quickly maturing the nascent ideological division between Federalists and Republicans. The first partisan fight was over neutrality. Under the 1778 Franco-American alliance France could call on the United States to defend its New World possessions. Hamilton, then secretary of the treasury, argued to Washington that the alliance was null and void because in 1792 France had illegally changed its form of government. Jefferson, the secretary of state, countered that America was bound to abide by the alliance because treaties were between nations rather than governments.[32] Both men wanted official U.S. neutrality, believing the young nation could not afford involvement in the European conflagration. But each man, and the faction he headed, did sympathize with the side whose system of government approximated his own vision for the United States.

Although the British government wanted to prevent neutral powers from aiding the French, no one in Britain wanted another war against the United States, now British industry's biggest customer (averaging £3.6 million in sales per annum between 1790 and 1794). British manufacturers relied heavily too on exports to the West Indies (averaging £2.4 million per annum over the same period), exports that the United States could disrupt. Yet the Pitt government, believing it had signifi-

30. Elkins and McKitrick, *Age of Federalism,* 403–4.

31. Plumb, *England in the Eighteenth Century,* 155–62. See also Jerald Combs, *The Jay Treaty* (Berkeley: University of California Press, 1970), 110–11; and Samuel Flagg Bemis, *Jay's Treaty: A Study in Commerce and Diplomacy* (1923; reprint, Westport, Conn.: Greenwood, 1975), 95–96.

32. See the Hamilton-Jefferson exchange in Thomas G. Paterson, ed., *Major Problems in American Foreign Policy,* 2d ed. (Lexington, Mass.: D. C. Heath, 1984), 1:70–73.

cant leverage over the militarily weak Americans, pursued a harsh policy.[33] Pitt's mercantilist ideology gave him long-term reasons to do so as well: believing British might rested partly on continued dominance by the British merchant marine, he wanted to choke off the young American challenge.[34] The British cabinet calculated that it could bully the United States into cutting off the French. In June and again in November 1793, the cabinet issued Orders in Council authorizing the seizure of goods carried on neutral vessels to or from French ports. By November the British Navy had snatched up three hundred U.S. merchant ships in the Caribbean.[35]

The seizures inflamed American public opinion. Britain had already refused to comply completely with the decade-old Treaty of Paris that established American independence—failing, for example, to vacate many frontier posts in U.S. territory. Now, under Madison's leadership, Congress responded to the Orders in Council with a one-month trade embargo, passed by wide margins.[36] Federalists tried to dampen Republican war talk by noting U.S. naval weakness vis-à-vis Britain. The *Gazette of the United States* noted that Britain had twenty-one ships of war and eight gunboats in Martinique alone, while the United States had none of either. The U.S. Army numbered a mere 3,861 men, mostly in the northwest. Republicans scoffed at these fears, asserting that the United States could defeat England just as it had in 1783, and this time perhaps even conquer Canada. Federalists quaked, one Republican journal noted, "As if the experience of the last war, an established government, and the duplication of our numbers had enfeebled us, and rendered us less capable than we were in 1776 of resisting a nation evidently fallen from her former greatness."[37] Indeed, Britain had only 3,500 regular troops in North America in the middle of 1793, and frontier posts were severely undermanned. Americans outnumbered Canadians by fourteen to one.[38]

Despite the trade embargo, British provocations continued. Around the same time as news of the maritime depredations arrived, outrageous news arrived from Canada. In January 1794, Lord Dorchester,

33. Bemis, *Jay's Treaty*, 46–49.

34. Pitt was influenced by reports from Lord Sheffield and the Earl of Hawkesbury urging the British government to discourage development of the U.S. merchant marine. These reports were predicated on the notion that a loss for the U.S. carrying trade was a gain for Britain. The Sheffield and Hawkesbury reports were made much of by Madison in his anti-British arguments. Elkins and McKitrick, *Age of Federalism*, 379–82.

35. Combs, *Jay Treaty*, 139–41; Frank T. Reuter, *Trials and Triumphs: George Washington's Foreign Policy* (Fort Worth: Texas Christian University Press, 1983), 180–82; Bemis, *Jay's Treaty*, 35–37, 100.

36. Bemis, *Jay's Treaty*, 101; Combs, *Jay Treaty*, 120–21.

37. *General Advertiser*, 8 January 1794, quoted in Combs, *Jay Treaty*, 130–31.

38. Combs, *Jay Treaty*, 138.

the Governor General, told Indian leaders that the United States and Britain would soon be at war and that the Indians could then reclaim lands stolen by U.S. settlers. Within two months the British had established a new fort roughly sixty miles southwest of Detroit, on the Miamis River, clearly in U.S. territory.[39] In London reformist Whigs demanded explanations. In the House of Lords, Lansdowne attacked the Orders in Council as anti-American. The City of London, he said, "deprecated any rupture with America, as one of the greatest calamities which, in a political as well as commercial point of view, could happen to this country."[40] In the Commons, Sheridan moved that a copy of Dorchester's speech should be made public. A few days later Fox, in arguing for an end to the war with France, deplored war with America as well.[41] The Whig press echoed these sentiments. The *Morning Chronicle* said that if the government did not disavow Dorchester's speech, "it is hardly to be hoped that we can avoid the horrors of a war with our former brethren. Every feeling and every wise man will deplore the fatality."[42]

The Pitt government stood firm. The cabinet denied that Dorchester had made any such speech. The ministerial press assured the public that Americans would not seek war over the Orders. A false rumor was even circulated that Thomas Jefferson, known as a fanatical francophile, had arrived in London to negotiate a new treaty.[43]

Tory propaganda was not far from the truth. Washington had responded to British provocations not with hostilities, as many Republicans wanted, but by sending John Jay as special envoy to London in the spring of 1794. The president was convinced that the nation could not afford war with England. A reputed anglophile, Jay was not the man most likely to drive a difficult bargain with the British, especially after receiving secret instructions from Hamilton not to threaten any retaliation against the Orders in Council.[44] The resulting treaty heavily favored England. It allowed the British to trade anywhere in the United States but allowed Americans to trade only in certain parts of Canada; it disallowed U.S. cotton exports, and of course re-exports of West Indian goods to France; it did not prohibit impressment of U.S. sailors; it did not compensate owners for slaves carried away during the American Revolution; and finally, in the notorious article 12, it allowed only

---

39. Thomas A. Bailey, *A Diplomatic History of the American People*, 6th ed. (New York: Appleton-Century-Crofts, 1958), 70–72.

40. *Times* (London), 27 May 1794.

41. *Hansard's Parliamentary Debates* (Commons), vol. 31 (30 May 1794), col. 627.

42. *Morning Chronicle* (London), 26 April 1794, 2.

43. Combs, *Jay Treaty*, 143–45.

44. Ibid., 133, 148.

U.S. vessels of seventy tons or less to trade with the British West Indies.[45] The young U.S. merchant marine would be crippled by such a restriction.

Knowing the ideological prejudices of both Federalists and Republicans, President Washington disliked having to submit questions of national security to Congress, yet he was constrained by law to do so.[46] Upon reading the Jay Treaty in March 1795, the president knew Congressional approval would be difficult. He kept its contents secret from the public, thereby raising Republican suspicions. The Senate passed the treaty in July without a vote to spare, after expurgating article 12. Then a South Carolina senator leaked the treaty to Madison. Large segments of the American public exploded in fury upon reading the treaty. Jay was guillotined in effigy and riots broke out in Portsmouth, New York, Trenton, Philadelphia, Charleston, and Augusta; Hamilton was stoned from a podium in New York while defending the treaty; even the sacrosanct Washington was damned in toasts by embittered Republicans. The outrage nearly stopped Washington from implementing the treaty. Then, fortuitously, a scandal surfaced involving intrigues between the French minister and the new secretary of state, Edmund Randolph. With France momentarily less popular, Washington declared the Jay Treaty in effect. Yet it still remained for the House of Representatives to appropriate $90,000 to implement the treaty.[47]

Republicans prepared for a political battle royal. Jefferson, who had resigned from the cabinet out of frustration with Hamilton's interference, wrote to a friend, "I trust the popular branch of our legislature will disapprove of [the treaty] and thus rid us of this infamous act, which is really nothing more than a treaty of alliance between England and the Anglomen of this country, against the Legislature and people of the United States."[48] In Congress, Dwight Foster of Massachusetts argued that Britain was trying not only to "[crush] the rising liberties of France, but also [to extend] her views to America."[49] William P. Giles of Virginia charged that "most of the despots of Europe" were united to achieve "the total destruction of liberty," and that Britain was already turning its attention to the United States.[50] "As it has not been in the power of the United States to assist their Republican allies, when fighting in fact their

45. Ibid., 150–57. For excerpts of the treaty, see Paterson, *Major Problems*, 1:73–76.
46. The president complained to Hamilton of ideological biases on both sides: "It is not the opinion of *those* who were determined (before it was promulgated) to *support*, or *oppose* it, that I am sollicitous to obtain." Combs, *Jay Treaty*, 164.
47. Ibid., 160–70.
48. Bailey, *Diplomatic History*, 79–80.
49. *Annals of Congress*, 4th Cong., 1st sess., 26 April 1796, vol. 5, col. 1174.
50. Ibid., col. 1050.

battles," said John Page of Virginia, at least America should not treat with France's enemies.[51]

A letter submitted to Congress from the citizens of Bennington, Vermont, in December 1795 was characterized as follows: "The petitioners were apprehensive of being involved in European politics, and in a contest with the magnanimous Republic of France."[52] When the Senate was considering ratification of the Jay Treaty, one Philadelphia writer pointed out that, unlike Jay, "the American people overwhelmingly approved the French Revolution, while the treaty would replace France with Great Britain as America's most favored nation. It was an integral part of the vast British plot to exterminate freedom from the face of the earth." Much of the acerbity directed at Washington accused him and other "aristocrats" of conspiring to establish a monarchy in the United States. One Republican paper asked, "Will you support your representatives in Congress, or put all power in the hands of twenty Senators and the President?"[53]

Rumors of the fierce opposition reached England, but as in 1794, the government effectively quieted dissent from official policy. The *Times* admitted that some Americans, "consisting of the lower orders of the people, and of the fraudulent traders of *Virginia*," wanted no treaty; but the rest of the "commercial body of the nation . . . as well as the higher orders of the people," favored it. Even rejection, the paper said, would not lead to war.[54]

The Tories were proved correct, as the Federalists counterattacked in Congress and the press. In the House debate over implementation of the treaty, Rep. Fisher Ames of Massachusetts declared that England, not France, was the paladin of liberty. Ames lambasted those who said that "the world ought to rejoice if Britain was sunk in the sea; if where there are now men and wealth and laws and liberty, there was no more than a sand bank for the sea-monsters to fatten on."[55] The Federalists' most effective argument was that reneging on the Jay Treaty would provoke war against the British and Indians. As weeks passed, public opinion began to shift toward the treaty.[56] Staunch Republicans dismissed the possibility of war. One paper warned: "Beware! Beware! of British influence. You will be told the mournful *wornout* ditty of peace or war!—Believe them not. The question is—*Will you again be connected with your greatest enemy—or will you remain free and independent.*"[57]

---

51. Ibid., col. 1099.
52. *Annals of Congress*, 29 December 1795, col. 171.
53. Stewart, *Opposition Press*, 194, 196, 225.
54. *Times* (London), 20 May 1796.
55. *Annals of Congress*, 28 April 1796, col. 1249.
56. Combs, *Jay Treaty*, 171–87.
57. Ibid., 180.

But they were no match for the Federalists. Ames, probably the nation's best orator, conjured the horrors of war against the British and Indians, and is credited by many with swinging the House debate in favor of the treaty: "I can fancy that I listen to the yells of savage vengeance, and the shrieks of torture. Already they seem to sigh in the West wind; already they mingle with every echo from the mountains."[58]

Ames and the Federalists won the day. Anti-treaty votes trickled away, and in the end, by a vote of 51–48, the House decided the risk of a catastrophic war was too great. Some have also attributed the vote and the turn in public opinion in 1796 to the economic growth that came with renewed intercourse with Britain. Trade volume and commodity prices certainly increased greatly in 1795 and 1796. But real wages actually fell, at least in some cities, as the cost of living rose as well.[59] In any event, public opinion decided that the Republican anglophobic strategy for securing self-interest was in this case inferior to the Federalist anglophilic strategy. The Jay Treaty went into effect, deferring Anglo-American tensions until another day.

American Federalists perceived England as a fellow liberal state before and during the Jay Treaty crisis. They interpreted British actions as relatively benign, and favored conciliatory responses. Republicans saw England as a despotism and a menace before and during the crisis, and pushed for defiant U.S. responses. The Washington administration was constrained by the Republicans to slow acceptance of the Jay Treaty, but not from ultimately keeping Anglo-American peace.

In Britain, reformers and Radicals favored conciliation of America before and during the crisis despite even though the U.S. merchant marine was helping France. These dissenters had little effect on the British cabinet, however, because Britain lacked liberal governmental institutions.

THE FRANCO-AMERICAN CRISIS OF 1796–98

How Liberal Was France?

France in 1798 was governed under the Constitution of the Year III (1795). The five-member national executive was elected by the national legislature, which was in turn elected by primary assemblies. R. R. Palmer writes that the Directory, as the system was called, was "the

---

58. *Annals of Congress,* 28 April 1796, col. 1260.

59. Elkins and McKitrick, *Age of Federalism,* 443–44. America's terms of trade improved from 80.2 in 1794 to 123.6 in 1795, and the price of (e.g.) tobacco shot up from $4.83 per cwt. to $6.16. Yet, real wages in Philadelphia dropped from $.79 per diem to $.66. Ibid., 842–43.

first constitutional republican government on modern principles that France or Europe had ever seen." The legislature was divided into two chambers, the Ancients and the Five Hundred; the power to declare war was vested in the two houses. As these bodies elected the executive, the executive was constitutionally accountable to them. The rights of a free press and free assembly were upheld, although the legislature could suspend the former for one year. Slavery had been abolished in 1794.[60]

Yet the First Republic by this time cannot be called liberal. The executive controlled the legislature by unconstitutional means. Twice, members of the executive ordered coups d'état to preserve their power. The 1797 election brought a royalist majority to the legislature, and soon in response the staunch republicans, with help from Bonaparte, expelled two rightist members of the executive and declared 198 legislative seats vacant—the 18 Fructidor (4 September) coup d'état. Soon the centrists in the Directory began to fear the democratic left, and when the Jacobins won a huge number of seats in the March 1798 election, the executive soon nullified 106 of the elections. This was the coup d'état of 22 Floréal (11 May). As Palmer writes, "After Fructidor and Floréal no one could pretend that the Directory enjoyed a popular mandate of any accepted kind." In short, the First Republic by the time of the Quasi-War was governed not by law but by the will of those leaders who could gain the support of the military.[61]

How Did the French Perceive the United States?

The Directory's defiance of liberal institutions shows how moribund liberal ideology was in France. The original Directory in 1795 had committed itself "to wage active war upon royalism, stimulate patriotism, vigorously to crush all factions, extinguish partisan feelings and all desires for vengeance, and to make concord reign."[62] In 1797 the dominant Directors, Jean-François Reubell, Louis Marie la Reveillière-Lépeaux, and Paul F. N. Barras, were committed to continuing this intolerant program. This meant not only suppressing royalists and the Catholic Church, but also escalating the wars against the European powers. The triumvirate set up satellite republics in the Netherlands, Switzerland, and Italy, and made plans to invade England under Bona-

60. Palmer, *Age of the Democratic Revolution*, 2:214–17; Georges Lefebvre, *The Thermidoreans and the Directory*, trans. Robert Baldick (New York: Random House, 1964), 176–79; Lawrence C. Jennings, *French Reaction to British Slave Emancipation* (Baton Rouge: Louisiana State University Press, 1988), 1.

61. Palmer, *Age of the Democratic Revolution*, 2:255–59.

62. Leo Gershoy, *The French Revolution* (New York: Henry Holt, 1932), 80.

parte.[63] Reaction must be smashed, and whoever was not for them was against them.

The triumvirate was opposed on the right by royalists and conservatives who wanted a return to fiscal solvency and peace. Those purged on 18 Fructidor, led by Lazare Carnot and François Barthélemy, were closer to this camp. Purged on 22 Floréal were far leftists such as the proto-Marxist "Gracchus" Babeuf.[64] Although American Republicans did not recognize it at the time, there were few liberals left in France in 1796.

There were moderates and conservatives who favored good relations with the United States, although it is not clear that they did so out of any affinity with American-style liberalism. As for the radicals, the considerable solidarity they had felt for the United States had largely worn away by this time. It was the Jay Treaty that turned so much French opinion against the United States. Republicans still admired the Jeffersonians in America, but were convinced that under Federalist government the United States had been subverted by monarchism. "In vain have we hoped for some time," wrote one French journalist, "that gratitude, or at least self-interest, would make of that federal republic a loyal ally of France. Now Washington has concluded with our most implacable enemies a treaty wholly inimical to our interests."[65] The French retaliated by confiscating U.S. cargoes, seizing 316 merchant vessels in 1795.[66] When the 1796 U.S. election brought John Adams to the presidency, and Jefferson to the vice presidency, the *Décade Philosophique* speculated, "France will have in these two men an evil genius and a good genius; but unfortunately the evil genius is the more powerful of the two."[67] By 1797, Reubell and LaRevellière saw Adams and America as English stooges.[68]

Actions, Interpretations, Reactions

In March 1797, hoping to stop U.S. ships from supplying Britain, the Directory decreed that French warships should bring into French ports all neutral vessels carrying British goods and that U.S. ships must have

63. Ibid., 79–90.

64. Palmer, *Age of the Democratic Revolution*, 2:255–59.

65. Alexander DeConde, *The Quasi–War: The Politics and Diplomacy of the Undeclared War with France 1797–1801* (New York: Charles Scribner's Sons, 1966), 9–10.

66. Ibid., 8–10.

67. Durand Echeverria, *Mirage in the West: A History of the French Image of American Society to 1815* (Princeton: Princeton University Press, 1957), 221.

68. Albert Hall Bowman, *The Struggle for Neutrality: Franco-American Diplomacy during the Federalist Era* (Knoxville: University of Tennessee Press, 1974), 315–16.

lists of crew and passengers ready for French inspection on the high seas.[69] Americans were again caught in the middle of the European war.

Adams loathed the French government, but not to the point of wanting war. Not only were French military victories too daunting, but there was in America, as Hamilton put it, "a general and strong desire for peace—and, with a considerable party, still a particular repugnance to war with France."[70] Hamilton was now a private citizen but exercised great control over Timothy Pickering, the secretary of state, Oliver Wolcott, the treasury secretary, and James McHenry, secretary of war. Hamilton warned Wolcott "that a suspicion begins to dawn among the friends of government, that the actual administration [Hamilton's disciples] is not much averse to war with France. How very important to obviate this!" Hamilton urged his men to persuade Adams to send a mission to Paris similar to that of Jay to London. "This will meet [the Republicans] on their own ground and disarm them of the argument that all has not been done which might have been done towards preserving peace."[71]

News that the French had refused to receive the U.S. minister to Paris angered Adams. In May he delivered a message to Congress accusing the French of trying to separate the American people from their government, stir up revolution, and endanger U.S. independence. Pursuing a double strategy, the president sought increased military and naval spending but, following his cabinet's advice, decided also to send Elbridge Gerry, John Marshall, and Charles Cotesworth Pinckney to France as special envoys.[72]

Like the British before them, the French government concluded that the United States could be exploited. Yet, the Directory had already been criticized for its harsh policies toward the United States. In the Five Hundred the conservative Marquis de Pastoret denounced the executive for "mak[ing] real aggressions" against the United States without consulting the legislature, which alone had the power to declare war. Another legislator argued: "We believe we take vengeance on the English. We serve them. To embitter the United States, is that not to cause them to lean towards Great Britain? To ruin American commerce, is that not to increase the strength of Great Britain?"[73] Louis-Guillaume Otto, a diplomat, wrote the foreign ministry that "the two nations whose relations should naturally be friendly" had been poisoned by inept French diplomacy. Calling Americans "undoubtedly the greatest

69. DeConde, *Quasi-War*, 17.
70. Ibid., 21–22.
71. Ibid., 19.
72. William C. Stinchcombe, *The XYZ Affair* (Westport, Conn.: Greenwood, 1980), 20–21.
73. Bowman, *Struggle for Neutrality*, 300–301; DeConde, *Quasi-War*, 37–38.

navigators of the earth," Otto warned against handing over American maritime skill to England. He also attacked the persistent notion that the U.S. government had betrayed the American people in accommodating Britain. The Directory must stop assuming that "most of the American people were devoted to France and only the government was sympathetic toward England," since the United States "had the freest elections in the world." More numerous than either the "French" or "English" parties in America was the "American" party.[74]

The triumvirate of Reubell, LaRevellière, and Barras was able to squelch this conservative opposition. In the legislature their ally Joseph F. M. Riou accused Pastoret of favoring England and "the Americans, who, since their treaty of alliance and commerce with Great Britain, make amends every day for the crime of having vanquished liberty."[75] These anti-American views were actually supported by Jefferson, who sent a letter to a Frenchman decrying Federalist autocracy, and by Thomas Paine (now a Paris resident), who publicly blasted Washington and encouraged the Directory not to receive the American envoy in 1797.[76] Soon the militants called the coup d'état of 18 Fructidor, purging Pastoret and his ilk from the government. Now genuinely short of funds, and incensed at Adams's May 1797 speech, the Directors wanted to punish the United States. Rather than negotiate a harsh treaty, however, the triumvirate directed the foreign minister, Charles Maurice de Talleyrand-Périgord, to extort millions of dollars from the Americans first. Talleyrand sent anonymous representatives, known as W, X, Y, and Z, in turn to Gerry, Marshall, and Pinckney to demand massive bribes. The shocked Americans refused to pay.[77]

When rumors of the XYZ Affair reached American shores, Jefferson and many Republicans refused to believe it.[78] Yet, anti-French sentiment began to rumble. Adams began to consider whether war with France was necessary to vindicate America's reputation. On 13 March 1798 the president drafted a message to Congress denouncing the Directory and stating that American honor and commerce demanded a full-scale war. "All men will think it more honorable and glorious to the national character when its existence as an independent nation is at stake that hostilities should be avowed in a formal Declaration of War,"

74. James A. James, "French Opinion as a Factor in Preventing War between France and the United States, 1795–1800," *American Historical Review* 30 (October 1924), 45, 53–54; Bowman, *Struggle for Neutrality*, 298.

75. Ibid., 311.

76. Bernard Faÿ, *The Revolutionary Spirit in France and America*, trans. Raymond Guthrie (New York: Cooper Square, 1966), 380–83, 401–4.

77. DeConde, *Quasi-War*, 46–51.

78. Elkins and McKitrick, *Age of Federalism*, 549–50.

he wrote. The draft message explicitly denied that the French Revolution had anything in common with the American.

Large segments of the public now called for war. "Millions for defense, not one cent for tribute!" became the cry. Pinckney's brother Thomas argued that France had shown it could not be trusted to uphold fellow republics, citing Napoleon's recent overthrow of the five-hundred-year-old Venetian Republic.[79] Republicans were verbally attacked without mercy, as Federalists stirred up fears of Jacobin lawlessness, atheism, libertinism, Freemasonry, and abolitionism.[80] High Federalists, predisposed to favor England over France, typically appealed to America's need to answer French humiliations. Some mentioned the possibility of wresting New Orleans and the Floridas from France's ally Spain.[81] Among the most violent was Pickering, who "longed to mount a grand crusade against the hideous menace of jacobinism, licence, and disorder, and [saw] the logical way to do it [as making] common cause with England, the more fully and explicitly the better."[82]

Nonetheless Republicans in and outside government stood staunchly by their fellow republicans in France. They vehemently disagreed with Adams as to the meaning of French actions and how America should respond, and largely blamed their own government for the friction. Jefferson commented after Adams's 1797 anti-French speech: "Thus we see two nations who love one another affectionately, brought by the temper of their executive administrations, to the very brink of a necessity to imbue their hands in the blood of each other." The vice president even hoped that France would, as rumored, invade England and "republicanize that country," so that "all will be safe with us."[83] The Boston *Independent Chronicle* averred that "'our Pharaohs' still wishfully looked for the downfall of the Republic and were ready to 'lend a hand to effect it.'" The New York *Diary* said of the Federalists: "The tory faction will endeavour to torture fact, in order to excite our feelings against the cause of liberty and the revolution. . . . Let us be calm."[84]

Adams never submitted his war message. Rather, he resorted to a series of hostile measures short of war amounting to a "state of limited hostilities against France." Adams authorized the arming of U.S. merchant vessels and planned to seek further provocative policies.

79. *Annals of Congress,* 5th Cong., 2d sess., 27 March 1798, cols. 1336–38.
80. DeConde, *Quasi-War,* 82–88.
81. "We can buy at a price cheap to ourselves the full co-operation of the British navy," relieve French pressure on England, take New Orleans and the Floridas, and "free ourselves from a troublesome neighbor," i.e., Spain, Robert Goodloe Harper of South Carolina told his constituents. DeConde, *Quasi-War,* 26–27.
82. Elkins and McKitrick, *Age of Federalism,* 583–84.
83. DeConde, *Quasi-War,* 34; Stinchcombe, *XYZ Affair,* 118.
84. Stewart, *Opposition Press,* 286–90.

Whether he hoped that the resulting "quasi-war" would result in incidents that would lead to full-scale war is not clear.[85] Between March and July 1798 Congress passed a number of laws designed to punish France. The laws procured ships and guns, embargoed France and its dependencies, abrogated all treaties with France, and finally authorized the navy and privateers to capture French ships anywhere they could be found.[86] Even Federalists who wanted war had to acknowledge that the Republican opposition blocked it. As Rep. Joseph McDowell of North Carolina announced in May to the House, "nothing could induce him more to oppose a war with France, than the strong conviction with which his mind was impressed that the certain consequence will be an alliance with Great Britain—a Government which he looked upon as the worst upon earth."[87]

Knowing Federalist attitudes toward France, Republicans were smart enough to base most of their arguments in Congress on the destructiveness of a French war and the danger to the lives of Gerry, Marshall, and Pinckney rather than on solidarity with the French republic.[88] Republicans were trying to convince the brokers who stood in the middle, i.e., the moderate Federalists. Moderates were wary of outright war, fearing that the United States was too divided to fight the French outright. As one put it after the defeat of a test vote in the House in July 1798, "we should have war; but he did not wish to go on faster to this state of things than the people of this country, and the opinion of the world would justify."[89]

When the XYZ allegations became public in France, Talleyrand was engulfed in scandal. Rather than defend the policy, both he and the Directors denied the extortion allegations. To the French public, the United States was still a powerful symbol of republicanism. Bernard Faÿ writes that ties with the United States were a source of prestige for the Directory, whose legitimacy was questionable.[90] There were moreover some economic ties between the two countries, though not as strong as those between the United States and Britain. Americans bought wine, brandy, vinegar, ribbons, silks, linens, and porcelain from

85. Adams's genuine anger at France and his drafting of the war message suggest he wanted war but was simply constrained by Republicans in Congress from asking for it. On the other hand, in 1799 Adams sent another peace mission to France that was ultimately successful. Elkins and McKitrick argue that this mission was in part motivated by Adams's fear that Hamilton was using the conflict with France to build the U.S. military and become general. Elkins and McKitrick, *Age of Federalism*, 614–17.

86. DeConde, *Quasi-War*, 67–106.

87. *Annals of Congress*, 23 May 1798, col. 1801.

88. *Annals of Congress*, 27 March 1798, cols. 1329 et seq.

89. DeConde, *Quasi-War*, 106.

90. Faÿ, *Revolutionary Spirit*, 382–83, 428–29.

France. The government also derived much-needed revenue from duties on U.S. tobacco imports.[91] Since the Directors had fallen into the habit of using the military to suppress opposition, however, they were relatively unconstrained by public opinion. Ironically, the American Republicans' concern for limited government led them to support a country whose government had broken away from all limits. Their fear of monarchy caused them to prefer dictatorship in France, yet also helped prevent a full Franco-American war.

American perceptions of France were a reverse image of those of Britain. Federalists were suspicious of France, and many called for full-scale war after the XYZ Affair. Republicans gave France the benefit of the doubt even when there was little doubt left. Adams pursued strict policies toward the French, but was constrained from hostility in part by the Republican opposition in Congress.

In France it is difficult to identify any liberals, and the Directory was a dictatorship, so we leave aside the question of liberal perceptions and constraints there.

THE ANGLO-AMERICAN CRISIS OF 1803–12

There had been no significant institutional change since 1798 in the United States. Both Congress and the Presidency were now controlled by the Republicans.

How Did Americans Perceive Great Britain?

The ideological map in America contained the same two camps, Federalists and Republicans. Federalists continued to envisage America as a commercial empire on the Hamiltonian model, with the moneyed class controlling a strong central government. Most Republicans maintained their vision of a more egalitarian, agricultural society.[92]

The mainstream of each party carried on with its foreign policy strategy from the previous decade as well. Federalists loathed France more than ever, and wanted harmony with England. The accession of Napoleon Bonaparte soured many Republicans on France as well, to the point where some (the so-called Quids, including John Randolph of

---

91. E. Wilson Lyon, "The Directory and the United States," *American Historical Review* 43 (April 1938), 525.

92. A prominent exception was Albert Gallatin, the treasury secretary. See Ray Walters, *Albert Gallatin: Jeffersonian Financier and Diplomat* (New York: Macmillan, 1957), esp. 181–84. I thank Stephen Rosen for pointing this out to me.

Virginia) now even supported England in the war. Still, most Republicans maintained their strong fear of Britain, conceding that although France was no longer a friendly sister republic, it was still less dangerous than the government of George III. Jefferson believed that "the nature of England's government unfit that country . . . 'for the observation of moral duties,' and nothing would prevent it from making a separate peace with Napoleon and exposing the United States to his wrath were this country to join forces with England." France's government, meanwhile, even under Bonaparte, made it more trustworthy: "A republican emperor, from his affection to republics, independent of motives of expediency, must grant to ours the Cyclop's boon of being the last devoured."[93] The foreign policy strategies of the Federalists and Republicans were essentially the same as the had been in the 1790s.

How Did the British Perceive the United States?

British institutions had changed little since the 1790s, and so, objectively, Britain remained only semiliberal. As before, there were those who actively sought liberal reforms in British politics. Reformers were animated by either or both of two motives. First, manufacturers and merchants in the north wanted to break the hold of the agricultural and maritime interests on public policy. Their cities were grossly underrepresented in Parliament, and trade was hampered as a result. Second was the group calling itself the "friends of peace." These were religious Dissenters who believed the established church and aristocracy were barriers to progress. The middle classes should have the vote, the friends of peace believed, and religious nonconformists should have full liberty.[94]

Reformers tended to view the United States as a model of liberty; many even wished to see a republican Britain. One member of Parliament, Samuel Whitbread, looked upon the American Revolution "with reverence and admiration."[95] Henry Brougham was an Edinburgh Whig steeped in the Scottish Enlightenment that produced David Hume and Adam Smith. A radical reformer, active in his twenties in the anti-slavery movement, Brougham openly admired the leveling tendencies

93. Robert W. Tucker and David C. Hendrickson, *Empire of Liberty: The Statecraft of Thomas Jefferson* (New York: Oxford University Press, 1990), 329–30. Bradford Perkins writes that despite their feelings that Napoleon had betrayed the French Revolution, they considered Britain the greater threat and "often wished Napoleon well." Perkins, *Prologue to War* (Berkeley: University of California Press, 1961), 63.

94. J. E. Cookson, *The Friends of Peace: Anti-war Liberalism in England, 1793–1815* (Cambridge: Cambridge University Press, 1982), 1–29.

95. Reginald Horsman, *The Causes of the War of 1812* (Philadelphia: University of Pennsylvania Press, 1962), 18–19.

of American democracy.[96] Jeremy Bentham, the utilitarian philosopher, had soured on democracy because of the French Revolution, but the American example persuaded him to become a democrat. Bentham complained bitterly in 1809 that while America already had a rational constitution, and "nothing but what is good, results from it," anyone proposing reform in Britain was attacked as subversive.[97]

More conservative Britons, who resisted reform, had hardened their views of the United States. Especially the Tories who held power for most of the 1803–12 period regarded Thomas Jefferson and other Republican leaders as "sycophants of France through sympathy or through fear."[98] One pamphlet attributed American affinity for France to "the excessively democratic nature of the American government, from the universal suffrage and elective magistracy, which are its distinguishing features, and the violent party contentions by which such a government must always be agitated."[99] Like the reformers, the conservatives saw the American question as integrally linked with the question of liberalism in Britain. Closer relations with America would mean encouragement for those who wanted to overthrow the established order in England.

Actions, Interpretations, Reactions

The Treaty of Amiens in 1801 brought peace between Britain and France, but war began again in 1803 with a new intensity. Believing their islands to be in immediate danger of invasion, the British stepped up impressment, the practice of seizing suspected British deserters from American merchant ships. Up to 1803, according to unofficial figures, England had impressed 2,410 seamen from ships sailing under the American flag; between 1803 and 1806 alone, the figure was 2,798.[100] Napoleon then courted U.S. sympathies by reopening France's West Indian colonies to U.S. vessels. The carrying trade proved extremely lucrative to the American merchant marine.[101]

96. Robert Stewart, *Henry Brougham, 1778–1868: His Public Career* (London: The Bodley Head, 1985), 3–5, 18–19; *Hansard's Parliamentary Debates*, 1st ser., vol. 23 (16 June 1812), cols. 514–15.

97. Jeremy Bentham, *Plan of Parliamentary Reform* (1809), quoted in Jon Roper, *Democracy and Its Critics* (London: Unwin Hyman, 1989), 132.

98. Perkins, *Prologue to War*, 7–8; Horsman, *Causes of the War of 1812*, 190–93.

99. Samuel MacCormack, *A View of the State of Parties in the United States of America*, 2d ed. (Edinburgh: James Ballantyne & Co., 1812), 4–5, 103–6.

100. Horsman, *Causes of the War of 1812*, 26–28.

101. While in 1792 U.S. ships had carried 1,112,000 lbs. of sugar to Europe, in 1804 the figure was 74,000,000 lbs.; in 1792 the figure for coffee was 2,136,742 lbs., while in 1804 it was 48,000,000 lbs. Horsman, *Causes of the War of 1812*, 30–31.

British impressment at first elicited no official U.S. response. Thomas Jefferson, now President, even toyed with the idea of an alliance with Britain as late as 1805. But in May of that year a British court ruled American transport of French goods illegal. Under the Pitt government, the British Navy began seizing cargoes carried by U.S. merchant ships. The main argument for British policy was found in James Stephen's 1805 pamphlet *War in Disguise; or, the Frauds of Neutral Flags*. Stephen pointed out that America was supplying the "sinews of war" to Napoleon and asserted that the Americans would surely not respond to British policy with war, since they knew that "the subjugation of England, would be fatal to the last hope of liberty in Europe."[102]

Stephen was correct that war was not yet to come, and also that many Americans believed that England was fighting for freedom. Not only Federalists but also Quid Republicans sympathized with England over Napoleonic France. Rep. John Randolph asked fellow Congressmen: "How far is it impolitic in the United States to throw their weight into the scale of France at this moment . . . to jeopardize the liberties of mankind?"[103] Still, in early 1806 Congress passed the Nonimportation Act, which would begin limiting British imports at the end of 1807.[104]

In early 1806 Pitt died, to be replaced at the premiership by Charles James Fox, the aging liberal reformer and friend of America. Fox helped pass an American Intercourse Bill permitting neutral vessels to carry goods from the Caribbean to Britain. When Napoleon responded with his Berlin Decree prohibiting all neutral trade with England, it appeared the United States and Britain were headed toward a cooperative arrangement. But Fox's death in January 1807, and the coming of a Tory government in March, reversed Anglo-American relations. In June a British ship fired on the U.S. frigate *Chesapeake*, killing three and wounding eighteen. Americans were seething for war, but Jefferson averted hostilities by allowing the Nonimportation Act to go into effect. In November the British cabinet issued more extreme Orders in Council prohibiting neutrals from almost all trade with Britain's enemies. Napoleon responded with the Milan Decree, stating that any ship searched by the British, or which visited a British port or paid a British duty, was liable to French seizure.[105]

In December 1807 Jefferson took the most extreme measure yet, asking Congress to pass a total embargo that would confine American ships to American ports. The Embargo Act passed the Senate 22–6 and

---

102. Perkins, *Prologue to War*, 76–80; Horsman, *Causes of the War of 1812*, 39–43, 254–58.
103. *Annals of Congress*, 9th Cong., 1st sess., 6 March 1806, vol. 15, col. 559.
104. Horsman, *Causes of the War of 1812*, 63–78, 90–94.
105. Ibid., 95–121.

the House 82–44 after two days of debate.[106] The embargo appeared evenhanded, but since Britain had effectively severed the U.S. merchant marine from France, it was bound to affect Britain more. Some historians argue, in fact, that Jefferson intended the embargo as a first step to war with England. In any event, Jefferson's policy clearly tilted toward France. Burton Spivak argues that "the bias reflected a lingering anglophobia that defined Republicanism itself."[107]

Concerned about the embargo, Whig reformers in England began a campaign to repeal the Orders in Council. In 1808 Alexander Baring published his *Inquiry into the Causes and Consequences of the Orders in Council,* in which he argued that the orders damaged the balance of trade at a time when England could ill afford it.[108] Baring also publicly averred that too many Britons' views of America were colored by resentment of U.S. independence and prosperity.[109] Baring's advocacy was doubtless motivated by financial interest, as his family's banking house had large amounts invested in the United States.[110] Also damaged by the orders were northern industrialists now denied the lucrative U.S. market. Liverpool manufacturers hired Henry Brougham, a young liberal lawyer, to petition Parliament for repeal. Conservatives resisted, however. The landed interests wanted to keep U.S. agricultural products out. They also feared that conciliating the United States would strengthen republicanism and Bonapartism in their own country. Seeing Jefferson as a sycophant of Bonaparte, the *Leicester Journal* was driven to inelegance:

> NAPOLEON's example to copy he strives,
> And NAPOLEON, it seems, at his project connives;
> He would quarrel with Britain, I'm sure if he durst,
> For the Corsican's friend is this—THOMAS THE FIRST.[111]

Conservatives won in 1808, and the orders continued in force.

106. Ibid., 109–10.

107. Burton Spivak, *Jefferson's English Crisis: Commerce, Embargo, and the Republican Revolution* (Charlottesville: University Press of Virginia, 1979), 124. Spivak adds that "the obvious fact that British oppression was greater, more insulting, and of a longer run" also contributed to the tilt toward France. Yet, considerations of British strength alone would suggest that America follow Federalist advice and "bandwagon" with Britain. Republican anglophobia is necessary to account for Jefferson's policy.

108. Cookson, *Friends of Peace,* 66–67.

109. Horsman, *Causes of the War of 1812,* 194.

110. Baring was also married to an American woman (a daughter of a senator from New York) and had lived for years in Philadelphia. As one historian writes, "Barings were constantly preoccupied by the bad relations between Britain and the United States. The problem was personal . . . but it was also, and more immediately, a business one." Philip Ziegler, *The Sixth Great Power: Barings 1762–1929* (London: Collins, 1988), 73.

111. Horsman, *Causes of the War of 1812,* 190–93.

By the end of the year it was clear that the U.S. embargo had not only failed to coerce either belligerent into respecting neutral trade but had also deeply damaged the U.S. economy. Still reluctant to resort to war, Congress in March 1809 passed the Nonintercourse Act, which embargoed only France and Britain and allowed the president, now James Madison, to rescind the embargo for either belligerent at his discretion.[112] Madison did so when the British minister, David Erskine, signed an agreement ending the Orders in Council. It appeared that liberal statecraft had triumphed. But then George Canning, the British foreign secretary, repudiated the Erskine Agreement. Madison renewed nonintercourse with England.[113]

Now resolutions from around the United States began calling for war with England. In May 1810 Congress passed the weakest measure of retaliation yet. Macon's Bill No. 2 was an effort in reverse psychology: it repealed all nonintercourse, but promised that if either belligerent rescinded its trade sanctions, the United States would renew nonintercourse with the other.

Apparently rising to the bait, Napoleon notified the United States in August that as of 1 November the Berlin and Milan decrees would be null and void and that France would cease interfering with U.S. commerce on the high seas. Bonaparte was lying, but Madison chose to believe him, and on 11 March America once again cut itself off from England.[114]

Again in England reformers mounted a vigorous campaign for repeal of the Orders in Council. This time the northern manufacturers were rallied by rank-and-file religious Dissenters who gathered petitions. The Dissenters not only wanted a government more responsible to the public and policy friendlier to peace and "commercial principles." They also objected particularly to a war with the United States, a country, as J. E. Cookson writes, "some of them admired . . . above their own for its egalitarianism, democracy and religious toleration."[115] The petitions often referred to Anglo-American commonalities. Glasgow merchants urged that "America, where our most extensive market, and, from the nature of her government, and the manners of her people, our best allies may be expected, should not be added to the already too numerous list of our enemies."[116]

Conservative Tories and Whigs continued to resist the reformers' arguments, maintaining that the justifications for the Orders had lost

112. Ibid., 109–10, 140–42.
113. Ibid., 149–52.
114. J. C. A. Stagg, *Mr. Madison's War: Politics, Diplomacy, and Warfare in the Early American Republic, 1783–1830* (Princeton: Princeton University Press, 1983), 55.
115. Cookson, *Friends of Peace*, 217.
116. *Hansard's Parliamentary Debates*, 1st ser., vol. 23 (21 May 1812), col. 248.

none of their original force. In 1811 Spencer Perceval's Tory government ordered another pamphlet, John Wilson Croker's *A Key to the Orders in Council,* arguing that "if the Orders were repealed, the United States would become carrier of the world, and the British shipping interest would be annihilated."[117] But the aristocracy resisted good relations with the United States out of fear that American republicanism was metastasizing across the Atlantic. At the same time, conservatives believed the American Republicans weak and unpopular in their own land. Conservatives were in fact victims of skewed intelligence. Naturally enough, the Americans with whom they communicated were mostly Federalists, who as partisans for the British cause sent articles to England portraying their opponents as weak. The anti-British Republicans rarely sent material to Britain.[118]

This time, however, the British liberals were to win the government over. The U.S. embargo was wreaking economic havoc in northern England and Scotland. By early 1812 between 20,000 and 25,000 Birmingham men were working only half-time.[119] Upper-class fears of riots and revolts brought the orders to the brink of repeal. A political accident pushed them over. In May a madman assassinated Perceval, an adamant supporter of the orders. The reformers' great triumph came with the complete rescission of the Orders in Council on 23 June 1812.[120]

It was too late. While British liberals were agitating for peace, the American Republicans they admired were agitating for war. So-called "malcontents" had been pushing Madison since 1809 to prepare for war,[121] in spite of the nation's strong economic ties with the United Kingdom. Trade with England averaged $14.8 million per annum between 1800 and 1812; the comparable figure with France was only $5.3 million.[122] The port cities of Boston, New York, Philadelphia, and Baltimore were heavily interested in British commerce. Farmers, too, were interested: in 1811, of 62 million pounds of cotton exported from the U.S., 38 million went to Britain.[123] Yet by that year most Republicans

117. Horsman, *Causes of the War of 1812,* 255.

118. Ibid., 190–93.

119. Ibid., 101–2.

120. Cookson, *Friends of Peace,* 234–37.

121. Stagg, *Mr. Madison's War,* 48–61.

122. Averages calculated from U.S. Bureau of Statistics, *Statistical Tables Exhibiting the Commerce of the United States with European Countries from 1790 to 1890* (Washington: Government Printing Office, 1893), xv, xviii. The French figure includes no trade in the year 1809.

123. Norman Sydney Buck, *The Development of the Organisation of Anglo-American Trade 1800–1850* (New Haven: Yale University Press, 1925), 31, 34 (Buck concedes that he cannot vouch for the veracity of all the figures he lists); Stuart Bruchey, ed., *Cotton and the Growth of the American Economy: 1790–1860* (New York: Harcourt, Brace & World, Inc., 1967), Tables 3A and 3F.

had begun to see their country's repeated humiliation as a threat to national sovereignty and to republicanism itself. France too was abusing the United States, but as historian Roger Brown shows, Jeffersonians believed the stakes were larger than simply seized cargoes. Republicans began fearing a "change of men" in government, meaning a Federalist electoral victory arising out of their own foreign policy failures. Such a change, Republicans believed, would lead to an alignment with England and possibly a restoration of monarchy in America.[124]

Richard Rush, Comptroller of the Treasury, wrote privately: "Being the only republick, the destinies of that sort of government are in our keeping. Should we stand by and see it longer debased by submission, or sordid avarice, its cause is gone forever."[125] John Campbell, a Virginia state legislator, wrote: "Time will soon test the durability of republican governments and shew the truth or falicy of the maxim that man is incapable of self-government." The *National Intelligencer* averred, "Not only the rights of the Nation, but the character of the government," the very future of republicanism, were at stake.[126] Madison himself felt these fears.[127] William Plumer of New Hampshire, a former Federalist, wrote a colleague that if England did not desist, "one of two things will follow, Congress will declare war, or the government of our Country will be *degraded*—degraded so that *hosts of tories* will emphatically *be* found *in private life*."[128]

Madison's December 1811 address recommended arming the nation. The new Congress of 1811, dominated by Henry Clay and the so-called War Hawks, was ready. Clay, John C. Calhoun, and others believed a government that did not protect its citizens would forfeit the right to govern.[129]

The country was certainly not unanimously in favor of war with England. Opposition was so fierce in fact that many New Englanders threatened secession. Federalists held two views of the goals of Jefferson and Madison, summed up by one critic: "That the Administration is bent on checking the spirit of Commerce, and gradually undermining it I have no doubt. That it is favorably disposed towards the French Government I more than Suspect."[130] They lambasted the Republicans as madmen with no business sense. The *New York Herald* declared that

124. Roger Brown, *The Republic in Peril: 1812* (New York: Columbia University Press, 1964), 73–76; Stagg, *Mr. Madison's War*, 61–63.

125. Brown, *Republic in Peril*, 83–84.

126. Ibid., 76–77.

127. Robert A. Rutland, ed., *Madison's Alternatives* (Philadelphia: J. B. Lippincott, 1975), 142–48; Ketcham, *James Madison*, 530.

128. Brown, *Republic in Peril*, 82.

129. Ibid., 76–79.

130. Abraham Van Vechten, quoted in ibid., 163.

"nothing was ever so universally execrated as is the projected war by every man . . . who possesses the means of earning a decent subsistence."[131] The Boston *Columbian Centinel* predicted that its city's wealthy residents would "lend no money to the ruling faction, for the same reason that they would not lend swords to the tenants of a lunatic hospital."[132]

More was at stake than profits, the Federalists believed. For them, England was fighting the world's fight against Napoleonic despotism, and the Republicans were Napoleon's fifth column in America. Leonard White of Massachusetts wrote that "what is more than all to be dreaded & feared is an alliance with the Emperor of France which must naturally & most assuredly be the consequence of this measure."[133] War with England, declared one North Carolina Federalist, was "Democratic folly and wickedness."[134]

Also afraid of aiding France were the Quid Republicans, led by Randolph of Virginia. Upon being challenged by a fellow Congressman for his open pride in America's English heritage, Randolph retorted: "Could that gentleman repose his head upon his pillow without returning thanks to God that he was descended from English parentage? Whence but from that origin came all the blessings of life, so far as political privileges are concerned? To what is it owing that we are at this moment deliberating under the forms of a free representative Government?"[135] Other Republicans opposed war because they felt the Northeast was exposed to Canada. Still others, headed by George and De Witt Clinton of New York, opposed war as part of their obsession with ending Virginian domination of the White House.[136]

Madison and the War Hawks had their way, however. The war vote in the House was 79–49, and in the Senate, 19–13. Even with some in their party voting against them, the Republican leaders got their war declaration. Why now but not in 1794 or 1796? Republican ideology had gained strength in the United States since the 1790s. Historians assert that this is because the Federalists had proved too elitist. During the Quasi-War with France, the Federalist-dominated Congress had enacted the Alien and Sedition Acts, which made it more difficult for foreigners to become citizens and criminalized libels against federal officials. Congress also made plans for a huge standing army, under the command of Alexander Hamilton himself. More and more Americans began to see the Federalist program as the twin of that of Pitt the

---

131. *New York Herald,* 19 May 1812, quoted in Perkins, *Prologue to War,* 395.
132. *Columbian Centinel* (Boston), 6 May 1812, quoted in ibid., 389.
133. Brown, *Republic in Peril,* 174–75.
134. Joseph Pearson, quoted in ibid., 175.
135. *Annals of Congress,* 12th Cong., 1st sess., 16 December 1811, vol. 23, col. 536.
136. Brown, *Republic in Peril,* 131–33, 141–56; Stagg, *Mr. Madison's War,* chap. 2.

Younger and George III.[137] The Republican Presidential victory in 1800, sometimes called the second American revolution, signaled a nation ready for Jeffersonian liberalism, and paved the way for the Anglo-American war that George Washington had averted in 1794–96.

With the exception of a few Republicans, perceptions of Britain (and France) by the two American parties were the same as they had been in the 1790s. Federalists interpreted British actions kindly, while Republicans saw them as menacing and imposed economic sanctions that in effect were more damaging to the British than to the French. Federalists helped constrain Jefferson and Madison from more hostile policies, but in the end Madison and the War Hawk Congress were able to declare war.

British liberal affinity for the United States was more in evidence now than in the 1790s. Reformers perceived a beleaguered United States that ought to be accommodated, while their conservative opponents wanted to punish America for helping the French. Surprisingly, given the insulation of the government from public opinion, in the end the reformers had some effect, as the British cabinet agreed to rescind the Orders in Council, albeit too late to prevent Anglo-American war.

In large measure, domestic ideology produced the perceptions Americans and British had of each other's country. The same divisions in both countries were to affect Anglo-American relations in the 1840s and 1860s as well, and would affect American perceptions of Mexico as well.

137. Elkins and McKitrick, *Age of Federalism*, 590–99.

[4]

From the Oregon Crisis
to the Civil War

*A line of separation, as yet not fully disclosed, has thus been drawn be-
tween England and America, on the one hand, and the antagonistic systems of the old world, on the other, which promises to endure as long as
anything that depends upon the will of the action of man, and thus interests of the greatest magnitude have become the subject of common and
equal concern to the two former Nations. Every assault upon those interests, whether immediately directed against them in Great Britain or in
the United States, must be regarded as an attack upon both and will, it is
to be hoped, be met with equal spirit by both.*

Martin Van Buren,
after the British Great Reform Act of 1832

*There never was a State in the world less capable of aggression with re-
gard to Europe than the United States of America. I speak of its Government, of its confederation, of the peculiarities of its organization; for the
House will agree with me that nothing is more peculiar than the fact of
the great power which the separate States, both of the North and South,
exercise upon the policy and course of the country.*

John Bright in the House of Commons,
30 June 1863

The War of 1812 left the United States in a period of relative national
unity, an "Era of Good Feelings," but competing visions for the country
remained. These visions diverged more sharply in the 1820s and 1830s,
until by the 1840s they stood in sharp relief. The Democrats, direct heirs
of the Jeffersonians, clung to the view of a society of yeoman farmers,
equal in standing, and a weak central government. The Whigs, indirect
heirs of the Federalists, held a vision of an urban, industrial, hierarchical
nation with a strong central state. This philosophical division had reper-

cussions for domestic and foreign politics. Favoring agriculture, Democrats tended to be expansionist and proslavery, while proindustry Whigs (and later Republicans) were wary of expansion and slavery.

Each faction's vision for America also colored its perceptions of foreign countries, in particular of Britain. Most Democrats were as hostile toward England as Jefferson had been, while Whigs (and certain Democrats such as Martin Van Buren, quoted above) tended to admire the mother country as Hamilton had done. The Democrats' perceptions combined with their policy prescriptions to bring about the first two war-threatening crises studied in this chapter. In the mid-1840s, expansionist Democrats were determined to acquire Texas, New Mexico, California, and Oregon for the Union. These ambitions collided with the perceived interests of many British, who claimed these territories for themselves. War with England over Oregon was narrowly averted, in part because Whigs and some Democrats blocked it. But the United States fought and won a controversial war against Mexico in 1846–48, as the expansionists argued that their southern neighbor was about to fall into monarchy.

Leaders and elites in Mexico and Britain in the middle of the nineteenth century likewise had incompatible visions for their own countries—liberal and conservative, republican and monarchical—and those visions affected their views on the desirability of war with the United States in the 1840s. Even more dramatically, the British struggle over whether liberalism was compatible with (or required) democracy heavily influenced the question of whether to intervene on the side of the Confederacy during the Civil War. The Union and Britain teetered on the brink of war three times between 1861 and 1863 but drew back each time. Once Abraham Lincoln demonstrated through the Emancipation Proclamation that the Union was fighting to free the slaves, British Liberals and Radicals threw their support behind the Union. Helping the Confederacy became politically unthinkable for the British cabinet.

THE ANGLO-AMERICAN CRISIS OF 1845–46

How Liberal Was the United States?

Popular sovereignty had been strengthened by a widening of suffrage since 1812.[1] The United States again earns a high liberal rating.

1. The franchise had been expanded in most states to include all adult white males, giving more citizens leverage over the government. Most states had eliminated voting restrictions on white males by 1845. See Marchette Chute, *The First Liberty: A History of the Right to Vote in America, 1619–1850* (New York: E. P. Dutton, 1969), 313; Chilton Williamson, *American Suffrage: From Property to Democracy 1760–1860* (Princeton: Princeton

How Did Americans Perceive Great Britain?

Americans were again divided into two main parties. As in the 1790–1812 period, both are properly labeled liberal. Yet, like the Federalists and Republicans before them, the Whigs and Democrats had distinct and incompatible visions for the country.

The Democratic Party was directly descended from the Jeffersonian Republicans; but as its change of name implies, it had become even more egalitarian since the days of Jefferson and Madison. Andrew Jackson, elected president in 1828 and 1832, represented the small farmers and artisans who gained the vote in large numbers in the 1820s. Democrats firmly believed in the future progress of the United States through territorial expansion, free trade, and equality of opportunity. They organized in opposition to the illiberalism they perceived in the ideas of Henry Clay, under which the federal government would guide the nation to prosperity through a strong central bank, public works projects, and the tariff. As president, Jackson vetoed the reinstitution of the "Monster Institution," the Bank of the United States (BUS), as a violation of states' rights and a ploy to concentrate power in the hands of an oligarchy.[2] Jacksonians, including James K. Polk, president during the Oregon and Mexican crises, held to the Jeffersonian vision of an America of yeoman farmers. As Thomas Hietala writes, they feared that the urbanization and industrialization of the Northeast would lead to a loss of republican virtue. They favored free trade and territorial expansion as ways to keep America rural and free.[3]

Jackson's veto of the BUS led Clay, Daniel Webster, and John C. Calhoun, three powerful senators, to organize the Whig Party (Calhoun returned to the Democrats in 1838). Claiming that Jackson was becoming "King Andrew" and arrogating excessive power to himself, the Whigs named themselves for the English gentry party that had opposed monarchical aggrandizement. Whigs considered the greatest threat to personal liberty an untutored mob in the hands of a demagogue. They held that the key to national progress was technological advancement directed by an enlightened central government. Daniel Walker Howe writes that the Whigs saw themselves as moderates guiding the nation "between the dangers of anarchy and the pressures of despotism." It was the duty of government to improve the condition of the governed,

University Press, 1960), viii. Yet slavery continued in the Southern states, and persecution of Indians continued unabated. See Robert Weil, *The Legal Status of the Indian* (1888; reprint, New York: AMS, 1975), 20–21.

2. Robert V. Remini, *Henry Clay: Statesman for the Union* (New York: W. W. Norton, 1991), 398.

3. Thomas R. Hietala, *Manifest Design: Anxious Aggrandizement in Late Jacksonian America* (Ithaca: Cornell University Press, 1985), 104–5.

they believed, which meant not only roads and canals and protection of industry but also moral legislation such as temperance and Sabbatarian laws. Whigs wanted a strong Congress and courts and a weaker President.[4]

Neither party can fairly be called more liberal than the other. All wanted prosperity, but there were two incompatible visions for achieving it. Democrats wanted free trade, laissez-faire, and local government. Whigs wanted the sure hand of the central government.[5] Democrats were more attached to "negative" liberty and were more supportive of unbridled competition, aggressive territorial expansion, and a powerful executive. Whigs elevated rational discussion over Darwinian competition, favored the tariff, and sought a more "positive" liberty.

The issue of slavery was much more divisive than it had been in earlier crises. Abolitionists, led in Congress by John Quincy Adams, tended to be Whigs. They were unlike other Whigs in that they were expansionist but only wanted free territory (i.e., territory that would expand the North). Apologists for slavery, led by John C. Calhoun, were mostly Democrats. They tended to want to expand Southern territory rather than Northern. As I show below, however, the Southerners' positions on war with Britain and Mexico cannot be reduced to a wish to annex Texas rather than Oregon.

Given their different visions and favored institutions, it is no surprise that Democrats and Whigs held widely divergent perceptions of England. Whigs tended to admire the British, particularly after the Great Reform Act of 1832, which, they claimed, restored the proper balance between aristocracy and bourgeoisie.[6] Daniel Webster identified a common commitment to liberty in the two countries in a speech in 1844: "I find at work everywhere, on both sides of the Atlantic . . . the great principle of *the freedom of human thought, and the respectability of individual character*. I find, everywhere, an elevation . . . of the individual as a component part of society. I find everywhere a rebuke of the idea, that . . . government is anything but an *agency* of mankind."[7] The American Whigs, like most Englishmen of the ruling classes, mistrusted mass opinion as a guide to politics. Their admiration of Britain affected their perceptions of the supposed British threat to U.S. security. In 1843 Clay publicly declared that, contrary to the fears of expansionist Democrats,

4. Daniel Walker Howe, *The Political Culture of the American Whigs* (Chicago: University of Chicago Press, 1979). See also Louis Hartz, *The Liberal Tradition in America* (New York: Harcourt Brace Jovanovich, 1955), chap. 4.

5. Daniel Walker Howe, ed. *The American Whigs* (New York: John Wiley and Sons, 1973), 4–5.

6. Howe, *Political Culture*, 77. The 1832 Reform Act is discussed below.

7. Quoted in John Dos Passos, *The Anglo-American Century* (New York: n.p., 1903), 63–64.

England neither threatened to swallow Texas nor to oppose U.S. claims to Oregon.[8]

A smaller group of Whigs, led by John Quincy Adams, the former President, admired England primarily for its leadership in the antislavery movement. For these abolitionists, the defining feature of liberal government was antislavery. They saw Britain as an ally in their struggle to emancipate the American slaves.[9]

Most Democrats, by contrast, carried on the Jeffersonian tradition of loathing Britain as a citadel of privilege and despotism. They either did not notice or were unimpressed by British constitutional reform.[10] Western Democrats in particular lambasted English greed and imperialism, the arrogance of the aristocracy, and treatment of the Irish.[11] As it had for the Jeffersonians, Britain epitomized for the Jacksonians precisely the society they feared most for their own country. "Like causes will produce like results," said one Congressman in a debate over expansion: unless the United States began favoring agriculture over manufacturing, it would become "like England, a nation of nabobs and paupers."[12] Democrats were confident that England was ripe for revolution because of its hierarchical society and government. For most of them, Great Britain was an aggressive empire as well as a symbol and source of the elitism, corruption, and instability they wanted to drive from American shores.

A major exception was the Southern Democrats, who tended to admire England for its ordered hierarchical society and its example of a strong aristocracy acting as a hedge against tyranny.[13] Another was Martin Van Buren, the Democrats' *éminence grise*, who had watched Parliament debate the Great Reform Act from the gallery in 1832 and was certain that Britain was now a fellow free country.[14]

How Liberal Was Great Britain?

Van Buren recognized that Britain was undergoing a fundamental governmental transformation. The main instrument of change was the

8. Remini, *Clay*, 628.

9. "[Adams] had come to view the British people, if not their actual Government, as leaders of the antislavery movement throughout the world, even as he felt himself to be leader of the American people against the expansion of slavery in the United States." Samuel Flagg Bemis, *John Quincy Adams and the Union* (New York: Alfred A. Knopf, 1956), 457–58.

10. William Brock, "The Image of England and American Nationalism," *Journal of American Studies* 5 (December 1971), 225–45.

11. Frederick Merk, *The Oregon Question* (Cambridge: Harvard University Press, 1967), 372.

12. Representative Alfred Stone of Ohio speaking in early 1845, quoted in Hietala, *Manifest Design*, 106.

13. Brock, "Image of England," 228.

14. See the the epigraph at the head of this chapter.

Great Reform Act of 1832. Immediate concrete results of the act were modest: the franchise increased by at most 250,000, the Commons still comprised mainly aristocratic members and the Lords remained hereditary. But the Reform Act's real importance for liberalism in Britain is difficult to overstate. The act redistributed seats in the House of Commons away from so-called "pocket" and "rotten" boroughs, which were overrepresented and corrupt. Industrial areas that had grown in population since the seventeenth century were now represented for the first time. Middle-class men were the main winners from the reforms, as property qualifications for voting were lowered.[15]

Furthermore, final decision-making responsibility had passed from the monarch to the cabinet. Most important, the cabinet became responsible to Parliament rather than to the monarch. After 1832, there was never an instance of a monarch dismissing a ministry, even though legally such could still take place; from then on, ministries fell because the Commons voted them out.[16] This parliamentary control over the executive meant that the executive was ultimately accountable to the electors, who could indirectly oust the cabinet through Parliament.

Other reforms contributed to liberalization as well. Equality before the law was strengthened in 1829 as Protestant Dissenters and Catholics were fully emancipated. Slavery was outlawed in 1833. Freedom of the press became protected by the courts in 1813 with Lord Ellenborough's law of "fair comment on matters of public concern."[17] The other civil rights enjoyed by Englishmen continued in effect, and the civil government remained sovereign over the military. According to this book's criteria, Britain moves from semiliberal to liberal status.[18]

How Did the British Perceive the United States?

Meanwhile, liberalism had seeped into mainstream thinking in both the Whig and Tory parties by the 1840s. Sir Robert Peel, a Tory, had been largely responsible for Catholic emancipation in 1829. Like the Jacksonians, the Peelites sought to help the poor through attacking the paper money system and the financial speculation that led to harsh

15. Robert Livingston Schuyler and Corinne Comstock Weston, *British Constitutional History since 1832* (Princeton: D. Van Nostrand, 1957), 26–33.

16. Ibid., 34–44.

17. James Walvin, *England, Slaves, and Freedom 1776–1838* (Houndsmills, England: Macmillan, 1986), 44; Louis Edward Ingelhart, *Press Freedoms* (New York: Greenwood, 1987), 167.

18. Michael Doyle considers Britain to have become a liberal state in 1832. Doyle, "Liberalism in World Politics," *American Political Science Review* 80 (December 1986).

business cycles.[19] Mainstream Whigs such as Palmerston and Lord John Russell had tended to support reform in 1832 and were sympathetic to liberal movements in Europe, in defiance of the conservative system set up by the Concert of Europe. But for them, liberalism implied neither democracy nor republicanism. Both parties practiced an aristocratic liberalism that believed liberty would be best preserved for all if political power were withheld from the general public. Peel and his followers had opposed the 1832 reform bill as too democratic. Popular opinion, so often inconstant and imprudent, would no longer be checked by the other branches of government under the bill, Peel reasoned.[20]

As in 1812, however, there were Radicals who advocated greater rights for Dissenters and extension of the franchise. The working-class Chartist movement begun in the 1830s failed to achieve universal male suffrage, equal electoral districts, and the other reforms it sought. Yet it represented a segment of the population that agitated through the press and exerted some pressure over the government.

Both Tories and the ruling-class Whigs tended to hew to the old English view that the United States was excessively democratic and liable to behave recklessly toward other nations. Individual Tories or Whigs may have admired individual Americans, but as a whole the leadership of both parties saw America as a concrete example of the sort of government they were trying to stave off in their own country, one where the common man ruled. They were hostile to its republicanism, fearful of its democracy, and especially threatened by these features because of its success.[21] The Whig leader Viscount Palmerston was especially hostile to the United States.

On the other hand, the middle and working classes tended to see the United States as a model for Britain, where even a man without property could vote. The Radical *Chartist Circular* stirringly proclaimed: "From beneath the annihilating hoof of oppression . . . has sprung a nation—the bright luminary of the western hemisphere whose radiance will extend across the Atlantic's broad expanse and light the whole world to freedom and happiness."[22] Andrew Jackson was lionized, George Washington virtually worshipped, the Declaration of Indepen-

19. Charles Stuart Parker, ed., *Sir Robert Peel* (London: John Murray, 1899), 324; Robert Kelley, *The Transatlantic Persuasion* (New Brunswick, N.J.: Transaction Publishers, 1990), 186–89.

20. See Jon Roper, *Democracy and Its Critics* (London: Unwin Hyman, 1989), especially 137–47.

21. Merk, *Oregon Question*, 150.

22. *Chartist Circular*, 13 February 1841, quoted in G. D. Lillibridge, *Beacon of Freedom: The Impact of American Democracy upon Great Britain 1830–1870* (Philadelphia: University of Pennsylvania Press, 1955), 40.

dence taken as holy writ. Chartists constantly cited America as a land that showed how the absence of privilege led to universal prosperity and happiness.[23] Radical speeches and articles in the 1830s and 1840s brimmed with often exaggerated litanies of American achievements. Jeremy Bentham, the utilitarian philosopher, had written to Jackson that he was "more of a United States man than an Englishman." Benthamites commended U.S. political and legal institutions as rational replacements for their antiquated English counterparts. Both the middle and working classes saw U.S. institutions as the route to the political and social prestige and material comfort they so wanted.[24] In an 1837 flare-up over private American attempts to help discontented Canadians achieve independence from Britain, Radicals were strikingly pro-American, calling on their government to let Canada be absorbed by the United States and thereby prosper under republican institutions.[25]

Actions, Interpretations, Reactions

For James K. Polk, America's new president in 1845, the United States had been content too long to let the enormous areas of Texas, California, and Oregon languish under foreign sovereignty. Polk had won the presidency partly on the slogan "Fifty-four Forty or Fight!" referring to the northernmost latitude of the Oregon territory. The "fight," as everyone knew, would be against Great Britain, which also claimed Oregon. Jointly held by the two nations under an 1827 treaty, Oregon comprised what are now Washington, Oregon, Idaho, parts of Montana and Wyoming, and half of British Columbia. Americans were beginning to settle the territory in increasing numbers, and American and British fur traders had begun to clash. Polk and other expansionist Democrats also coveted California, then part of Mexico.

The British had strong incentives to oppose Polk. The Hudson's Bay Company in Britain wanted to preserve its control over the Oregon fur trade. More centrally, many British perceived a strong national interest in limiting U.S. power, especially over Canada. Most Englishmen knew of and cared little for Oregon, but most were noticing the rise of American power. As seen below, however, those who feared U.S. power were also those who feared U.S. institutions. Reformers did not feel menaced by rising American power.

Polk threw down a rhetorical gauntlet in his inaugural address of March 1845, proclaiming, "Our title to the country of Oregon is clear

23. Ibid., 40–58.
24. Frank Thistlethwaite, *The Anglo-American Connection in the Early Nineteenth Century* (Philadelphia: University of Pennsylvania Press, 1959), 40–43.
25. Lillibridge, *Beacon of Freedom*, 59–65.

and unquestionable." The *Times* thundered back that Polk's "pretensions amount, if acted upon, to the clearest *causa belli* [*sic*] which has ever yet arisen between Great Britain and the American Union," but added that "the same democratic folly which makes [the Americans] arrogant in the cabinet, makes them habitually feeble in . . . the field." Palmerston's *Morning Chronicle* expressed respect for Polk's boldness but demanded a vigorous response from the Tory government.[26]

Peel and Lord Aberdeen, the foreign secretary, gave a firm response. Aberdeen announced in the Lords, "I can only say that we possess rights which, in our opinion, are 'clear and unquestionable,' and by the blessing of God and your support, those rights we are fully prepared to maintain." One historian writes that this was "practically the only occasion in his life when Aberdeen sat down amidst 'loud and general applause.'" Peel made similar statements in the Commons, to similar acclamation.[27]

In America a few Democratic papers, especially in the western states, responded by baiting the British. "Why should we fear a conflict with Great Britain? . . . The Canadas are ripe for rebellion, and the single states of Ohio and New York could . . . reduce them to subjection in six weeks," claimed the Louisville *Daily Democrat*. Eastern and Southern editors were more conciliatory. The New York *Evening Post* took the line of John C. Calhoun, suggesting that the country let Oregon lie for a while. Polk himself interpreted the British response as an effort to test American nerve.[28]

Peel and Aberdeen did not want a war with the United States, especially over Oregon. This was not because of any admiration for the U.S. system of government, but was probably instead a result of apprehension that a Franco-American entente, similar to that of the 1780s, could come with war. Ever since the Peel cabinet assumed office in 1841, Aberdeen had been determined to improve British relations with both the United States and France, relations that Palmerston himself had roiled during his tenure as foreign secretary. The government's Oregon policy became one of deterrence and negotiation, building up British defenses even as it began suggesting third-party arbitration.[29]

Aberdeen felt domestically constrained, however, as the truculence of Polk and the expansionist Democrats had raised the hackles of those British already contemptuous of American republicanism. With help

26. David M. Pletcher, *The Diplomacy of Annexation: Texas, Oregon, and the Mexican War* (Columbia: University of Missouri Press, 1973), 237–38.

27. Lucille Iremonger, *Lord Aberdeen* (London: Collins, 1978), 173–74; Muriel Chamberlain, *Lord Aberdeen* (London: Longman, 1983), 336; Pletcher, *Diplomacy of Annexation*, 239.

28. Ibid., 240–41.

29. Ibid., 20–21.

from the U.S. minister to London, Edward Everett, Aberdeen engineered a propaganda campaign for peace. Soon the London *Examiner* and the *Edinburgh Review* were carrying articles stressing that the British economy would be helped by compromise on Oregon, both because it would break the fur monopoly of the Hudson's Bay Company and because it would restore investor confidence.[30] Everett also implored Lord John Russell, a leader of the Whig opposition, not to stir up public opinion against a forty-nine degree compromise. Russell agreed, but his colleague Palmerston did not.[31]

By the end of the year, certain that the U.S. Congress and public overwhelmingly favored a tough stance, Polk heightened the tension.[32] In a December 1845 address, the president not only recommended that Congress abrogate the 1827 Anglo-American treaty of joint occupation, but he also called for placement and protection of U.S. settlers there, creation of an Oregon Indian Bureau, and construction of forts along the Oregon trail. "Oregon is part of the North American continent," Polk declared, "to which, it is confidently affirmed, the title of the United States is the best in existence." He then invoked the Monroe Doctrine. Europe's attention was being drawn by America's rapid growth, "the expansion of free principles, and our rising greatness as a nation," the president proclaimed. This meant that the old European principle of "balance of power" threatened to encroach upon the New World. But that could not be allowed: American peoples must be left to decide their own destinies.[33] Polk wrote in his diary that "the only way to deal with John Bull is to look him straight in the eye."[34] Expansionist Democrats roundly congratulated the president.

Meanwhile, the Peel government fell because of opposition within its own Tory Party to the repeal of the protectionist Corn Laws. The Whigs were unable to form a replacement cabinet, however, and the Tories formed another government. Days after Peel resumed office, Polk's speech arrived in England. Press organs predisposed against America ridiculed Polk's use of the Monroe Doctrine but did not call

---

30. Merk, *Oregon Question,* 284–96.

31. Ibid., 258–61.

32. The president's diary records his telling his secretary of state that there was "not one in ten of the members [of Congress] whom I had seen who were not roused on the Oregon question and were going the whole length." When Buchanan suggested the country should wait and see whether war with Mexico materialized, Polk answered that "we should do our duty towards both Mexico and Great Britain and firmly maintain our rights, and leave the rest to God and the country." James Knox Polk, *The Diary of a President,* ed. Allan Nevins (New York: Longmans, 1952), 29 (entry for 29 November 1845; see also entry for 26 August, pp. 3–4).

33. Pletcher, *Diplomacy of Annexation,* 305–9.

34. Polk, *Diary,* 42.

for war. Several suggested that repeal of the Corn Laws would solve the matter by placating Western U.S. farmers. The *British Quarterly Review* put the case in liberal cosmopolitan terms:

> Let England repeal her corn-laws, and cease to interfere with the peaceful progress of the Anglo-Saxon race over the continent of North America, and the irritation and jealousy of the United States may mitigate and die away. In all else the democratic tendency is in our favour. It is the aristocracy, and not the democracy, it is the capitalists, and not the working millions of these great States, that are the patrons of restrictive tariffs. . . . Let us hope that a mere point of honour as to the ownership of the Oregon, or the ultimate destinies of the Mexican Provinces, may not be suffered to exasperate and increase these feelings of hostility.[35]

Thus the argument went: the United States is popularly governed and therefore would want peace if only England would also follow the will of its people and liberalize grain imports. In Parliament, Russell, Lord Morpeth, Lord Clarendon, Sir James Graham, and Charles Buller made the same point.[36]

Americans paid close attention to the tariff debate in England, for U.S. farmers stood to benefit from an opening of British agricultural markets. But Westerners thwarted the predictions of the British free traders. "Free trade I love dearly," announced Sen. Edward Hannegan of Indiana, "but never will it be bought by me by the territory of my country. He who would entertain such an idea is a traitor to his country."[37] Repeal of the Corn Laws did not move the war party.

The British were greatly disappointed. An exasperated *Manchester Guardian* reporter wrote from Washington:

> The news of Sir Robert Peel's great economical scheme has not tended to allay the zeal of the western members for war as much as might have been expected. . . . [Messrs. Breese, Cass, Allen, and Hannegan] have addressed the senate in their usual strain, and endeavoured, as much as possible, to oppose the pacific views of the majority of that body. It would be impossible to name four states so likely to be benefited by Sir Robert Peel's measure as those which these persons represent; indeed, that measure seems to be framed expressly for them.

In June, after Parliament formally ended the Corn Laws, the western Democrats stood firm in rejecting any compromise over Oregon. Im-

35. *British Quarterly Review*, February 1846, 233, quoted in Pletcher, *Diplomacy of Annexation*, 313.

36. Merk, *Oregon Question*, 317–18.

37. Ibid., 330–31.

mediate economic interest was superseded by a subtler notion of interest, shaped by liberal ideology.[38]

Aberdeen disagreed with this diagnosis, writing privately to Everett, "The truth is that everything depends on the real disposition of the President, and of the people by whom he is directed, whether Ministers, or Mob."[39] Still hoping for peace, Aberdeen continued his propaganda, this time apparently persuading the Yankee-baiting *Times* to call for moderation. Britain's most respected newspaper suddenly asserted that the "relations of commerce—the affections of kindred—identity of origin, of language, of laws—the common prevalence of similar sentiments, and the common deference to the same principles of moral action—bind the two nations together by ties which it would be atrocious to sever by the sword."[40] At the same time, Peel allowed Aberdeen to use temperate language toward the United States in Parliament.[41] Richard Pakenham, British minister to Washington, continued to propose third-party arbitration to Buchanan.

In December Polk's cabinet definitively voted against arbitration. These men saw the proposal as a British ploy, in part because they believed that any arbiter would likely be a European monarch, by nature biased against the American republic. John L. O'Sullivan, propagator of the manifest destiny doctrine, wrote in the *New York Morning News*, "There must be no arbitration but at the cannon's mouth!" American Whigs, meanwhile, deplored Polk's stubbornness, believing even a biased arbitration better than war with Britain over Oregon.[42]

Still intent on peace, Aberdeen now saw that a bit of deterrence was in order. He sent thirty ships of the line and several steamers to Canada. Liberals were still granting the Americans the benefit of the doubt. Radicals, meanwhile, supported American claims to Oregon, and in fact predicted peaceful U.S. annexation of land from the St. Lawrence to Venezuela.[43]

The coming of the thirty British warships gave Polk pause. He remarked in his diary that the British government's attitude "was not altogether of so pacific a character as the accounts given in the English

38. Ibid., 330–32. Scott C. James and David A. Lake argue that the Corn Law repeal and the resolution of the Oregon question paved the way for a U.S. tariff reduction in 1846; they do not argue that the Corn Law repeal led to resolution of the Oregon question. Scott C. James and David A. Lake, "The Second Face of Hegemony: Britain's Repeal of the Corn Laws and the American Walker Tariff of 1846," *International Organization* 43 (Winter 1989), 22–23.

39. Wilbur Devereux Jones, *Lord Aberdeen and the Americas* (Athens: University of Georgia Press, 1958), 79–85.

40. Merk, *Oregon Question,* 302.

41. Pletcher, *Diplomacy of Annexation,* 317.

42. Merk, *Oregon Question,* 217–32.

43. Lillibridge, *Beacon of Freedom,* 63.

newspapers had led me to believe." He informed Aberdeen through diplomatic channels that he would submit to the Senate a forty-nine degree compromise proposal, which the Senate would probably approve.[44] In February Congress took up Polk's request that it abrogate the 1827 treaty of joint occupation. All agreed that the treaty should be jettisoned; debate centered on the question of whether the wording of the resolution should be conciliatory or bellicose toward England. Western Democrats pushed for the latter, and revealed their strong anglophobia. In an address lasting two days, Sen. William Allen of Ohio blasted those Americans who would allow Britain to control 640,000 square miles of North American territory sixty-three years after U.S. independence—especially since tyrannical England was now too weak to fight. The British were bent on crippling America: "Tell [the American people] that arrogant England—their hereditary enemy, the enemy of all free governments—is seeking to snatch it from them, to fence us out from the Pacific Ocean."[45] Representative John S. Chipman of Michigan roared that the people of his state would take Canada by themselves in ninety days: "If conflict should come between republican and monarchical systems [I] would be glad to see it in [my] day."[46]

Many Democrats amplified the theme that Oregon was primarily about the struggle between republicanism and monarchy. Sen. Lewis Cass of Michigan reassured his colleagues that republicanism would win in a military contest and that the United States would continue to be "a landmark, inviting the nations of the world, struggling upon the stormy ocean of political oppression, to follow us to a haven of safety and of rational liberty."[47]

In the press, too, these notions were articulated with vigor. It was during the Oregon dispute that the term *manifest destiny* first appeared. The U.S. claim to Oregon, wrote John L. O'Sullivan in the *Democratic Review*, "is by the right of our manifest destiny to overspread and possess the whole of the continent which Providence has given us for the development of the great experiment of Liberty and federated self-government entrusted to us."[48] One New Yorker wrote that "war was desirable to spread the 'Egis of Republicanism' and revolutionize Europe."[49]

---

44. Charles S. Campbell, *From Revolution to Rapprochement: The United States and Great Britain, 1783–1900* (New York: John Wiley and Sons, 1974), 69–70; Pletcher, *Diplomacy of Annexation*, 344–49.

45. Pletcher, *Diplomacy of Annexation*, 333.

46. Frederick Merk, *Manifest Destiny and Mission in American History* (New York: Alfred A. Knopf, 1970), 38.

47. *Congressional Globe*, 29th Cong., 1st sess., 30 March 1846, appendix, 430.

48. Pletcher, *Diplomacy of Annexation*, 320.

49. Ibid., 333–34.

To the delight of Jacksonians and the horror of most Whigs, the war hawks were joined by the abolitionists, led by John Quincy Adams and Joshua Giddings of Ohio. Adams went so far as to claim that the United States had a biblical title to all of Oregon.[50] The abolitionists' main goal was adding free territory to the country so as to hasten the demise of slavery.

But the anglophilic coalition of Whigs and Southern Democrats fought back against the fifty-four forty men. Leading the Whigs was Daniel Webster, who was himself materially interested in peace.[51] Webster told a Boston audience that war between Britain and America was unthinkable because "the spirit of the age is against it!"[52] Yet he privately acknowledged to a member of Parliament that democracy in America might violate that spirit: "Popular Governments do, & I suppose always will produce such things, equally the ebullitions of wrong Principles, wrong feelings, & bad taste. Every good man in the United States would deprecate a War between us & England for such a subject as the Oregon dispute, as an act at once of stupendous folly and enormous crime."[53] Sen. Jacob Miller of New Jersey explicitly decried war because both nations were committed to "that great cause," "civil and religious liberty."[54] To the Whigs, the progress of history was at stake. Southern Democrats emphasized the same theme, tying progress explicitly to the trade disruption that would follow an Anglo-American war.[55]

Press organs also alluded to a common commitment to rational progress. The *National Intelligencer* asked, "Cannot Governments—Governments, too, of Christian and kindred nations—be guided by the dictates of reason and common sense which regulate the disputes of individual men?"[56] The *New York Journal of Commerce* appealed to rationality: "It would be a shame for these two greatest of Christian nations,

---

50. Merk, *Oregon Question*, 227–29.

51. Webster had served as legal council to Baring Brothers, a British banking house with huge sums invested in the United States. Howe, *Political Culture*, 223.

52. Daniel Webster, speech at Faneuil Hall, 7 November 1845, in *The Writings and Speeches of Daniel Webster* (Boston: Little, Brown, 1903), 13:310–17.

53. Webster to John Evelyn Denison, 26 February 1846, from Charles N. Wiltse, ed., *The Papers of Daniel Webster* (Hanover, N.H.: University Press of New England, 1984), 6:126.

54. *Congressional Globe*, 29th Cong., 1st sess., 26 March 1846, appendix, 568–72.

55. John C. Calhoun, leader of the Southern bloc, told his Senate colleagues that "powerful causes are now in operation, calculated to cement and secure a lasting—I hope a perpetual—peace between the two countries, by breaking down the barriers which impede their commerce, and thereby uniting them more closely by a vastly enlarged commercial intercourse, equally beneficial to both." Moreover, war with England would require such a national militarization that American democracy itself would be threatened. *Congressional Globe*, 29th Cong., 1st sess., 16 March 1846, appendix, 474–75.

56. Quoted in *New York Journal of Commerce*, 27 March 1846, 2.

now in the nineteenth century, to go to war—It would turn the current of civilization, now setting gloriously on, backward towards barbarism."[57] The threat of war with Britain did not darken the anglophiles' view of England, but instead led them to denounce the "mob" in their own country who called for war.

The heated American debate made an impression on British of all political stripes. Conservatives took it as confirmation of democratic recklessness. The Tory *Blackwood's Magazine* sarcastically titled an article on the Oregon question "How They Manage Matters in 'The Model Republic.'" "The *prestige* which America and her institutions once undoubtedly enjoyed in many parts of Europe is rapidly fading away, as each successive post brings fresh evidence of her vices and her follies," asserted the writer with glee.[58] Clearly, in the minds of conservatives, more was at stake in the debate than the fate of Oregon.

Some admirers of America glumly conceded the point that American truculence reflected badly on American government. Yet, liberals defended their model country. The *Spectator* explained that the U.S. Congress and President were outspoken because they were "from the people." "The legislature of America is to the legislature of England as a man who thinks aloud is to one who matures his ideas in silence before he speaks."[59] The paper pleaded with the Americans to abide by the rule of reason: "It was as a guarantee of the progress of such maxims of state policy, that the foundation of the experimental republic of the old Thirteen was hailed with joy in every clime by the philanthropists of the last century."[60] *Tait's Magazine* agreed: "The electors in England, and in the United States, can compel their governments to keep the peace. The electors of England are willing to do so, and their rulers need no compulsion. The electors of England request of those in America, to exercise the same restraint upon their government, if it shall be found to need it."[61] Liberals still abhorred the idea of an Anglo-American war, and desperately wanted America to prove worthy of their trust.

57. Ibid., 30 March 1846, 2.
58. *Littell's Living Age*, 16 May 1846, 320.
59. Ibid., 21 March 1846, 578.
60. Ibid.
61. The editors of *Tait's* also argued that Americans ought not to worry so about monarchism in the New World: "The citizens of the United States may regret, and may regret with justice, that there should be people on their continent who prefer, and may continue to prefer, unphilosophical monarchical institutions to their more scientific frame of government. . . . [But] if the republican institutions of America are really more conducive that those of our monarchies, to promote the virtue, greatness, and happiness of societies, cannot they trust to the silent eloquence of their example for extending their sway?" "War with America: Are We Not Brethren?" reprinted in *Littell's Living Age* 8, no. 96 (14 March 1846), 489–92.

The conciliators won the day. In April the Senate passed a gently worded termination of the 1827 treaty of joint occupation. The next month, as described below, Congress declared war on Mexico over a skirmish near the Rio Grande. In June, Britain offered a forty-nine degree compromise. The once pacific Buchanan was now inclined to reject the offer, as was Polk himself. But the rest of the cabinet persuaded the president to submit it to the Senate and abide by that body's decision. The Senate approved the compromise by a 38–12 vote, and the Oregon crisis was over.

Before the Oregon crisis, Jacksonian Americans perceived Britain as illiberal, while Whigs and some other Democrats categorized Britain as liberal. These prior perceptions held through the crisis. Jacksonians read British arbitration offers as threatening and believed the United States could defeat Britain in a war. Whigs and others took the opposite view. Without this opposition, it would have been much easier for Polk, a Jacksonian, to take the country into war. In Britain, Radicals, Liberals, and conservatives all held to their prior views of the United States as well. Radicals and Liberals made excuses for American belligerence, while many conservatives said the United States was a dangerous republic that should be taught a lesson. The British cabinet wanted no war for reasons of its own, and would have sought peace even without Liberal backing.

THE MEXICAN-AMERICAN CRISIS OF 1845–46

How Did Americans Perceive Mexico?

Americans tended to group Mexico with the rest of Latin America. Many saw these countries as actual or potential fellow liberal states. Others saw them as hopelessly backward.

The Latin American independence movements of the early nineteenth century were seen by leading Jeffersonians as part of their own republican revolution. Furthermore, a republican Western Hemisphere was to their minds essential to U.S. national security. Henry Clay, the leading War Hawk of 1811–12, had told Congress in 1816 that the United States should foster an "American system" and help the peoples to the south to protect itself from the reactionary Holy Alliance in Europe:

> Everyone has heard of the proceedings of the Congress of European potentates in Vienna; we heard, too, that their ideas of legitimate government were carried to an extent destructive of every principle of liberty. . . .
> Do we know whether we shall escape their influence? . . . This opinion I

boldly declare . . . it would undoubtedly be good policy to take part with the patriots of South America. . . . I consider the release of any part of America from the dominion of the Old World as adding to the general security of the New.[62]

Jefferson, Madison, and James Monroe agreed that the fate of republicanism in Latin America was important to U.S. security. "In the great struggle of the Epoch between liberty and despotism," Madison wrote to Jefferson, "we owe it to ourselves to sustain the former in this hemisphere at least."[63] The Monroe administration was one of the first governments in the world to recognize Mexican independence. The following year, in 1823, Monroe announced his famous foreign policy doctrine declaring the New World off-limits to any political ambitions of the European monarchies.[64]

Others, including Daniel Webster, Edward Everett, and John Quincy Adams, saw the Latin nations as irrelevant to U.S. interests. Adams responded to Clay's vision: "As to an American system, we have it— we constitute the whole of it . . . there is no community of interests or of principles between North and South America." The New Englanders tended to discount the republican potential of Hispanic, Roman Catholic societies.[65]

In fact, from the start, Mexico was a rickety republic at best. The hero of the 1821 revolution, Agustín de Iturbide, soon became Emperor Agustín I.[66] By the 1830s, when dictators such as Antonio López de Santa Anna seemed little better than monarchs, American confidence in Mexican republicanism was low. Just as the United States had appeared to British conservatives in the 1790s as a cipher for Revolutionary France, Mexico now began to appear to Jacksonians as a potential outpost for European monarchism, and the thought that it was most useful as a source of territory to strengthen their own republic took

62. *Annals of Congress*, 14th Cong., 1st sess., 20 January 1816, col. 724; 29 January 1816, col. 790. Quoted in Arthur Preston Whitaker, *The United States and the Independence of Latin America* (New York: Russell and Russell, 1962), 190.

63. Ralph Ketcham, *James Madison: A Biography* (New York: Macmillan, 1971), 631.

64. Monroe recognized Mexico on 12 December 1822. Whitaker, *United States and the Independence*, 390. Monroe was a lifelong antimonarchist. After his election to the presidency in 1816 he explained to Andrew Jackson that he would have no Federalists in his cabinet because they had wanted to establish a monarchy. Harry Ammon, *James Monroe: The Quest for National Identity* (New York: McGraw-Hill, 1971), 370–71. For an argument that the positions various politicians took on the Monroe Doctrine were a product of domestic political ambition rather than ideology, see Ernest R. May, *The Making of the Monroe Doctrine* (Cambridge: Harvard University Press, 1975).

65. Lester D. Langley, *America and the Americas: The United States in the Western Hemisphere* (Athens: University of Georgia Press, 1989), 41; Karl M. Schmitt, *Mexico and the United States, 1821–1973: Conflict and Coexistence* (New York: John Wiley & Sons, 1974), 34.

66. Schmitt, *Mexico*, 34–35.

hold.[67] In addition, the Texans' struggle for independence, especially Mexican brutality at the Alamo, generated much American ill will toward Mexico. American sympathy for Texas was strengthened by the fact that Texas set up a U.S.-style government.[68] The arrival of the Republic of Texas made Mexico look less liberal by comparison.

Yet, many Americans still desired friendship with Mexico. Martin Van Buren, president from 1837 to 1841, strove to reestablish diplomatic relations even while continuing to recognize Texas.[69] Clay now spoke less about Western Hemispheric solidarity, but he still openly opposed immediate annexation of Texas because, he said, he wanted no Mexican war.[70] John Quincy Adams wanted peace with Mexico and no annexation of Texas primarily because he stridently opposed the extension of slave territory. In fact, one liberal faction became more pro-Mexican as time passed: the abolitionists.[71] Mexico had outlawed slavery in 1829, and Texas, a state dominated by slave-holding Anglo-Saxons, had seceded from that country in part because the 1836 Mexican constitution centralized authority and thus made enforcement of abolition in Texas more certain (see below). American abolitionists used the Mexican example to try to shame their own nation into eradicating slavery.

How Liberal Was Mexico?

Primarily because of its political instability, Mexico earns an illiberal rating in the mid-1840s. The nation went through fourteen different presidents between 1829 and 1844.[72] It is not clear today—nor, significantly, was it clear at the time—under what constitution Mexico was operating in 1846. The relatively liberal 1824 constitution, setting up a federal system, was superseded by the centralist 1836 constitution called the Seven Laws. In 1843 Santa Anna imposed a new constitution centralizing power even further. Santa Anna was overthrown the following year, and in 1845 the government of José Joaquín de Herrera called for a return to federalism. Herrera was himself overthrown in December of that year by General Mariano Paredes y Arrillaga,

67. Ibid., 42–44.

68. Edward A. Moseley, "The United States and Mexico, 1810–1850," in T. Ray Shurbutt, ed., *United States-Latin American Relations, 1800–1850: The Formative Generations* (Tuscaloosa: University of Alabama Press, 1991), 147.

69. Ibid., 159–60.

70. Remini, *Clay*, 628–29.

71. Justin H. Smith, *The War with Mexico* (New York: Macmillan, 1919), 1:117–19; Bemis, *Adams and the Union*, 496–98.

72. Gene Brack, *Mexico Views Manifest Destiny, 1821–1846* (Albuquerque: University of New Mexico Press, 1975), 53.

who oscillated between liberal federalism and monarchism. Paredes claimed to be a republican even while ordering the nation's leading monarchist, Lucas Alamán, to draft a new constitution.[73]

The 1843 Constitution, like its predecessor, was intolerant of any religion other than Catholicism. At the same time, the 1843 document prohibited slavery, and declared freedom of conscience. In practice, freedom of the press was often curtailed. Only adult male citizens with an annual income of two hundred dollars or more could vote. Congress comprised a Chamber of Deputies, elected by the Electoral Colleges, and a Senate, two-thirds of whose members were chosen by the Department Assemblies, and one-third by the Chamber of Deputies, the President, and the Supreme Court. The President was elected every five years by the Departmental Assemblies.[74]

It is important to note that the 1843 constitution was less liberal than that of 1836—most tellingly by shifting the power to declare war from Congress to the president.[75] Regardless of which constitution was in force, in practice the civilian government was controlled by the military, or, more precisely, by whichever general had gained the upper hand most recently. All three Presidents after 1843—Santa Anna, Herrera, and Paredes—came to office through military insurrections. These dictators protested that they were republicans; but under none of them could Mexico's government be called liberal.[76]

How Did Mexicans Perceive the United States?

Traditional historiography has divided Mexicans in the early republic into two factions, liberals and conservatives. More recent studies have identified three factions: conservatives, moderate liberals, and radical liberals.[77]

The conservative faction, which had largely grown out of the Scottish Rite Masonic Lodges, had backed Mexican independence only when

73. See George Lockhart Reeves, *The United States and Mexico 1821–1848* (New York: Charles Scribner's Sons, 1913), 1:42–43, 262–63; Hubert Howe Bancroft, *History of Mexico* (San Francisco: A. L. Bancroft, 1885), 5:144–46; Arthur Howard Noll, *From Empire to Republic: The Story of the Struggle for Constitutional Government in Mexico* (Chicago: A. C. McClurg, 1903), 139–58; José Fernando Ramírez, *Mexico during the War with the United States*, ed. Walter Scholes, trans. Elliott B. Scherr (Columbia: University of Missouri Press, 1950), 12. Ramírez was a moderate liberal who kept a detailed journal on Mexican politics during this period. Scholes states that the 1843 constitution was in effect in early 1846.

74. Noll, *Empire to Republic*, 139–43.

75. Bancroft, *History of Mexico*, 5:144; Noll, *Empire to Republic*, 140–42; Brack, *Mexico Views Manifest Destiny*, 142.

76. Pletcher, *Diplomacy of Annexation*, 357–59.

77. Donald Fithian Stevens, *Origins of Instability in Early Republican Mexico* (Durham: Duke University Press, 1991), chap. 3.

Spain itself became convulsed by a liberal uprising. Led by the intellectual Lucas Alamán, conservatives wanted a Mexico with a strong central government committed to property rights, Catholicism, mercantilism, and order.[78] In the 1840s they began calling for the establishment of a European prince as head of state. Alamán and the conservatives believed that its lack of unity and progress since independence in 1821 showed that Mexico must return to monarchy.[79] Paredes, the general who became President after a coup d'état in late 1845, was a conservative.[80]

Liberals had their origins in York Rite Masonry and valued individual liberty over order. In contrast to conservatives, liberals wanted a constitutional Mexico, with freedoms of the press and association and equality before the law for Indians. But liberals were divided between a moderate and a radical faction. Moderates were less inclined to throw out all of the colonial past. They were not staunch antimonarchists; they wanted to reduce the power of the Church, but slowly; they wanted a weak central government; and they wanted suffrage limited to property owners and in general held to middle-class views of property rights.[81] Herrera, president from late 1844 until his overthrow in late 1845, was a moderate liberal.[82]

Radical liberals were adamant republicans who sought to overturn virtually every feature of the colonial past. Like Conservatives, Radicals wanted a strong central government, but for very different purposes. For Radicals, the state should actively help the poor masses of Mexico by seizing Church property, raising taxes, and forming a strong national army while eliminating provincial militias. They were less committed to liberal procedural correctness than to egalitarianism.[83]

In the first decade after independence from Spain, when the conservative-liberal fissure was relatively shallow, Mexicans tended to look on the United States as a model because of its republican success. In an exhaustive study of the Mexican press, Gene Brack finds enormous admiration among Mexican elites for U.S. political institutions and economic prosperity in the early years after Mexican independence. One newspaper noted that the U.S. example showed that frequent elections were a way of preventing revolution.[84] José María Luis Mora wrote that

78. Brack, *Mexico Views Manifest Destiny*, 30; Stevens, *Origins of Instability*, 29.

79. Miguel E. Soto, "The Monarchist Conspiracy and the Mexican War," in the Walter Prescott Webb Memorial Lectures, *Essays on the Mexican War*, ed. Douglas W. Richmond (College Station: Texas A&M University Press, 1986), 69–70. See also Charles A. Hale, *Mexican Liberalism in the Age of Mora, 1821–1853* (New Haven: Yale University Press, 1968), 15–22.

80. Pletcher, *Diplomacy of Annexation*, 172.

81. Stevens, *Origins of Instability*, 30–36.

82. Pletcher, *Diplomacy of Annexation*, 174.

83. Stevens, *Origins of Instability*, 30–37.

84. Brack, *Mexico Views Manifest Destiny*, 17–25.

the U.S. constitution had "brought glory and prosperity in a firm and stable manner to the freest people of the universe."[85] As Charles A. Hale summarizes, "In general, the Mexican liberals of the pre-Reforma generation approached North American society uncritically. . . . To Mexican liberals the United States was a utilitarian dream world. . . . Tadeo Ortíz, one of the most enthusiastic of the Mexicans, referred to the United States as 'the classic land of liberty and order and the refuge of all the social virtues.'"[86]

Most liberals had come to believe by the 1840s that Mexico's social structure and history were too unlike those of the United States to permit slavish imitation, and that the theories and experience of continental liberalism were more relevant to their nation.[87] Related to that shift was a general souring of Mexican opinion regarding the giant northern neighbor, beginning with the Conservatives. In the 1820s the U.S. minister and British chargé to Mexico competed to be the first to arrange a commercial treaty with the new nation. Alamán was foreign minister at the time, and given his conservative vision for Mexico he naturally leaned toward monarchical, conservative Britain rather than republican, liberal America. An Anglo-Mexican treaty was approved in 1826, while a U.S.-Mexican treaty was delayed until 1831.[88] In the meantime, the U.S. minister, Joel Poinsett, openly interfered in national and state politics on the side of the York Rite lodges.[89]

In the 1830s Alamán, who continued to admire U.S. power, began warning his countrymen that federalism and Enlightenment philosophy, both associated with America, were foreign to Mexico and should be eradicated. Soon he became alarmed at evident U.S. designs on Texas. Alamán was joined in 1840 by José María Gutiérrez de Estrada, a former liberal who admitted in an article that while he had once been "sincerely addicted to the dominant principles of our neighbors," it was now evident that Mexico was hierarchical by nature.[90]

Other liberals repudiated Gutiérrez's call, but many of them too had by now become unsettled at the American threat. The event that galvanized the opinions of many liberals against the United States was Texas independence in 1836. When the Mexican government passed the cen-

85. Hale, *Mexican Liberalism*, 194. Mora's journal *Seminario politico y literario* reprinted basic U.S. documents, including the Articles of Confederation, the Declaration of Independence, the Constitution, and two of Washington's speeches, for Mexican readers.

86. Hale, *Mexican Liberalism*, 198–99.

87. Ibid., 195–97, 206–7.

88. Brack, *Mexico Views Manifest Destiny*, 28–38; Pletcher, *Diplomacy of Annexation*, 39–40. Brack notes that Mexican Conservatives held political views similar to those of old American Federalists (see Chapter 3 above) and that like the Federalists they were pro-British.

89. Brack, *Mexico Views Manifest Destiny*, 31–37.

90. Hale, *Mexican Liberalism*, 212–13; Pletcher, *Diplomacy of Annexation*, 37.

tralist 1836 Mexican Constitution, Texans (particularly the growing population of Anglo-Saxons), fearing an unacceptable loss of state autonomy, declared an independent republic; the rebellious Texans defeated Santa Anna at San Jacinto and forced him to agree to Texas independence. Washington recognized the Republic of Texas the next year. But Mexicans of all political stripes were adamant that Texas was still a part of their country.

It was becoming obvious to liberals as well that their Anglo-Saxon neighbors wanted not only Texas but also New Mexico and California. The leading Radical Gómez Farías now wrote that if Texas were to fall into U.S. hands, America would eventually stretch "from sea to sea," thus ruining Mexico's future.[91] Now the interest that Mexican liberals had seen in good relations with the United States became outweighed for many by the clear and present danger of the loss of vast tracts of sovereign Mexican territory. Mexican writers began emphasizing the more disturbing aspects of the American polity, such as slavery and persecution of Indians. Brack writes that "anti-Americanism became an obsessive, transcendent issue, one by which all Mexican administrations after 1836 would be measured."[92] The United States, once appealing, became appalling.

Interestingly, some liberals even then sustained hopes of good relations with the United States. Lorenzo de Zavala actually settled in Texas and joined in the Anglo-Saxon revolt against Mexico, becoming vice president of the Republic of Texas.[93] As we shall see, President Herrera favored conciliation even after the United States had annexed Texas. Moderates continued to favor compromise with the United States even during the war itself.[94]

Actions, Interpretations, Reactions

As a Jacksonian Democrat, Polk believed that territorial expansion was needed to maintain American virtue and prosperity. He campaigned as an expansionist and evidently entered the American presidency wanting to annex California as well as Oregon.[95] Mexicans had fervently hoped that Henry Clay, a Whig who despite his equivocations was antiexpansionist, would defeat Polk in the 1844 campaign. All Mexican governments since 1836 had insisted that Texas independence was

91. Brack, *Mexico Views Manifest Destiny*, 119.
92. Ibid., 54–56; see also 60–61.
93. Hale, *Mexican Liberalism*, 202–3.
94. Pletcher, *Diplomacy of Annexation*, 484.
95. John H. Schroeder, *Mr. Polk's War: American Opposition and Dissent, 1846–1848* (Madison: University of Wisconsin Press, 1973), 3–4. Opposing this view is Smith, *War with Mexico*, chap. 1.

illegal and made it clear that the United States was not to annex the state. John Tyler, Polk's nominally Whig predecessor, had finally made an offer to annex Texas the night before Polk was to take office. When Polk stood by Tyler's offer, Mexico broke relations with Washington.[96]

Upon taking office, Polk ordered military and naval movements ostensibly to defend Texas against possible Mexican attack. In mid-June he sent General Zachary Taylor to move his "corps of observation" from Louisiana into Texas. Taylor moved his 4,000 men toward the Nueces River, located between San Antonio and the Rio Grande, where they remained for four months. On 4 July 1845, Texas officially accepted the U.S. annexation offer.

Most of the Mexican press was livid at news of annexation. Liberal factions differed passionately on how to respond. *Puros*, members of the doctrinaire wing, believed that acquiescence would only increase the American appetite for California and New Mexico. *Moderados*, the practical men of affairs, still wanted to accommodate the Americans.[97] A *moderado* newspaper, *El Siglo XIX*, pointed out that war with the United States would cost five million pesos a month, money the government did not have. Moreover, European support for Mexico was in doubt.[98] Realizing the country's difficult situation, the Mexican Congress balked at declaring war.

In November Polk, assuming that Mexican silence implied capitulation, sent John Slidell as an envoy to offer renewal of diplomatic relations and payment of up to $25 million for California. An odd anti-U.S. coalition of monarchists and *puros* made ready to charge Herrera, a *moderado*, with treason if he received Slidell. Herrera's own minister of war called for all-out war, arguing that victory would come easily: the Americans comprised "some miserable colonists, a few hundred adventurers, and a handful of speculators from New Orleans and New York." Sensing capitulation, newspapers denounced "that vile gang of hypocrites and philosophers" in the National Palace. Nonplused, the president played for time, asking Slidell for better credentials and requesting advice from Mexican state governors.[99]

At this point Bermúdez de Castro, the Spanish minister to Mexico, decided the time was ripe to carry out Madrid's long-standing plans to place a Spanish monarch at the head of Mexico. Working with Alamán, Bermúdez enlisted the conservative General Paredes to over-

96. Pletcher, *Diplomacy of Annexation*, chap. 7.

97. Cecil Robinson, ed., *The View from Chapultepec: Mexican Writers on the Mexican-American War* (Tucson: University of Arizona Press, 1989), xx–xxi; Pletcher, *Diplomacy of Annexation*, 174–75.

98. Ibid., 254–60.

99. John Edwards Weems, *To Conquer a Peace: The War between the United States and Mexico* (New York: Doubleday, 1974), 95–97; Pletcher, *Diplomacy of Annexation*, 353–57.

throw Herrera and act as a transitional ruler. Paredes demanded as his price war with the United States. The general believed Mexico would win such a war, given the strength of Mexican public opinion and obvious divisions within the United States. On 18 December Paredes launched a rebellion, accusing Herrera "of trying to give away national territory by negotiating the cession of Texas to the United States and with that, trying to avoid a 'glorious and necessary war.'" On 2 January 1846, Paredes marched into Mexico City and Herrera resigned.[100] Paredes quickly tried to please both his monarchist and his *puro* supporters. He appointed a few liberals to his cabinet and called himself a republican, yet he also had the monarchist Alamán write his new constitution.[101]

As noted in the *New York Herald*, Paredes proclaimed that only the Mexican Congress could declare war.[102] In Washington, however, Polk and Buchanan were more than suspicious that Paredes was carrying out a monarchical plot with the aid of the British and French. As Buchanan wrote privately to Slidell in March:

> Should Great Britain and France attempt to place a Spanish or any other European Prince upon the throne of Mexico, this would be resisted by all the power of the United States. In opposition to such an attempt, party distinctions in . . . [the United States] would vanish and the people would be nearly unanimous . . . the United States could never suffer foreign powers to erect a throne for a European Prince on the ruins of a neighboring Republic, without our most determined resistance.[103]

For months, U.S. editors had been clamoring about a monarchical plot in Mexico. The *Herald* announced: "Europe is adverse to liberty in Europe, and it belongs to us, the greatest republic in the whole world, to watch with zealous care, that her enmity to liberty, which reigns in her own regions, be not actively transferred to this hemisphere."[104]

In the meantime, Polk had ordered Taylor to march to the north bank of the Rio Grande. On 28 March the men camped across the river from the Mexican town of Matamoros, announcing pacific intentions to the Mexican commander there. The Mexicans saw the U.S. move as an incursion into their territory, and Taylor set up a fort with four eighteen-pound guns. Days later, Mexican Gen. Pedro Ampudia arrived at Matamoros with reinforcements and ordered the Americans to march north to the Nueces within twenty-four hours. Taylor responded by

---

100. Soto, "Monarchist Conspiracy," 67–73.
101. Ibid., 74–75.
102. *New York Herald*, 17 April 1846, p. 2
103. Soto, "Monarchist Conspiracy," 78.
104. *New York Herald*, 25 March 1846.

asking a U.S. naval auxiliary to blockade the mouth of the Rio Grande—normally done only in wartime.[105]

In Mexico City, Paredes proclaimed a "defensive war" against the U.S. "invaders." On 25 April the fighting began. A reconnaissance patrol of sixty-three American soldiers was ambushed by several hundred Mexicans. Sixteen Americans, including the captain in command, were killed or wounded. Taylor reported to Washington, "Hostilities may now be considered as commenced."[106]

By now calls for war in Mexico drowned out all dissent. Gómez Farías, a *puro*, began a "federation and Texas" movement. In a pamphlet Gómez Farías wrote that "expansionists in the United States were almost all from the slave states of the South . . . [they] sought to make of Mexican territory a vast emporium for the buying and selling of slaves." The conservative *El Defensor de las Leyes* concurred, publishing a letter saying in effect that "Mexico must counter force with force, for if they permitted an invasion they would exchange their liberty for slavery."[107]

Polk had decided to wait until Slidell returned to Washington before acting, hoping that the *moderados* would force a compromise and wanting to deal with the Oregon crisis first. Upon his return Slidell recommended war, and the president prepared a war message. Word of the Matamoros skirmish led the cabinet to vote unanimously to send the message to Congress. Polk's message declared that war already existed "by act of Mexico" and took pains to emphasize that Mexico was no longer a republic. Contrasting "General Paredes" with "President Herrera," Polk announced: "The Government of General Paredes owes its existence to a military revolution, by which the subsisting constitutional authorities had been subverted. The form of government was entirely changed."[108] In other words, the U.S. Congress need not wait for its Mexican counterpart to declare war. The dictator of Mexico had already done so.

The House of Representatives easily approved the war resolution by a vote of 174–14, the only opposition coming from abolitionist Whigs led by John Quincy Adams. Resistance in the Senate was stronger at first. A central issue was whether Mexico was still a republic: if it was, many argued, war was out of the question. On the Senate floor Thomas Hart Benton, a Missouri Democrat from the Van Buren wing of the party, read part of a speech from Paredes where the general had proclaimed that only the Mexican Congress could declare war. Benton read the passage "with a view to show that the door was open for an adjustment of our

105. Weems, *To Conquer a Peace*, 103–12.
106. Pletcher, *Diplomacy of Annexation*, 373–77; Weems, *To Conquer a Peace*, 113–14.
107. Brack, *Mexico Views Manifest Destiny*, 135–36, 142.
108. *Congressional Globe*, 29th Cong., 1st sess., 11 May 1846, 15:783.

difficulties." Leading the doves was John C. Calhoun, who argued similarly that the Mexican Congress might still disavow war.[109] The argument that Mexico was still a fellow republic, constrained by its own laws from reckless war, was potentially a powerful one to Americans.

Sen. John J. Crittenden, a Kentucky Whig, lamented the possibility of a war as a violation of Henry Clay's vision.

> This country had regarded [the Latin American revolutions] as an imitation of our example—as a new creation of republics, united by a strong affinity, and warm sympathy. They were regarded as a portion of that great system of republics which were to stand forth in proud contrast with the Governments of the Old World. . . . It was not in the amount of precious blood that had been shed that consisted the importance of [the proposed war]. No; it was the great political consequences—the bad example—the evil consequences to liberty and republicanism in every place. The hand of one republic stretched out in hostility against another!

Making the hostilities still worse for Crittenden was that Mexico was struggling even then not to fall back "into the hands of despots, and that monarchical system from which we saw her, with pleasure, arise."[110] Before the tension had escalated into a crisis, the *New York Evening Post* had cautioned that real winners of a Mexican-American war would be the monarchies of the Old World: "One democracy set to fight against another would cause John Bull to rub his hands with glee."[111] Yet Polk's argument that Mexico was no longer a republic was too strong, as expansionists wore down the doves. Sen. Sam Houston of Texas asserted, "A declaration of war has been made by the President, or, rather, the usurper of Mexico." Sen. Ambrose Sevier of Arkansas replied to Crittenden: "This country had reared [Mexico] up, fostered her, protected her, as it had the republics of South America. Was she a republic to-day? How long had she been a republic? How long since she had an emperor on her throne?"[112] Sen. Lewis Cass of Michigan ridiculed his dovish colleagues for taking the Mexican constitution seriously. "It is not for us to stop in the middle of our deliberations to turn over the pages of the last, so-called, constitution of Mexico, and to seek how the powers of Government are divided among its various functionaries, nor to inquire what is the last *pronunciamento*, or who is the present Dictator of that unhappy country."[113] Other Senators echoed the argument that Mexican disarray was a reason for, not against, war.

109. Ibid., 15:789, 796–97.
110. Ibid., 15:788.
111. Pletcher, *Diplomacy of Annexation*, 265.
112. *Congressional Globe*, 11 May 1846, 15:787–88.
113. Ibid., 12 May 1846, 15:800–802.

Newspapers continued the theme that Mexico was about to plunge into monarchism. The *New York Herald* declared: "It is time for the chief magistrate of this great people . . . to begin this great movement, which will prevent a relapse of a sister republic into the arms of a monarchy, as is threatened by the English government."[114] One magazine declared that "the question of extending *constitutional republican institutions* over this whole continent is one of the broadest, noblest and most important that was ever presented to any nation."[115]

The antiwar forces in the Senate were too few and too unconvincing. Benton switched his vote under enormous pressure from Polk; Calhoun and the Whigs tried several legislative maneuvers; but the fact that American blood had been shed on what may have been American soil caused opposition to wither away. With Calhoun and two others abstaining, the war resolution passed 40–2.

American perceptions of Mexico correlated fairly closely with perceptions of Britain. Whigs and elitist Democrats labeled Mexico a fellow republic and saw its erratic policies as a cause for sympathy rather than hostility. Jacksonians perceived in Mexico an incipient monarchy and interpreted its policies as hostile and threatening. Polk was constrained by the opposition to try to negotiate with Mexico and knew that, for Congress to declare war, he had to show that Mexico was no longer a republic. In the end, however, Polk forced Congress to make the declaration via the Matamoros incident.

Mexican liberals disagreed over whether the United States was liberal. Purists had become anti-American in the previous decade, and during the crisis they interpreted every U.S. move darkly and insisted that Mexico would win a war should it come about. Moderates continued to look at the United States as a republican model, and thought accommodating America better than fighting a war Mexico would surely lose. In any event, Mexican governmental institutions by now were a shambles, and Paredes was unconstrained from war.

THE ANGLO-AMERICAN CRISES OF 1861–63

How Liberal Was the United States?

During the Civil War, although supporters of the Union would deny that the Southern states were a separate political and legal entity—indeed, that is why they were fighting—the British dealt with the Union

---

114. *New York Herald*, 18 April 1846.

115. Letter from Parke Godwin to Harbinger magazine, quoted in Pletcher, *Diplomacy of Annexation*, 390.

and Confederacy separately. Although no foreign nation recognized the Confederacy as a sovereign state, Queen Victoria did recognize it as a belligerent. Thus I treat the Union only in considering how liberal the United States was in the years 1861–63.

Few political institutions had changed in the Northern states since 1846. As so often happens during wartime, however, certain civil liberties were in abeyance during the Civil War. Most important, Lincoln's suspension of habeas corpus allowed the military to make an estimated 14,000 arbitrary arrests. Opposition newspapers were also seized at post offices. Lincoln and his cabinet portrayed these unconstitutional actions as violating the law in order to save it, and as sanctioned by the will of the people. Furthermore, the president allowed national elections in 1862 and 1864 despite the possibility that Democrats would win and sue for peace with the South. (The army interfered in the 1862 elections in a few states.) Even so, we must conclude that the U.S. government was less liberal than it had been in 1846, and we should expect governmental decision making to be less responsive to the will of the electorate.[116]

How Did Americans Perceive Great Britain?

Slavery and sectionalism had changed the partisan landscape since the 1840s. In 1854 a group of northern Whigs and Democrats had formed the Republican Party as a direct response to the "slave power," the apparently increasing dominance of the Southern slave owners in national politics. The Kansas-Nebraska Act of that year opened up all remaining territories of the Louisiana Purchase to slavery, thus superseding the Missouri Compromise of 1820. A group of innovators, including Carl Schurz, William Seward, Thurlow Weed, and Abraham Lincoln, propagated the idea that Northerners had a common interest in the spread of "free labor," as opposed to expansion of the Southern "slavocracy," into new territories. Arguing that the Democratic Party had abandoned the tradition of Jefferson, which sought to limit slavery, the new party took the original name of Jefferson's faction.[117]

116. Lincoln claimed that public opinion supported him in these emergency measures and that his actions were moreover to preserve the rule of law itself. Mark E. Neely, Jr., *The Fate of Liberty: Abraham Lincoln and Civil Liberties* (New York: Oxford University Press, 1991), 65–68, 234; see also Brian Jenkins, *Britain and the War for the Union* (Montreal: McGill-Queen's University Press, 1974–80), 1:182–85.

117. Robert Kelley, *The Cultural Pattern in American Politics: The First Century* (New York: Alfred A. Knopf, 1979), 196–99. Eric Foner, *Free Soil, Free Labor, Free Men: The Ideology of the Republican Party before the Civil War* (New York: Oxford University Press, 1970), esp. chap. 1. For a discussion of the dialectic of ideas and interests in group formation, see Chapter 1 above.

Lincoln and the Republicans won all Northern states in the 1860 election, and their party dominated the North during the Civil War. From the start, however, the party was divided between conservatives, who wanted to win the war without drastic measures such as slave emancipation, and radicals who pushed for abolition and a social revolution in the South. Lincoln began as a conservative.[118] Democrats meanwhile included War Democrats, who wanted a restored Union that tolerated slavery, and Peace Democrats or Copperheads who sympathized with the South and pushed for a negotiated peace and recognition of the Confederacy. In both parties were vociferous critics of Lincoln who feared the president was setting up a dictatorship through his violations of civil liberties.

This case study pays particular attention to three New York editors who represent the radical Republican, conservative Republican, and War Democrat factions respectively. Horace Greeley, editor of the *New York Tribune*, was a radical Whig/Republican who had long defended the common man, but unlike the Democrats he included blacks as men. Henry Raymond, editor of the *New York Times*, was a centrist Whig/Republican who believed Greeley advocated too strong a role for the state. In a serial debate in 1846 Greeley had called for "a true social state [guaranteeing] the right of every individual to such labor as he is able to perform, and . . . the fair and equal recompense of his labor." Raymond had responded that "we are not of those who 'feel personally responsible for the turning of the earth upon its axis,' nor do we deem it our special 'mission' to reorganize society."[119] James Gordon Bennett, editor of the *New York Herald*, was a fiery defender of the Democratic tradition of egalitarianism via laissez-faire, including toleration of slavery.[120]

Before the war, Radical Republicans and abolitionists heaped praise on England for abolishing slavery and working for the end of the slave trade. Sen. Charles Sumner of Massachusetts, the most prominent Radical, was nicknamed "the Earl" for his anglophilia.[121] Greeley's antimonarchism and hostility to free trade[122] were counterbalanced by his appreciation of British antislavery. When the Prince of Wales visited the

118. Foner, *Free Soil*.

119. Coy F. Cross II, *Go West Young Man! Horace Greeley's Vision for America* (Albuquerque: University of New Mexico Press, 1995), 21; Francis Brown, *Raymond of the Times* (New York: W. W. Norton, 1951), 54–56.

120. Douglas Fermer, *James Gordon Bennett and the New York Herald: A Study of Editorial Opinion in the Civil War Era 1854–1867* (New York: St. Martin's, 1986), 44–45.

121. Kelley, *Cultural Pattern*, 202–3.

122. Henry Luther Stoddard, *Horace Greeley: Printer, Editor, Crusader* (New York: G. P. Putnam's Sons, 1946), 146; Jeter Allen Iseley, *Horace Greeley and the Republican Party 1853–1861* (New York: Octagon Books, 1965), 214–15.

United States in October 1860, Greeley criticized the governor of Arkansas for still "seeing in Great Britain the implacable enemy of our republican institutions and rising greatness." In fact, "the British Nation and Government" no longer posed any threat to America, Greeley wrote.[123]

Mainstream Republicans also tended to admire Britain, although more for its ordered liberty than its abolitionist activism. Raymond of the *New York Times* even chided noted British Radical John Bright for pushing his country to imitate American democracy a bit too precipitously.[124]

Democrats, however, were still typically anglophobic. Bennett routinely used the pages of the *New York Herald* to hector England. A Catholic Scot by birth, Bennett carried his resentment of British hierarchical society to America.[125] He was temporarily caught up in the enthusiasm surrounding the Prince of Wales's visit in 1860, even declaring that "henceforth the giant leaders of Liberty in the Old World and in the New are united in impulse and in aim for the perpetuation of Freedom and the elevation of man."[126] In general, however, the *Herald* was consistently hostile toward Britain, to the point of seeming bent on fomenting Anglo-American conflict.

How Liberal Was Great Britain?

Little political reform had taken place since 1846. The Chartist movement, which had sought equal political rights for working-class men, had faded away, but its proposal to eliminate property requirements for members of Parliament was finally adopted in 1858.[127] The electorate in 1861–63 looked much the same as in 1845–46. Thus Britain rates as a liberal state.

How Did the British Perceive the United States?

Most Britons supported the reforms of 1832 and should thus be regarded as liberal. But as in previous episodes, there were those who

123. "British Influence," *New York Daily Tribune*, 18 October 1860, 4.

124. "[John Bright] seems to think that an extension of the suffrage is the one great panacea for all the evils with which the [British] empire is afflicted, but he surely forgets that there is a large number of concomitants needed, without which universal, or even household suffrage, is a positive mockery." "The Ballot in England," *New York Times*, 13 January 1859.

125. Fermer, *Bennett and the Herald*, 45.

126. *New York Herald*, 12 October 1860, quoted in Martin Crawford, *The Anglo-American Crisis of the Mid-Nineteenth Century: The Times and America, 1850–1862* (Athens: University of Georgia Press, 1986), 10.

127. Schuyler and Weston, *British Constitutional History*, 34–35.

sought more reform in Britain, and those who did not, at least not yet. Those who did not, whose numbers included both Tories and Whigs, continued to fear further democracy as a harbinger of the mob rule they believed they saw in the United States.

Even some who sought further reform and rationalization were wary of democracy. John Stuart Mill's concern about the tyranny of the majority (see Chapter 1) led him to propose a complicated scheme to insure minority representation. Walter Bagehot, editor of *The Economist*, feared the lower classes would seek their particular interests over those of society as a whole. Matthew Arnold wrote, "The central idea of English life and politics is the *assertion of personal liberty*"; he dreaded that the working classes would impinge on this principle.[128] Politicians who fell into this Whig-Liberal camp included Lord John Russell, who offered limited but failed reform bills in 1852 and 1854, and William E. Gladstone, who sought some expansion of the franchise in 1864.[129]

The Philosophical Radicals wanted more reform. Richard Cobden, John Bright, and William E. Forster were among the leaders who saw little or no tension between democracy and liberalism. The failure of Chartism had demoralized the working class, but now the middle class began calling for full democracy. As the *New York Times* noted with concern, manhood suffrage for these men was "the only panacea for the world's evils."[130]

For decades, virtually all British had agreed that slavery was an evil and wasteful institution. The evangelicals, Unitarians, and Quakers who had led the abolitionist movement earlier in the century had persuaded their countrymen that the interests of the nation as a whole were served by emancipation. God had ordained a harmonious order to the world, and if a nation conformed to that order, it would do good and do well. Slavery violated that order. Hence slavery was irrational and inefficient as well as morally wrong. Playing on themes dear to liberals, emancipationists argued that free labor and prosperity went together. Slaves were less motivated and productive than free laborers; slavery exhausted the soil and was resistant to new technology.[131]

128. Roper, *Democracy and Its Critics*, 149–61.

129. Michael Winstanley, *Gladstone and the Liberal Party* (London: Routledge, 1990), 38–40. Decades later, Russell's grandson Bertrand Russell wrote that Lord John was "the type of aristocratic reformer whose zeal is derived from the classics, from Demosthenes and Tacitus, rather than from any more recent source. They worshipped a goddess called Liberty, but her feathers were rather vague." Philip Van Doren Stern, *When the Guns Roared: World Aspects of the American Civil War* (Garden City, N.Y.: Doubleday, 1965), 22.

130. Lillibridge, *Beacon of Freedom*, 88.

131. David Turley, *The Culture of English Antislavery, 1780–1860* (New York: Routledge, 1991), 17–47. The quotation is from p. 35.

These arguments helped persuade Parliament to end slavery throughout the British Empire in 1833.

Tories and conservative Whigs respected U.S. power but not U.S. institutions and society. Palmerston continued to loathe the United States as the prime example of why England should not extend suffrage to the working classes. For Palmerston and other conservatives, republics such as the United States were *more* warlike than monarchies, for in republics "the masses influence or direct the destinies of the Country [and] are swayed much more by Passion than Interest."[132]

As in the 1840s, the Radicals, on the other hand, were famous, or infamous, for their paeans to America. Radicals constantly compared the United States favorably to Britain, and the comparisons extended to foreign affairs. Britain intervened in European troubles and had to maintain a national government at five times the cost of the American; at the same time, the British government was responsible only to a small fraction of the Queen's subjects, while the U.S. government was beholden to the masses. Bright tirelessly cited American success in his 1858 campaign for parliamentary reform.[133]

The centrist Whig-Liberals were inclined to admire the United States but worried about the tyranny of the majority. Despite fear that American sectionalism was confirming their doubts about full democracy, in the years before the Civil War Whig-Liberals increasingly held the United States in esteem.[134] The *Times*, the nation's leading newspaper, spoke for a large segment of the public when it repeatedly expressed a paternal admiration for the United States coupled with a concern for American imprudence in the decade before the Civil War. In 1857 the newspaper commented that the failure of "English ideas"—i.e., liberalism—on the continent of Europe necessitated Britain to look to the United States as "an enormous counterpoise to the despotism which sullenly lords it over the southern and eastern portion of the Old World."[135]

Liberals and Radicals were bothered by America's inability to emancipate its slaves. In fact, those who most admired U.S. institutions were the most vehement in attacking U.S. slavery. Joseph Sturge commented, "So long as slavery and the distinction of colour exist, America will always be pointed at with the finger of scorn for her flagrant violation of all truth and consistency."[136] Indeed, as seen below, conservative British taunted Liberals and Radicals that the Union, being a

132. Jenkins, *Britain and the War*, 1:83–84.

133. Ibid., 1:69–70.

134. Ibid., 1:71; Roper, *Democracy and Its Critics*, 146–50; Arnold Whitridge, "British Liberals and the American Civil War," *History Today* 12 (October 1962), 688–95.

135. Crawford, *Anglo-American Crisis*, 49. Note that the *Times* had softened its view of the United States since the 1840s.

136. Howard Temperley, *British Antislavery 1833–1870* (London: Longman, 1972), 194.

mere democracy, was no more opposed to slavery than was the Confederacy.

Actions, Interpretations, Reactions

Early in the war the Lincoln administration and Congress seemed to bear out the taunts of British conservatives. The president announced in his first inaugural address: "I have no purpose, directly or indirectly, to interfere with the institution of slavery in the States where it exists. I believe I have no lawful right to do so, and I have no inclination to do so."[137] Britons were shocked at this disavowal, but took Lincoln at his word: if the war was about crude national interest, then Britain would treat it that way.[138] With ideology an uncertain guide, two other moves by the Union ensured that many British would side with the Confederacy. First, in 1861 Lincoln declared a naval blockade of the seceded states that was to continue for the remainder of the Civil War. Second, in February Congress passed the Morrill Tariff, which shrank British exports to the Union. These moves, together with the war itself, put the British government in a difficult situation. Textile manufacturers had enormous interests in the continuation of the flow of cotton from the Southern states. Cotton manufacture was the largest industry in the United Kingdom, with 2,650 factories employing 900,000 workers; 80 percent of the cotton came from the American South.[139] Although stockpiles of the raw material were high, the potential for distress in the northern districts was great, much like that in the years leading up to the War of 1812.

On 13 May Queen Victoria declared Britain neutral in the conflict, thereby recognizing Confederacy as a belligerent in a war. Palmerston's government pointed out that the queen had not recognized the South as an independent nation, and claimed that neutrality was intended to prevent British subjects from participating in the war. Still, the Union government was enraged. For Lincoln and William Henry Seward, the secretary of state, Britain had legitimized the Confederacy and implied that the war was more than a domestic affair. Seward instructed Charles Francis Adams, the new minister to London, to quit Britain the minute the queen recognized the Confederacy as a nation.[140]

137. Ephraim Douglass Adams, *Great Britain and the American Civil War* (New York: Longmans, Green, 1925), 1:50.

138. Betty Fladeland, *Men and Brothers: Anglo-American Antislavery Cooperation* (Urbana: University of Illinois Press, 1972), 387.

139. Gordon H. Warren, "The King Cotton Theory," in Alexander DeConde, ed., *Encyclopedia of American Foreign Policy: Studies of the Principal Movements and Ideas* (New York: Charles Scribner's Sons, 1978), 515–25.

140. Jenkins, *Britain and the War*, 1:92–95; Howard Jones, *Union in Peril: The Crisis over British Intervention in the Civil War* (Chapel Hill: University of North Carolina Press, 1992), 26–31.

Public resentment in the Union was summed up by the pen of James Russell Lowell:

> We know we've got a cause, John,
> Thet's honest, just, an' true;
> We thought 'twould win applause, John,
> Ef nowheres else, from you.[141]

The anglophilic *Boston Daily Evening Transcript* was incredulous: "A constitutional government, like that of Great Britain, which shows itself so eager to injure the only other great constitutional government in the world, and give aid and comfort to its enemies, should receive a lesson"—the lesson being a hanging of any British subjects caught privateering.[142] Raymond blamed the governing classes for Britain's failure to support the Union but predicted that the English electorate would constrain the country from intervening on behalf of the Confederacy.[143] The *Chicago Tribune* agreed that the people to whom the British government was responsible would "deal with the American question not as one merely of dollars and cents but as one that concerns civilization and constitutional freedom all over the earth."[144] Bennett in the *New York Herald*, by contrast, held to his previous view that only republicanism could liberalize Britain, and suggested that the British ruling classes feared a U.S.-inspired revolution similar to that which rocked France in 1789.[145]

The first real threat of war came in November, when the U.S.S. *San Jacinto* seized the H.M.S. *Trent*, a mail boat. The *Trent* had been carrying two Confederate emissaries, James Murray Mason and John Slidell, to Europe to work for British and French recognition of the Confederacy. The *San Jacinto* spirited Mason and Slidell to Boston. Northerners were at first elated at the kidnapping. Most Britons were enraged, however. An angry Palmerston told the cabinet, "I don't know whether you are going to stand for this, but I'll be damned if I do!"[146] The harshest reactions were by those ideologically predisposed to hate America. The London *Morning Chronicle* clamored for war against the "upstart Republic which has insulted us" and asserted that such lawlessness validated "the fact that

141. Thomas Bailey, *A Diplomatic History of the American People*, 6th ed. (New York: Appleton-Century-Crofts, 1958), 320.

142. *Boston Daily Evening Transcript*, 1 June 1861.

143. "The Sympathies of England," *New York Times*, 28 May 1861; "The House of Lords on American Affairs," ibid., 31 May 1861.

144. "Position of England," *Chicago Tribune*, 29 May 1861.

145. "The Perplexities of England with Regard to This Country," *New York Herald*, 30 May 1861.

146. Howard Jones, *Union in Peril: The Crisis over British Intervention in the Civil War* (Chapel Hill: University of North Carolina Press, 1992), 84–85.

Englishmen greatly prefer a limited monarchy to a despotic republic."[147] The *Manchester Guardian* took the opportunity to lambaste Cobden and Bright: "The country which, from their point of view, if from no other, ought to be peace-loving, long-suffering, and just, has given a wanton insult to a friendly nation," adding days later, "It is difficult to understand that any candid observer of the struggle can believe that either the government of the United States, or the mob who rule over them, have the slightest intention of emancipating the negroes."[148]

Even so, Radical leaders toiled to keep the peace. Bright declared to his home district of Rochdale that even though there may be those in Britain "who dislike democracy, and who hate a republic . . . if all other tongues are silent, mine shall speak for that policy which gives hope to the bondsmen of the South." Forster publicly declared that "a war between these two countries would be the same as a civil war."[149]

In the middle was the circumspect *Times*, clinging to its admiration of the United States, expressing the hope "that our people will not meet this provocation with an outburst of passion, or rush to resentment without full consideration of all the bearings on the case."[150] Palmerston sent eleven thousand troops to Canada and prepared a harsh ultimatum demanding immediate release of Mason and Slidell. The night before it was dispatched, Prince Albert softened the ultimatum, using language from the *Times* editorial, allowing Lincoln to say that the captain who seized the *Trent* had not acted under instructions. Palmerston and Russell approved of Albert's wording.[151]

Lincoln at first was inclined to hold on to Mason and Slidell and submit the question to arbitration. Many in Congress and the press denounced any capitulation to England. Rep. Clement L. Vallandigham, a Copperhead later to be imprisoned for pro-Southern conspiracy, introduced a resolution calling on the president to stand firm against Britain.[152] Bennett's *New York Herald* pronounced that "the enterprise has so far succeeded as to give to the feudal oligarchy of England a new lease of that power which was slipping through their fingers, from the moral influence of our successful popular institutions." Declaring that "England cannot afford to go to war with us," Bennett called for no compromise.[153]

Less anglophobic elites were more circumspect. The *Boston Daily Evening Transcript* lamented that Britain had "exhibited no sympathy

147. *Morning Chronicle* (London), 2–3 December 1861.
148. *Manchester Guardian,* 6 and 10 December 1861.
149. *Manchester Guardian,* 5 and 2 December 1861.
150. Quoted in Norman B. Ferris, *The "Trent" Affair: A Diplomatic Crisis* (Knoxville: University of Tennessee Press, 1977), 47.
151. Ferris, "Trent," 51–52, 150.
152. *Congressional Globe,* 37th Cong., 2d sess., 16 December 1861, 1: 101.
153. *New York Herald,* 16–17 December 1861.

with the only other constitutional government in the world in a struggle for national existence," but the newspaper trusted "our mother-country" to be reasonable.[154] Raymond and Greeley both blamed the Tories for whipping up public outrage in England and hoped for a peaceful and honorable resolution.[155] As days passed, it became apparent that the seizure of Mason and Slidell had in fact been illegal. Charles Sumner, chairman of the Senate foreign relations committee, visited Lincoln almost daily during the crisis, trying to persuade him to hand over Mason and Slidell.[156] Sumner scolded the president: "Now, Mr. President, if you had done your duty earlier in the slavery matter, you would not have this trouble on you. Now you have no friends, or the country has none, because it has no policy upon slavery."[157] The *New York Times* quickly advised compromise: "If the act of Capt. Wilkes was not in conformity with public law, it will be disavowed."[158] Seward himself helped talk Lincoln into releasing the envoys with a statement noting that Wilkes had inadvertently broken international law and that Washington was pleased that the rights of neutrals on the high seas, championed by Americans since the 1790s, were finally being acknowledged by the British. Despite the absence of an explicit apology, the response satisfied the British cabinet.[159]

In the ensuing months Union sympathizers in Britain, exuberant at the resolution of the *Trent* affair, went to work. John Stuart Mill published "The Contest of America" in *Fraser's Magazine,* in which he argued that the war was indeed about slavery, even if the Union's motives were alloyed. Letters from Harriet Beecher Stowe to prominent Britons were published arguing the same point. The economist John Elliott Cairnes and the historian Goldwin Smith published articles condemning British sympathy for the South.[160]

Within a year, the two countries were near a crisis again. From the opening of the Civil War, various officials in Britain and France had considered making a joint offer to mediate between Union and Confederacy. Seward had clearly implied that the Union would declare war on any European power that made such an offer, since it would

---

154. *Boston Daily Evening Transcript,* 16 December 1861.

155. *New York Tribune,* 17 and 19 December 1861; *New York Times,* 16–18 December 1861.

156. On Christmas Day Sumner read the president letters from his friends Cobden and Bright warning that Britain would go to war if not satisfied. David H. Donald, *Charles Sumner and the Rights of Man* (New York: Alfred A. Knopf, 1970), 30–39; Adams, *Great Britain and the Civil War,* 1:231–33; Jenkins, *Britain and the War,* 1:226.

157. Donald, *Sumner,* 46.

158. *New York Times,* 16 and 20 December 1861.

159. Ferris, "*Trent,*" 168–84; H. C. Allen, *Great Britain and the United States: A History of Anglo-American Relations (1783–1952)* (London: Odhams, 1954), 469–71.

160. Fladeland, *Men and Brothers,* 394–97.

amount to recognition of the Confederacy as a sovereign state.[161] In the summer and fall of 1862 Louis Napoleon peddled an armistice proposal to all the European powers, reasoning that the Union would dare not make war on such a combination.[162]

Russell and Gladstone began lobbying Palmerston to consider the French proposal in the fall. Gladstone, a Liberal who in the previous decade had expressed strong aversion to Anglo-American war,[163] now was dismayed at the heightening slaughter in America and thought the Confederacy might win the war. Like many, he was also concerned at the distress in the cotton-starved Lancashire textile district. In a notorious speech at Newcastle in October the chancellor declared, "Jefferson Davis and the other leaders of the South have made an army; they are making, it appears, a navy; and they have made what is more than either—they have made a nation."[164] Russell too believed Southern independence a fait accompli and that the Union was not going to eradicate slavery in any case. The cabinet considered the Russell-Gladstone intervention proposal in November.

Most adamant in opposing the proposal were George Cornewall Lewis, secretary for war, and the Duke of Argyll, lord privy seal. Argyll wrote Gladstone that slavery, not empire, was the central issue of the Civil War, and that England should allow the war to continue until emancipation.[165] Lewis argued to the cabinet that the Confederacy had not yet established its own independence, and therefore recognition of the Confederacy would be premature: under international law foreign recognition was supposed to be a consequence rather than a cause of independence. Thus British intervention would be a virtual alliance with the South, and war with the North was bound to follow.[166]

Palmerston was nonplused. On his mind were no doubt the arguments of Lewis, and the knowledge that with Robert E. Lee's retreat from Maryland after the battle of Antietam the case for Southern independence was weakening. Yet the premier admitted he was also hesitant because of a major announcement Lincoln had made two months earlier: the preliminary Emancipation Proclamation. On 22 September, Lincoln had announced that as of 1 January 1863 all slaves in the rebellious states would be declared free. While at first Palmerston himself and other British elites sneered at the proclamation as hypocritical and

161. Adams, *Great Britain and the Civil War*, 2:35–36.
162. Jones, *Union in Peril*, 1–9.
163. When U.S. troops had occupied San Juan Island in 1859, Gladstone had argued that even were the American action illegal, war would not be justified. Crawford, *Anglo-American Crisis*, 8.
164. Jones, *Union in Peril*, 180–86.
165. Ibid., 158.
166. Ibid., 212–17.

likely to start a Southern race war, an inexorable shift in British public opinion began to take place.[167]

On 6 October the Radical *Morning Star* announced, "The inevitable has come at last. Negro emancipation is formally and definitively adopted as the policy in war and peace of the United States."[168] Evangelical Christian and other emancipation groups were energized, and John Bright stated that the "anti-slavery sentiment" of his country was finally being "called forth." The *Daily News* predicted that "the most audacious Secessionists" would shy away from proposing recognition of the "confederated Slave States."[169] Rallies and mass meetings began all over Britain in which middle- and working-class Englishmen passed resolutions pledging support for the Northern cause. The shift in working-class opinion was most remarkable because the Northern blockade of Southern cotton continued in force—that is, intervention remained in the immediate material interests of the workers, but most now opposed it. This shift to Union sympathy was precisely what Lincoln had hoped for in issuing the proclamation. As he wrote to a Chicago emancipation group, "No other step would be so potent to prevent foreign intervention."[170]

In recent years some historians have challenged the traditional view (first articulated by Karl Marx) that the British working class did in fact begin to support the Union at this point. Mary Ellison argues that in fact they continued to follow their short-term material interests and support the Confederacy and intervention.[171] But Philip S. Foner challenges Ellison's study as tendentious. She assumes rather than demonstrates that all pro-Union labor meetings were contrived and all pro-Confederate meetings genuine. By contrast, Foner contends that the workers were courted by both sides and by 1863 had come down decisively on the side of the Union.[172]

In any event, Palmerston had already written privately to Russell that slavery was now England's "great difficulty" in trying to put together peace terms. Could the British government, he asked, "without offence to many People here recommend to the North to sanction Slavery and to

167. Palmerston called the proclamation "trash," while the *Times* accused Lincoln of trying to stir up slaves to make war on their masters. Stern, *When the Guns Roared*, 156–57. By this time the *Times* was mainly in the hands of pro-Confederate writers; see Crawford, *Anglo-American Crisis*, 130–33.

168. Jenkins, *Britain and the War*, 2:152.

169. Ibid., 1:215–16.

170. Lincoln, "Reply to Emancipation Memorial Presented by Chicago Christians of All Denominations," 13 September 1862, quoted in Jones, *Union in Peril*, 172.

171. Mary Ellison, *Support for Secession: Lancashire and the American Civil War* (Chicago: University of Chicago Press, 1972).

172. Philip S. Foner, *British Labor and the American Civil War* (New York: Holmes & Meier, 1981), esp. 19–24.

undertake to give back Runaways, and yet would not the South insist upon some such Conditions after Lincoln's Emancipation Decree[?]" The French were readier to intervene, he wrote, because they were freer from the "Shackles of Principle and of Right & Wrong on these Matters, as on all others than we are."[173] The prime minister may have disdained public opinion, but he admitted to being constrained by it: as he had told the Russian ambassador the previous year, there were "two Powers in this Country, the government & public opinion, and that both must concur for any great important steps."[174] Without Palmerston's support, the cabinet dropped the proposal. Intervention was to be proposed again several more times, but never again was the cabinet to entertain the idea seriously. As Henry Adams, son of the U.S. minister, wrote in his diary, "The Emancipation Proclamation has done more for us here than all our former victories and all our diplomacy. It is creating an almost convulsive reaction in our favor all over this country."[175]

The third major Anglo-American crisis came when the Laird shipyard in Scotland began building ironclad vessels or "rams" for the Confederacy. British law prohibited such sales, but Laird claimed the ships were not destined for the South, and the government could not prove otherwise. In the summer of 1862 the *Alabama* steamed away from the shipyard, soon to do great damage to the Union as a commerce raider. Adams had protested loudly at the British government's failure to prevent the "escape" of the *Alabama*. Laird was building two more rams to run the Northern Blockade but claimed that these were for sale to Egypt.[176]

In April 1863 Russell seized the *Alexandra* as it was being fitted. In the summer, however, Adams learned that another ironclad had been launched, and he genuinely began to fear Anglo-American war. As he pointed out to Russell, a Confederate publication had boasted that the ironclads would enter the ports at New York, Boston, and Portland and "[inflict] a vital blow upon the enemy. The destruction of Boston alone would be worth a hundred victories in the field." Adams warned Russell: "It would be superfluous in me to point out to your lordship that this is war."[177] Even pro-Confederate British papers opposed the release of the ironclads. The *Times* admitted that the public was firmly

---

173. Jones, *Union in Peril*, 191, 206.

174. Ferris, "*Trent*," 158.

175. Bailey, *Diplomatic History*, 342.

176. Allen, *Britain and the United States*, 487; Jenkins, *Britain and the War*, 2:121–22, 278. Bitterness over the *Alabama* persisted for years after the Civil War; in 1871 a five-nation arbitration commission assessed damages at $15.5 million, and the next year Britain paid this amount to the United States. R. B. Mowat, *The Diplomatic Relations of Great Britain and the United States* (New York: Longmans, Green and Co., 1925), 213–20.

177. Jenkins, *Britain and the War*, 2:277–78; Thomas G. Paterson, ed., *Major Problems in American Foreign Policy* (Lexington, Mass.: D. C. Heath, 1984), 1:298–99. Ironically, Adams

against it and argued that a bad international legal precedent would be set if they were released.[178]

Significantly, by this time even Britain's traditional defenders in the Union were turning against the mother country and recategorizing it as illiberal. The *New York Times* solemnly announced that, although it deplored the thought of Anglo-American war, the English government was "laying up wrath against the day of wrath." If war were to come, the British public would have to blame it not on Americans but on "their own class rulers."[179] The *Boston Daily Evening Transcript*, once anglophilic, now took Bennett's line that all European monarchs and aristocrats wanted the Union to fail so as to defeat democracy in their own countries.[180] Like Mexican liberals who turned against the United States in the late 1830s, Union liberals who had once admired England were now forced by repeated evidence of hostility from London to relabel Britain a despotism.[181]

Even before Adams had sent his stern note, however, Russell had seized the ironclads, ending the crisis. By now the foreign secretary was firmly opposed to any British intervention in the war, writing to his minister to Washington, "If we have taken part in interventions, it has been in behalf of the independence, freedom and welfare of a great portion of mankind. I should be sorry, indeed, if there should be any intervention on the part of this country which could bear another character."[182] His former partner Gladstone was to declare in Parliament two months later, in response to another intervention proposal by pro-Confederates, "A war with the United States would be dangerous to us on several grounds. It would be dangerous to our commerce, and it would be dangerous to Canada; but it ought to be unpopular on far higher grounds, because it would be a war against our own kinsmen for slavery."[183]

Northern Americans who had always hated Britain for ideological reasons interpreted British actions throughout the war in the harshest

---

was now pushing the position he had denied, that the Civil War was a war, while the British government was acting as though it were not a war even though the queen had recognized it as such in 1861.

178. Jenkins, *Britain and the War*, 2:286.

179. *New York Times*, 7 March 1863.

180. *Boston Daily Evening Transcript*, 6 March 1863.

181. Charles Sumner was so enraged that after the war he insisted that Britain pay a $4 billion indemnity to the United States, by which he meant hand over all of Canada. Allen, *Britain and the United States*, 510.

182. Jenkins, *Britain and the War*, 2:241. Jenkins notes here that Russell "did acknowledge at that time, albeit indirectly, the success of the Emancipation Society. Its demonstrations had lent force to Palmerston's warning that any interference which appeared to benefit the cause of slavery would give offence to many people."

183. *Hansard's Parliamentary Debates*, 3d ser., vol. 171 (30 June 1863), cols. 1805–6.

possible light. Americans who for ideological reasons had been in-clined to favor England before the Civil War gave it the benefit of the doubt during the war, seeking accommodation during the *Trent* crisis. By 1863, however, even these had relabeled Britain an illiberal state and spoke of the possibility of war later. Lincoln was persuaded by his cab-inet to capitulate about the *Trent*, but had he followed the bellicose ad-vice of Democrats, he would have had difficulty gaining public sup-port for Anglo-American war.

British who had been anti-American before the war remained that way. Those who had been pro-American before the war were divided on whether to back the Union or the Confederacy at first, perceiving the two to be equally liberal. Despite Radical peace agitation during the *Trent* crisis, the country would have clearly supported war had Lincoln not acquiesced. After the fall of 1862, however, Liberals and Radicals shifted toward pro-Unionism, seeing the North as a natural friend de-serving support. Evidence is strong that public opinion helped prevent the Palmerston government from intervening in the war on the side of the South.

In the middle of the nineteenth century, then, elites in the United States, Britain, and Mexico perceived foreign states in light of their de-sires for their own country. These perceptions affected Anglo-American and Mexican-American relations, although there were times when the quality of the relations themselves could feed back and alter the per-ceptions. Similar dynamics were to be at work in the latter decades of the century in U.S. diplomatic crises involving Spain, Chile, and Great Britain.

[5]

From the Virginius Affair to the Spanish-American War

Three nations were the founders of American liberty, France, Spain, &
the United States; the three are now republics. . . . [T]he world will bless
our arrangements which without humiliation to anybody keeps [sic] the
peace between republican peoples and gives [sic] security and consolida-
tion to our republic.

Letter from seven Spanish Deputies to Charles Sumner,
November 1873

American expansionists' ambitions to acquire or influence more of the
Western Hemisphere did not end with the Civil War. Twice, American
interest in Cuba brought a crisis with Spain; in 1873 war was averted,
in 1898 it was not. In between these two Spanish-American crises, the
United States had war-threatening disputes with Chile in 1891–92 (the
Baltimore affair) and with Britain in 1895–96 (the Venezuelan border
crisis).

Liberalism influenced all four cases. As in earlier periods, ideology
and domestic politics are arguably partly responsible for U.S. expansion
and foreign reactions to that expansion.[1] But to reiterate, my argument
has to do not with general drives toward expansion but with attitudes
subjects held toward particular foreign states. In 1873 Spain was a fragile republic, and liberals in that nation and in the United States explicitly
cited republican solidarity as a reason not to fight. In 1898, liberalism
prodded the United States in the opposite direction, as Spain was again
a monarchy. In the Chilean affair as well, many American elites were
loath to fight their fellow republic. In the Venezuelan affair, as in earlier

[handwritten margin note: public opinion trumps int. system]

1. For an influential treatment of domestic drives toward U.S. expansion, see Walter
LaFeber, *The New Empire: An Interpretation of American Expansion 1860–1898* (Ithaca: Cornell University Press, 1963).

[139]

Anglo-American crises, American liberals were divided over whether England was a fellow liberal state. Yet in both nations liberal ideology and institutions helped hold the governments back from war.

THE SPANISH-AMERICAN CRISIS OF 1873

How Liberal Was the United States?

The United States became more liberal than ever in the years after the Civil War. The thirteenth amendment to the Constitution outlawed slavery; the fifteenth prohibited denial of suffrage on the basis of "race, color, or previous condition of servitude." Now, all inhabitants were eligible for citizenship, and basic civil rights were guaranteed from encroachment by the federal government, if not yet the states. By 1873, however, whites in many Southern states had already regained power and were finding ways of subverting blacks' right to vote. Methods ranged from ballot theft and fraud to outright violence. The federal courts generally allowed these violations of the Constitution.[2] In addition, women continued to lack the franchise, and Indians were persecuted. Yet since discussion was free and elections were regular and competitive, the United States earns a high liberal rating.

How Did Americans Perceive Spain?

Partisanship was high during the so-called Gilded Age, but with the slavery issue solved the two main parties' ideological differences had begun to cloud. Republicans were the dominant party, but they began slipping from the grasp of Charles Sumner's reformist wing and into the hands of social Darwinists. Mainstream Republican politicians vaunted the entrepreneur and became notorious for corrupt relationships with businessmen. The party's 1872 platform reaffirmed the commitment to civil rights for blacks (and to consider extending more rights to women), the tariff, and a vigorous national government.[3]

When the Republicans renominated the incumbent Ulysses S. Grant for president in 1872, the old reformist wing of the party formed the Liberal Republican party and nominated the radical editor Horace

2. Kirk H. Porter, *A History of Suffrage in the United States* (Chicago: University of Chicago Press, 1918), 196–202. By 1873, white Democrats had regained control of Georgia, North Carolina, Tennessee, Virginia, and Texas.

3. Robert Kelley, *The Cultural Pattern in American Politics: The First Century* (New York: Alfred A. Knopf, 1979), 248–50; Donald Bruce Johnson, ed., *National Party Platforms*, vol. 1, *1840–1956*, rev. ed. (Urbana: University of Illinois Press, 1978), 46–48.

Greeley, now a Democrat, for president. The Liberal Republicans and Democrats used the same platform in 1872, one affirming local government over centralization, the rights of labor, and a Congressional solution to the tariff question "wholly free from Executive interference or dictation." Those Democrats unable to stomach Greeley formed the "Straight-Out" Democrats, and reaffirmed states' rights. Grant won the election in a landslide.[4]

Thus, in general, Republicans followed the Federalist-Whig tradition of a strong central government, socioeconomic hierarchy, and moral rectitude. Democrats followed the Jeffersonian-Jacksonian tradition of local self-government, economic and cultural laissez-faire, and defense of the common people.

Spain was much discussed in the United States because of the Cuban rebellion, later called the Ten Years' War, that began in 1868. American sympathies generally went to the Cuban insurgents, not least because they were demanding the abolition of slavery. The issue was complicated by the fact that the rebellion had begun just as Spain itself began moving in the direction of republicanism. In 1868 Queen Isabel II was overthrown, and in 1870 a constitutional monarchy under Amadeo was established. In February 1873, thanks in part to the U.S. minister to Madrid, Amadeo abdicated and Spain set up its first republican government.[5] As Allan Nevins writes, "To most Americans 'republic' was a word more blest than Mesopotamia .... [a] host of Americans were loath to think that a republic would not solve all of Spain's problems," including slavery. In early March Congress passed resolutions congratulating the Spanish people, and the press joined the chorus.[6] The American predilection toward republics caused the United States to mute its criticisms of Spain.

Still, there remained many Americans who doubted that a Hispanic, Catholic, European nation could genuinely become republican, especially so quickly. The influential Republican E. L. Godkin of the *Nation* averred that Spain was merely a nominal republic.[7] Feeding this skepticism was Spanish conduct in the province of Cuba. Not only had Spanish governments all refused to abolish slavery there, but they were also putting down the liberal independence movement.[8] Still, in general, hopes were high at first for the young Spanish republic.

4. Johnson, *National Party Platforms*, 41–45; Kelley, *Cultural Pattern*, 250–51.

5. Richard Bradford, *The "Virginius" Affair* (Boulder: Colorado Associated University Press, 1980), 22–24.

6. Allan Nevins, *Hamilton Fish: The Inner History of the Grant Administration* (New York: Dodd, Mead, 1936), 635–36.

7. *Nation*, 20 November 1873, 334.

8. Bradford, "*Virginius*," 10–22.

How Liberal Was Spain?

The First Spanish Republic was never stable, and its legal status was in doubt throughout its twenty-two month existence. Immediately after its establishment, rebellions sprang up throughout the country as region after region declared independence from Madrid and monarchist plots were hatched by both supporters of the Bourbon Alfonso XII and the ultraconservative Don Carlos. Although the Cortes (national legislature) was democratically elected in May 1873, President Emilio Castelar ruled by decree between September 1873 and May 1874. As virtual dictator, Castelar suspended certain constitutional guarantees and used the army to put down the rebellions.[9] American perceptions at the time notwithstanding, Spain earns an illiberal rating. With Castelar ruling by decree, there were few institutional checks on foreign policy.

How Did Spaniards Perceive the United States?

Spain contained Republican and monarchist factions, both internally divided. Monarchists were either Alfonsists or Carlists. Moderate Republicans, led by Castelar, wanted a laissez-faire liberal order, with equality of opportunity for all but a weak economic role for the state. Castelar's republicanism was cosmopolitan. He was a staunch advocate of free trade and envisaged a league of Latin republics comprising Spain, France, Italy, and Portugal.[10] Radical Republicans, led by Francisco Pi y Margall, were socialistic, stressing that land redistribution was necessary to true democracy.[11]

In the 1860s the moderate and radical Republicans were allied in the hopes of ousting the monarchy; the Spanish Republican movement, like its counterparts in other countries, looked to the United States as a model.[12] Certain passages of the Constitution of 1869, heavily influenced by Republicans, appear to have been lifted directly from the U.S. Constitution. There was even a small movement in Spain that wished to sell Cuba to the United States. The nobility, the Catholic church, and many in the government, army, and bourgeoisie, however, tended to be hostile toward the United States. They not only were repulsed by American democracy and liberalism, but also felt threatened by U.S.

9. H. Butler Clarke, *Modern Spain 1815–1898* (Cambridge: Cambridge University Press, 1906), 337–88; C. A. M. Hennessy, *The Federal Republic in Spain: Pi y Margall and the Federal Republican Movement 1868–74* (Oxford: Clarendon, 1962), 234.

10. The 1867 Congress of Peace and Freedom in Geneva, headed by Italy's Garibaldi, foresaw a United States of Europe, modeled on the U.S. and Swiss examples of federal republicanism. Hennessy, *Federal Republic in Spain*, 23–25, 88–90.

11. Ibid., 20–23.

12. Ibid., 77, 89.

territorial ambitions.[13] In fact, Spaniards of all political stripes were adamant that the island was to remain in the Spanish Empire. Spanish suspicion of U.S. designs had been alive since the first days of manifest destiny and the Ostend Manifesto of 1854, in which a group of influential American Southerners said they would favor U.S. seizure of Cuba if necessary.[14]

Actions, Interpretations, Reactions

The first Cuban war of independence was begun in 1868 by ethnic Spaniards born in Cuba, or Creoles, who demanded abolition of slavery, lower taxes, and political, civil, and religious liberty for Cuba. The spread of the insurrection over the island prompted the Spanish government to organize a national guard, the Volunteers, whose mission to put down the rebellion overrode even loyalty to the Madrid government. Both the Volunteers and the Spanish Army committed atrocities on Cubans suspected of sympathizing with the rebellion. In January 1869, upon hearing that performers at a Havana theater were insulting the Spanish flag, Volunteers fired on the audience, killing or wounding dozens of people.[15] By 1872, 76,000 Spanish soldiers had gone to Cuba, and 46,000 casualties had been reported.[16]

Members of the Cuban revolutionary junta in New York and other eastern seaboard cities labored to involve the United States in the rebellion. Private filibusters from America supplied men and matériel to the rebels; members of Congress and the U.S. press openly sympathized. Hamilton Fish, the secretary of state, instructed Daniel Sickles, minister to Madrid, to insist that Spain free the 500,000 slaves in Cuba, or else there would follow "a marked change in the feeling and in the temper of the people and of the government of the United States." As a gesture, the Liberal government of Manuel Ruiz Zorilla freed the 50,000 slaves in nearby Puerto Rico. But when Fish's dispatch to Sickles was published, a political firestorm erupted in Spain. Conservatives accused the Zorilla government of taking orders from Washington. Just when it looked as though Grant would be forced by Congress to recognize Cuban belligerency, Spain was convulsed by revolution, King Amadeo abdicated, and the First Spanish Republic was set up.[17]

13. James W. Cortada, *Two Nations over Time: Spain and the United States, 1776–1977* (Westport, Conn.: Greenwood, 1978), 142–45.

14. Hennessy, *Federal Republic in Spain*, 92; Raymond Carr, *Modern Spain, 1808–1975*, 2d ed. (Oxford: Clarendon, 1982), 307; Frederick Merk, *Manifest Destiny and Mission in American History* (New York: Vintage Books, 1963), 211.

15. Bradford, "*Virginius*," 7–9.

16. Nevins, *Hamilton Fish*, 615.

17. Ibid., 615–33.

Sickles, a colorful former Union general in the Civil War, had aided the Madrid revolutionaries. While striding over to visit Estanislao Figueras, the new president, to announce U.S. recognition, Sickles was saluted by rows of infantry to the tune of "The Star Spangled Banner."[18] Sickles and Figueras made fraternal exchanges on liberty, democracy, and fraternity. Christin Martos, the foreign minister, assured the Cortes that the danger of U.S. annexation of Cuba was gone now that Spain was a republic: "we may consider as dissipated those shadows, those apprehensions that patriots may have felt as to the integrity of our territory; which if always protected by the valor and resolution of Spain, is now safer than ever by reason of the new-born affection of a nation which until today might have formed views hostile to our sovereignty."[19]

Martos had good reason to be hopeful. In Washington, Congress passed resolutions congratulating the Spanish people, with the press chiming in. In a marked change, Grant omitted any reference to the Cuban question in his March inaugural address. Now cabinet discussions were suddenly much more amiable toward Spain, touching on the hostility of the European powers to the Madrid republic, and the possibility of a revolution in Portugal. Grant indicated that he might oppose a hypothetical British attempt to overthrow the Spanish republic, since the future of republican government in Cuba and Puerto Rico was probably at stake.[20] In April, Fish urged the Colombian minister not to press Spain about Cuba at this historic moment; as he wrote in his diary:

> some of the most earnest and intelligent republicans of the present age had inaugurated the revolution in Spain, and were now endeavoring to establish permanently a republican government; . . . the future of a republican government in Spain and its dependencies was hanging upon this issue, involving not only the question of a republic for $1\frac{1}{2}$ [million] in Cuba but for 14 [million] in Spain, it behooves those who were considering this question to think of the effect of pressing Spain in the present emergency with questions such as he contemplated.[21]

The establishment of the First Republic gave Spain enormous breathing room in dealing with the United States.

Sickles soon became disillusioned with the Spanish republic, however, surmising that it would be no quicker than the monarchy to settle

18. W. A. Swanberg, *Sickles the Incredible* (New York: Charles Scribner's Sons, 1956), 343.

19. Nevins, *Hamilton Fish*, 635–36.

20. Ibid., 636.

21. James B. Chapin, "Hamilton Fish and the Lessons of the Ten Years' War," in Jules Davids, ed., *Perspectives in American Diplomacy* (New York: Arno, 1976), 150–51.

the Cuban question.[22] American filibusters to Cuba continued, including matériel sent in a U.S.-flagged ship called the *Virginius*. Among the Americans on board were the captain, Joseph Fry, a naval veteran, and William Ryan, an Irish-American mercenary. In October the vessel loaded up with men, weapons, and ammunition in Jamaica and Haiti and set sail for Cuba. The men hoped that the American flag would immunize the ship from capture, but the *Virginius* was apprehended by a Spanish corvette on 31 October. The Spaniards lowered the ship's U.S. flag and allowed it to be trampled on the ship's deck, raising the Spanish flag in its place.[23] Ryan and three Cuban junta officers had already been tried in a Spanish court and sentenced to death *in absentia*. Over the protests of the U.S. Vice Consul, General Don Juan N. Burriel, military commander at Santiago, had the four men executed before a firing squad.[24]

When word of the executions arrived in Washington on 7 November, Grant asked Fish whether it would not "be well to telegraph Sickles that the summary infliction of the death penalty upon the prisoners . . . will necessarily attract much attention in this country, and will be regarded as an inhuman act not in accordance with the spirit of civilization of the nineteenth century?"[25] Although the capture of the *Virginius* had taken place in international waters, making it illegal, Grant's cabinet decided on 11 November not to intervene in Cuba. Fish's diary notes that the cabinet agreed that war was now possible but not desirable. The secretary suggested an embargo of Cuba coupled with "expressions of kindness and sympathy with the present Republican Government in Spain, and the pointing out that the outrage and wrongs in Cuba are the result of a secondary insurrection against the power of Spain; viz., that of the Casino Espagnol and the Spanish Volunteers." On top of their concern for Spanish republicanism, Fish and others suspected that the *Virginius* had been improperly flagged.[26]

In Madrid, Castelar made clear to Sickles that he was on the side of ending oppression in Cuba. "How deeply I deplore the execution of the four prisoners at Santiago de Cuba!" he told the U.S. minister, adding that slavery was the true culprit. Castelar threatened legal proceedings against editors of leading Madrid newspapers unless they ceased attacking Sickles in print.[27]

On the day the news of Ryan's execution reached Washington, Captain Fry and his crew of thirty-seven were executed as well. When this

22. Swanberg, *Sickles*, 344–45.
23. Bradford, "*Virginius*," 36–43.
24. Ibid., 45–47.
25. Ibid., 57–58.
26. Nevins, *Hamilton Fish*, 668–69.
27. Bradford, "*Virginius*," 77–85.

news reached Fish on 12 November, he angrily cabled Sickles that if the report were confirmed the minister was to "protest in the name of this government and of civilization and humanity." During a heated session with José Polo de Barnabé, Spanish minister to Washington, Fish suggested that war could be avoided if Spain let the United States deal with Cuba. On the 15th Fish received a cable falsely stating that Burriel had executed fifty-three more passengers. Now convinced that Madrid had lost control of Cuba, the secretary cabled the U.S. ultimatum to Sickles: Spain would have to release the remaining passengers of the *Virginius*, salute the U.S. flag, and punish the responsible officials. But he added: "You will use this instruction cautiously and discreetly, avoiding all appearances of menace, but the gravity of the case admits of no doubt, and must be fairly and frankly met."[28]

Calls for wand public

The American public was outraged at the executions. The jingoistic *New York Herald* called for recognition of Cuban belligerency. Mass meetings in St. Louis, New Orleans, New York, Baltimore, and other cities called for vengeance. As one Southern newspaper summarized, "On no occasion for a quarter of a century have the people of all sections of the Union been so united upon a question as upon this of launching the power of our government against the Cuban authorities."[29] Rep. Samuel S. Cox of Brooklyn told a New York rally, "let our people go and come to and from Cuba, at their risk, if you please, to help liberty and defeat oppression."[30] United in hostility to Spain were the financiers of Wall Street, who hoped a war would wrench the nation out of the depression it had recently slid into.[31] Fish was anxious that the issue be resolved peacefully before Congress reconvened on 1 December.[32]

In Spain, both the republican and monarchical presses were intransigent. All Spaniards considered Cuba an internal affair, and had long resented U.S. interloping.[33] The *Epoca* solemnly declared, "The law has been applied. . . . Today nought remains to us but to desire peace for the dead, and to ask respect for the justice of the Spanish nation in the American provinces."[34] The monarchical *Diario Español* savagely attacked Sickles and urged that he be driven from Spain.[35] *El Imparcial* ran an extended refutation of U.S. claims concerning the *Virginius* and,

28. Ibid., 57–62.

29. Ibid., 65–66. Quotation is from *New Orleans Daily Picayune*, 14 November 1873.

30. *New York Times*, 18 November 1873.

31. One was quoted as saying that "the *Virginius* uproar was the best thing that could have happened, for it would boost business, relieve financial distress, give workers relief in shipyards which already were stepping up work on naval vessels." Bradford, "*Virginius*," 68.

32. Ibid., 61.

33. Hennessy, *Federal Republic in Spain*, 236 n. 2; Bradford, "*Virginius*," 80, 153 n. 14.

34. *Times* (London), 20 November 1873.

35. Ibid., 19 November 1873.

significantly, also doubted that America would dare push Spain very far, since "a majority of the American people desire the consolidation of the Spanish Republic."[36]

El Imparcial well understood American liberal ideology. While some Americans furiously called for intervention in Cuba, others called for understanding for Madrid's predicament in the name of republican solidarity. Charles Sumner had declined an invitation to speak at a "Free Cuba" rally in New York, instead sending a letter insisting "on waiting for evidence and on considerate treatment of the Spanish republic and its noble president."[37] As one historian writes, Sumner told the *New York Tribune* that "the first business of the United States should be to save the Spanish republic. The enemies of republicanism around the world would like nothing better than to see two of the world's republics destroy each other."[38] William M. Evarts, a former attorney general, did speak at the New York rally, but in a conciliatory tone, saying that Americans "desire the Republic to be upheld" and expect Spain to effect justice in Cuba.[39] Other prominent Americans who advocated conciliation, and thanked Fish and Sumner for their conciliatory acts and statements, included John Murray Forbes, Gouverneur Kemble, Reverdy Johnson, R. H. Dana, Jr., Caleb Cushing, Henry Wadsworth Longfellow, and J. R. Doolittle. The last wrote Sumner, "A war with the Republic of Spain if successful for us would result I doubt not in ending the Spanish Republic, and would surely endanger our own not less by a victorious result which would come to us I believe, than if we should be defeated. How the Despots and monarchists of the world would rejoice at the spectacle. I pray God the bloody cup may pass."[40]

Many newspapers sounded the same themes. The *New York World* noted, "The new Republican Government in Spain has pursued a most friendly course towards the United States since it came into power in March last, and President Grant seems to have no doubt that all the reparation which this Government may find it necessary to demand will be duly rendered in the present important controversy."[41] *Harper's Weekly* averred, "War may be necessary, but let us see what it means. War with Spain would be the overthrow of the Spanish republic by ours—a gleeful spectacle to every enemy of republicanism in the world!"[42] The *New*

36. Ibid., 15 November 1873.

37. Edward L. Pierce, *Memoir and Letters of Charles Sumner* (1894; reprint, New York: Arno, 1969), 4:573–74.

38. Bradford, "*Virginius*," 72.

39. *New York Times*, 18 November 1873.

40. Ibid.; Nevins, *Hamilton Fish*, 690; Sumner, *Papers*, 20 November 1873.

41. *Times* (London), 24 November 1873.

42. *Harper's Weekly*, 6 December 1873, 1082. *Harper's Monthly Magazine* had recently run a series of articles by Castelar on "The Republican Movement in Europe."

York Times sympathized with the Spanish government, headlining one article, "The Spanish Government Said to Be Friendly—the Republican Form of Government Shield."[43] But the *Times* was sometimes skeptical of Spain's capacity to control Cuba, and Godkin in the *Nation* pleaded for peace despite his belief that Spain was not truly a stable republic.[44] The *Chicago Daily Tribune* too pleaded for peace, but said republican solidarity in the end could not prevent war. The *Atlanta Constitution* pointed out that Americans were torn between two liberal causes: helping the Spanish republic and aiding Cuban independence and abolition.[45]

Upon receiving the U.S. ultimatum, Castelar glumly expected war unless England offered to arbitrate. The British minister to Madrid refused, suggesting that Castelar simply give in. Sickles by now genuinely desired war.[46] A group of Republican deputies in the Cortes asked for a special session to discuss the foreign crisis they alleged the Castelar government had brought on.[47] *La Discusion*, the ministerial paper, denied any discord between Cortes and government and blamed the crisis on the Cuban insurgents, whose refusal to compromise was especially wicked "now that the Republic offers them the liberty and Democracy which already exist in their neighbouring isle of Porto Rico."[48] But Castelar's government was itself divided, as the foreign minister, José de Carvajal, had now turned to warmongering and baiting Sickles.[49]

Ready to give in, Castelar decided to bypass Carvajal. After the British minister convinced the leader of the monarchical opposition not to oppose a compromise, Castelar notified a disappointed Sickles that Spain would meet the terms of the ultimatum, on the condition that it be shown that the *Virginius* had been flying the U.S. flag legally.[50]

Intent on not bringing about the fall of the Spanish republic, Fish took care not to humiliate Castelar.[51] Even so, he told Polo the offer was unacceptable. Spain must respect the U.S. flag regardless of suspicions about its being improperly flown. On authority from Madrid, Polo then offered to release the ship and remaining passengers and to delay the salute until the question of the flag could be resolved. Fish and Grant agreed.[52]

43. *New York Times*, 19 November 1873.
44. *Nation*, 20 November 1873, 334.
45. *Chicago Daily Tribune*, 17 November 1873; *Atlanta Constitution*, 22 November 1873.
46. Bradford, "*Virginius*," 80–85.
47. *Times* (London), 20 November 1873.
48. Ibid.
49. Bradford, "*Virginius*," 80, 85.
50. Ibid., 89–92.
51. Nevins, *Hamilton Fish*, 673–74.
52. Bradford, "*Virginius*," 92–93.

A few difficulties of timing remained, but the crisis was resolved. To the surprise of many, the new session of Congress raised no protests. Grant remarked that "he believed if Spain were to send a fleet into the harbor of New York and bombard the city the Senate might pass a resolution of regret that they had had cause for so doing and offer to pay them for the expense of coming over and doing it."[53]

Prior to the establishment of the Spanish Republic in February 1873 most Americans were hostile toward Spain and suspicious of its intentions in Cuba. Once a republic was declared, key U.S. elites perceived Spain as a fellow liberal state and became more accommodating. These perceptions held through the *Virginius* crisis. Had the Grant administration sought war, it is clear that it would have faced staunch opposition from these liberal elites. A central figure in keeping the peace was Fish, Grant's secretary of state.

In Spain, liberals (Republicans) were divided over the United States. The president and a number of legislators evidently believed in affinity among republics, and so took a cooperative stance. The Republican press, however, appears to have been hostile toward the United States over the Cuban question. The question of whether Castelar was domestically constrained is moot, since he effectively ruled by decree.

THE CHILEAN-AMERICAN CRISIS OF 1891–92

How Did Americans Perceive Chile?

The major political parties remained the Republican and Democratic. The party platforms from the 1888 and 1892 elections indicate that the major division was over the size and power of the federal government. Two particular disagreements were over the tariff—which Republicans continued to support and Democrats to oppose—and states' rights— which Republicans saw as the Democrats' excuse to disenfranchise blacks and Democrats upheld as the heart of free government.[54] Thus the Democrats remained within the Jeffersonian and Jacksonian traditions of laissez-faire economics and a relatively weak central government. The Republicans followed the tradition, traceable back through the Whigs to the Federalists, of a strong central government directing economic development.

Partisanship in the 1890s, however, was weaker than in previous times because the main political divide was *within* rather than *between* the parties. That divide was over the silver question. The Populist

53. Ibid., 97–99.
54. Johnson, *National Party Platforms*, 76–81, 86–91.

movement began in the late 1880s when poor farmers identified a common interest in a larger money supply. The gold standard, they believed, was a tool of Eastern and European banking interests; Populists demanded bimetallism, or a currency based in plentiful silver as well as gold, as a way of returning power to the "plain people." The currency controversy dominated U.S. politics in the 1890s, climaxing in William Jennings Bryan's unsuccessful 1896 presidential campaign.[55] The leaders of both parties—Harrison and William McKinley of the Republicans and Grover Cleveland of the Democrats—had differing visions for the American polity, but they agreed that the "free silver" movement was a menace.

American perceptions of the degree of liberalism in foreign states in the 1890s do not correlate well with party affiliation. There were Republicans and Democrats who perceived Chile, Britain, and to some extent Spain as liberal, and Republicans and Democrats who did not. Doubtless the fact that the divide between the parties was superseded by the Populist threat is largely responsible. In any event, as seen in the following cases, American perceptions of Chile, Britain, and Spain were constant before and during crises with those states.

The Republic of Chile did not loom large in the consciousness of most Americans in 1891. Yet Americans had perceptions of Latin American republics in general, and as in the 1810s, there were two conflicting views of the Western Hemisphere: that it was a region of republican solidarity, and that it was a meaningless construct. In 1881 James G. Blaine, the U.S. secretary of state, and others had followed the vision of Henry Clay (see Chapter 4) and begun what became known as the Pan-American movement. Blaine was concerned that conflicts among Latin American states would draw European intervention, that France's intention to build a canal across the isthmus of Panama was a troubling harbinger, and that U.S. manufacturing needed foreign markets.[56] Blaine had invited statesmen from the entire hemisphere to a general conference to set up a zone of peace among American republics, but the plan was cut short after President James A. Garfield was assassinated and replaced by Chester A. Arthur. Arthur replaced Blaine and canceled the conference. Congressmen and publicists kept the Pan-American movement alive during the 1880s. By the time Blaine was again secretary of state under Benjamin Harrison's presidency, another conference was scheduled for 1889, this one with the goal of establish-

55. James L. Sundquist, *Dynamics of the Party System: Alignment and Realignment of Political Parties in the United States*, rev. ed. (Washington: Brookings Institution, 1983), 127–42. See also Nell Irvin Painter, *Standing at Armageddon: The United States 1877–1919* (New York: W. W. Norton, 1987), esp. 115.

56. Arthur Preston Whitaker, *The Western Hemisphere Idea: Its Rise and Decline* (Ithaca: Cornell University Press, 1954), 74–75.

ing a customs union. The conference created a Commercial Bureau of the American Republics but utterly failed to create a Pan-American economic zone.[57]

The idea of international republican solidarity, then, was alive and well in the United States in 1891. Elites knew Chile as historically one of the more successful Latin republics. The Chilean revolution of 1891, described below, brought forth sympathetic comments. The *Baltimore Sun* wrote, "After having been for many years a model of order and prosperity for the other South American republics, Chili is now at length rent with a formidable rebellion, which may eventuate in a revolution."[58] The *New Orleans Times-Democrat* observed, "The situation is growing worse daily in Chili . . . one of the most prosperous [countries] in South America, which has been the most stable, quiet, orderly, and peaceable."[59] The civil war, fought between Chile's president and Congress, confused Americans. Some, including the U.S. minister to Santiago and probably Blaine himself, backed the president, José Manuel Balmaceda. Not only had Balmaceda stated a preference for U.S.-style presidential government over parliamentary, but he was trying to decrease British economic control over Chile. Others, including the above newspapers, backed the Chilean Congress.[60]

How Liberal Was Chile?

Before the revolution of 1891, Chile was indeed a model of stability. As one writer puts it, the Constitution of 1833 was designed to bring about "liberty without democracy." Equality before the law, the right to petition, freedom of the press, assembly, association, movement, and contract were upheld.[61] Yet, sovereignty was vested in a powerful executive nearly unchecked by Congress. The president was elected every five years and possessed enormous authority. He controlled the courts, bureaucracy, and to an extent Congressional elections. Departmental governors were responsible to him.[62] By 1891 the presidency

57. Among the strong advocates of Pan-Americanism was William McKinley of Ohio, later president before and during the Spanish-American War. Ibid., 76–85.

58. *Public Opinion*, 24 January 1891, 371.

59. Ibid., 514–15.

60. Henry Clay Evans, Jr., *Chile and Its Relations with the United States* (1927; reprint, New York: Johnson Reprint, 1971), 136–37; Fredrick B. Pike, *Chile and the United States, 1880–1962* (Notre Dame: University of Notre Dame Press, 1963), 69–70.

61. Anson Uriel Hancock, *A History of Chile* (Chicago: Charles H. Sergel & Co., 1893), 427–28; Harold Blakemore, *British Nitrates and Chilean Politics, 1886–1896* (London: Athlone, 1974), 7; Simon Collier, *Ideas and Politics of Chilean Independence 1808–1833* (Cambridge: Cambridge University Press, 1967), 347.

62. Maurice Zeitlin, *The Civil Wars in Chile* (Princeton: Princeton University Press, 1984), 33; Blakemore, *British Nitrates*, 3; Collier, *Chilean Independence*, 346.

had been weakened by several reforms. But Balmaceda's attempts to strengthen the executive by rigging elections and ignoring Congress led to civil war. After the Congressionalists won the war, they quickly passed laws weakening the presidency, including those prohibiting civil servants from serving in Congress, mandating popular election of the president, and turning over local elections to localities.[63] Suffrage was limited to married males twenty-one or older and unmarried males twenty-five or older.[64] By the time of the *Baltimore* affair, after the civil war was over, Chile rates as a liberal state.

How Did Chileans Perceive the United States?

Four distinct parties dominated politics. The Conservative Party comprised proclerical aristocrats who coalesced to combat liberalism. The National Party was also aristocratic and authoritarian but anticlerical. The Liberal Party, which urged democracy and the separation of church and state, aligned with the Conservatives against the Nationals in the 1860s, resulting in an eventual liberal offshoot called the Radical Party. Liberals and Radicals later worked together again and sought to lift up the poor through education and the franchise. They favored the laissez-faire approach over the paternalism of the Conservatives and Nationals.[65]

The Liberals nominated Balmaceda for president in 1886, causing the Radicals to split off again. As president, Balmaceda moved to abandon the liberal laissez-faire program and instead to implement state-directed growth through public works and deficit spending. Resistance from all parties, including a newly formed Democrat Party, led Balmaceda to lurch toward authoritarianism. Radicals declared that the president was violating the principles of parliamentary government. On 1 January 1891, Balmaceda announced he would implement his budget without Congressional approval. Six days later, the Radical leader Jorge Montt led the navy in a revolt of an anti-Balmaceda coalition dubbed "Congressionalists." The army sided with the president, and Chile entered nine months of civil war. The Congressionalists won, and parliamentary government and laissez-faire liberalism were reestablished.[66]

Frederick Pike has identified three traditions of attitude toward the United States in nineteenth-century Chile. First is anti-Yankee isolationism, which held that the Monroe Doctrine was an effort at Anglo-Saxon domination and that Chile should tie its future to Europe rather

---

63. Blakemore, *British Nitrates*, 6; Luis Galdames, *A History of Chile*, trans. I. J. Cox (New York: Russell & Russell, 1964), 362–63.

64. Hancock, *History of Chile*, 426; Galdames, *History of Chile*, 362–63.

65. Pike, *Chile and the United States*, 13–23.

66. Ibid., 40–46.

than to any Western Hemisphere vision. Second is anti-Yankee, pro-Latin solidarity. Propounded by radicals and conservatives alike, this tradition perceived that the United States had betrayed its early humanitarian promise and become materialist and imperialist. Interestingly, many who held this view were liberals and radicals, such as Manuel Antonio Matta. Third is a tradition parallel to Henry Clay's American system, where all Western republics share a common peaceful and prosperous destiny (see Chapter 4). This republican tradition held that common institutions in North and South America outweighed racial and cultural differences.[67]

Balmaceda belonged to the third tradition, and pointedly expressed his friendliness toward the United States.[68] The Congressionalists who won the civil war, however, had a long-standing anti-U.S. animus. An abortive effort by Blaine to mediate in the War of the Pacific in 1881, in which Chile was in the process of defeating Bolivia and Peru, had poisoned the attitudes of many liberals (Blaine was concerned that Chile was a proxy for British interests). The American refusal to support the Congressionalists in the civil war aggravated these perceptions. The administration of Benjamin Harrison was officially neutral. Still, a U.S. admiral allegedly notified Balmaceda of rebel troop movements; a U.S. company protected by U.S. ships cut the undersea cable linking rebel headquarters with the outside world while restoring the cable linking Santiago to Peru; and the U.S. minister to Chile, Patrick Egan, provided asylum to a number of Balmaceda's cronies after the president fell in September. Egan had already been known to be friendly with the deposed president.[69] Thus liberal Congressionalists entered the *Baltimore* affair highly suspicious of the United States.

Actions, Interpretations, Reactions

On 16 October 1891, the U.S.S. *Baltimore*, a dynamite cruiser, docked at Valparaiso and its crew took a twenty-four-hour shore leave. One small party of sailors ended up at the True Blue Saloon. Seaman Charles Riggin became involved in a fight with a Chilean sailor, and Riggin's comrade John Talbot intervened. A mob of Chileans began chasing the two Americans, and someone—a policeman, one American eyewitness claimed—fatally shot Riggin. At the same time, mobs attacked scores of

67. Ibid., 23–30. Pike writes that Chile was distinctive among Latin American nations in having liberal-positivists who were anti-U.S. (27).

68. Evans, *Chile and Its Relations*, 136–37.

69. Egan was an Irish émigré and rabid anglophobe who believed Balmaceda would break the British hold on Chile and open the door to U.S. business. Pike, *Chile and the United States*, 66–70; William F. Sater, *Chile and the United States: Empires in Conflict* (Athens: University of Georgia Press, 1990), 56–58.

other American sailors. William Turnbull was stabbed ten to fifteen times and died nine days later. Seventeen more sailors were injured, and thirty-one others were arrested by the Valparaiso police.[70]

Capt. Winfield Scott Schley of the *Baltimore* determined that the fault lay entirely with the Chilean populace and police. Still, reaction in the United States was muted. The *New York Times* attributed the riot to pent-up anti-Americanism and predicted, "It is improbable that any serious results will follow the incident." The *New York Daily Tribune* called the situation "grave and serious" but added, "We do not believe that the most progressive and enlightened State in South America will refuse to make proper reparation for the affront. . . . No war with Chili is probable."[71] The *New York Herald* asked for understanding: "[Chile] is in a condition of semi-anarchy just now, and more impetuous than she will be later on. . . . We desire that the amicable relations between the two republics shall continue."[72]

Secretary of State Blaine, long an advocate of Pan-Americanism, was ill at the time, and the Acting Secretary William Wharton enjoined Egan to demand an explanation from the Chilean government. But that government, still in disarray in the aftermath of its civil war victory, was slow to respond. On 26 October Egan sent a note to Manuel Antonio Matta, the foreign minister, reiterating Schley's findings and noting that Santiago had as yet expressed no regret.[73]

Matta, a Radical leader who had been feuding with Egan, replied that his government would withhold comment until it had completed its own investigation. The *Daily Tribune* played up Matta's defiance, and Chile's minister to Washington, Pedro Montt, labored to smooth relations. Montt told Blaine, whose health had improved, that Chile would punish the guilty parties in Valparaiso, and cabled Matta that Blaine was much more fair-minded than Wharton had been. "In Chile I am misunderstood. I do not want difficulties or questions, only peace and good friendship," Montt quoted Blaine as saying. The U.S. press was by now quiet. On 7 November the Congressionalist *Chilian Times*, still resenting U.S. support for Balmaceda, nonetheless advised "cool-headed patience . . . to release the strain on the relations between the huge and powerful Republic of North America and the small but vigorous Republic of South America."[74]

The Chilean governmental inquiry into the *Baltimore* incident dragged into December. President Benjamin Harrison decided to make the inci-

70. Ibid., 61; Joyce S. Goldberg, *The "Baltimore" Affair* (Lincoln: University of Nebraska Press, 1986), 1–19.

71. Ibid., 59–62.

72. *New York Herald*, 3 November 1891, quoted in *Public Opinion*, 7 November 1891, 101.

73. Goldberg, "*Baltimore*," 61–64.

74. Ibid., 64–70.

dent a centerpiece of his annual message to the nation. The president justified U.S. actions during the Chilean civil war and recounted the *Baltimore* incident in vivid language, noting that U.S. investigations placed the blame wholly on Chile. He therefore expected "full and prompt reparation" and concluded ominously: "If these just expectations should be disappointed or further needless delay intervene, I will, by a special message, bring this matter again to the attention of Congress for such action as may be necessary."[75]

The *New York Times* said that war was now possible. Some editors called for a tough line. The *St. Louis Globe-Democrat* told its readers that Chile was not a civilized republic like the United States, in that beneath the surface Chileans were as "the American aborigine or the African barbarian."[76] Soon after, a report of the secretary of the navy accused the Valparaiso police of aiding and abetting the murderers.[77]

Matta responded quickly and forcefully with a note to Montt in Washington. Calling Harrison's statements "erroneous or deliberately incorrect," the foreign minister blamed Egan for delays in the Chilean inquiry. He instructed Montt to deny all U.S. accusations "notwithstanding the intrigues which proceed from so low a source and the threats which come from so high a source." While Matta later claimed the abusive note had been private, it was read in the Chilean senate and Egan quickly sent it to Washington.[78]

Chileans felt insulted when Egan did not attend the December inauguration of Jorge Montt, their new president. The U.S.S. *Yorktown* arrived in Valparaiso harbor, where it came close several times to clashing with Chilean vessels. In Washington, Blaine met twice in December with John Trumbull, a Chilean politician of U.S. ancestry. Blaine asked for leniency toward the Balmacedists, blamed Britain for the U.S.-Chilean imbroglio, and made clear his strong desire for peace.[79] The *Nation* pleaded for understanding: in response to Egan's demand that Balmacedist refugees be allowed safe passage, the journal wrote, "This is probably the most curious of all the demands we have made on 'the sister Republic.' It might be a perfectly proper demand to make on the Chinese, or Turks, or Moroccans, but it is a very odd condition for one civilized, law-governed Republic to seek to impose on another."[80]

But by now Harrison, feeling personally insulted by Matta's note, now called the Matta circular, took the foreign policy reins from Blaine.

75. Ibid., 78–83.
76. *St. Louis Globe-Democrat*, 4 December 1891, quoted in *Public Opinion*, 12 December 1891, 220.
77. Goldberg, "*Baltimore*," 83.
78. Ibid., 84–85.
79. Ibid., 89–99.
80. *Nation*, 31 December 1891, 499.

In early January 1892 the results of the Chilean inquiry finally reached Washington. Portraying the incident as a brawl between drunken American and Chilean sailors that degenerated into a riot, the Chilean government expressed regret at the incident. The courts sentenced three Chileans and one American to prison. Harrison was unsatisfied.

To make matters worse, Pedro Montt now asked Blaine to replace Egan for the sake of "cordial and friendly relations" between the two republics. Harrison had Blaine instruct Egan not to reply.[81] Harrison's biographer writes that "Blaine alone prevented Harrison from sending an ultimatum" in the first three weeks of January. The rest of the cabinet, especially the navy secretary, wanted war.[82] But Blaine was again in ill health and Harrison was determined. On the 21st the reluctant Blaine sent an ultimatum to Santiago: unless the Chilean government withdrew the offensive parts of the Matta circular, and apologized publicly, Washington would break off diplomatic relations.[83] Harrison barely waited for Santiago's reply. Four days later he sent to Congress a lengthy message on relations with Chile. Blasting the Chileans for unfairness to Egan, blaming them for the *Baltimore* affair, and complaining of unreasonable delay in their investigation and the "grossly insulting" Matta circular, Harrison stated that the United States had to protect its flag and men in uniform. He invited Congress to take "such action as may be deemed appropriate"—effectively inviting them to declare war.[84]

Public reaction was cooler than Harrison had expected. Most agreed that Chile had been impudent, but Democratic papers called for forbearance, and Republicans called on Chile to give in.[85] The *New York Herald* declared, "The people of the United States do not want their official representatives at Washington to be exacting or domineering in this matter or to impose humiliating conditions upon a weaker sister republic just emerging from internal strife." The *Cincinnati Commercial Gazette* opined hopefully, "In a calm and considerate way [Harrison] dwells upon the former friendly relations between the two countries and does not lose sight of the fact that Chile is a sister republic with aims and aspirations like our own."[86] Still, some editors were less reluctant and apparently cared nothing for supposed republican solidarity. "The newspapers of Valparaiso and Santiago are clamoring for war against the United States," noted the *Atlanta Constitution*.[87] The *Boston*

81. Goldberg, "Baltimore," 100–101.
82. Harry J. Sievers, *Benjamin Harrison: Hoosier President* (New York: Bobbs-Merrill, 1968), 194–95.
83. Ibid., 195.
84. Goldberg, "Baltimore," 104–7.
85. Ibid., 108–9.
86. *Public Opinion*, 30 January 1892, 420–21.
87. Ibid., 12 December 1891, 220; 23 January 1892, 399.

Globe insisted that Chile's injuries and insults were intolerable, and responsibility for any rupture rested on Santiago.[88]

Congress took no immediate action, and Rep. William C. P. Breckinridge, Democrat of Kentucky, moved that the president be asked to notify Congress if Chile had yet responded. Breckinridge intoned:

> [War] is only the last resort, especially so when the war must be with a republic like our own, anxious for liberty, desiring to maintain constitutional freedom, seeking progress by means of that freedom; and this consideration is greatly strengthened by the fact that that Republic is in the midst of great internal trouble (having just overthrown a dictator), seeking congressional liberty under constitutional guaranties. All brave men, all generous men, all who love liberty will desire to bear and forbear with such a people passing through such a strait in the midst of such desperate conditions, as long as our honor will allow us to bear and forbear with her. [Applause.][89]

Even Harrison's own Republicans agreed that more information and a full debate would be necessary for a war declaration. Rather than debate war, the House sent the matter to committee, and the Senate requested more information from the president.

The U.S. Navy meanwhile prepared for hostilities, while Chile ordered massive quantities of war matériel from Europe. Chilean diplomats in Europe had already sought backing in vain from Germany and Britain. Now Matta's replacement in the foreign office, Luis Pereira, and President Montt decided that the stakes were not worth the risk. Pereira's capitulation arrived in Washington the same day Harrison sent his war request to Congress. The Chileans offered to pay reparations, with an arbitral tribunal or the U.S. Supreme Court to decide the amount; apologized for the offensive portions of the Matta circular; and promised not to demand Egan's recall unless Chile could give satisfactory cause. As one U.S. diplomat in Santiago wrote, it was "a very humiliating letter for these proud people to send." Yet send it they did, ending the crisis. In the end Chile paid a total of $75,000 to the *Baltimore* victims or their families.[90]

Americans were divided over whether Chile was a liberal state. Many said that it was, based on its history of constitutional government. Blaine, the secretary of state, was among these, as were some in Congress and the press. They argued for peace during the *Baltimore* crisis, but could not prevent Harrison from sending an ultimatum. Still,

88. Ibid., 30 January 1892, 420.
89. *Congressional Record*, 52d Cong., 1st sess., 26 January 1892, 23:550.
90. Goldberg, *"Baltimore,"* 108–31.

had Chile not yielded, Congressional balking suggests that Harrison might not have gotten his war.

Evidently most Chileans (apart from the ousted Balmacedists) regarded the United States as an unfriendly, even illiberal state. They were hostile and suspicious of U.S. gestures. Rather than cooperate with a fellow republic, they capitulated to superior U.S. power.

THE ANGLO-AMERICAN CRISIS OF 1895–96

How Did Americans Perceive Great Britain?

In the closing years of the nineteenth century many Americans, in particular those of Irish ancestry, held fast to the view that Britain was "perfidious Albion," the same aggressive monarchy it had always been. Populists commonly held the view that the British were co-conspirators with Wall Street to maintain the gold standard. Since the Civil War, however, more and more Americans, Democratic and Republican, had come to view Britain as a fellow democracy even though it was no republic. In 1867 and again in 1884–85, Parliament had passed reform bills further widening the franchise and rationalizing the electoral system (see below). Many American elites noticed these changes.[91] In 1886 Andrew Carnegie declared, "Henceforth is England democratic," and predicted that "British democracy is to be pacific, and that the American doctrine of non-intervention will commend itself to it."[92] During Victoria's Golden Jubilee the following year, U.S. editors noted approvingly how weak the Crown had become. "Political reforms have transformed the constitution of the government in substance by the extension of the franchise and the rising dominance of the popular branch," read the *Boston Advertiser*.[93]

Even the noted realist Alfred Thayer Mahan was having liberal visions of Anglo-American reunion, based inter alia on "a common inherited political tradition and habit of thought . . . [and] moral forces which govern and shape political development."[94]

When Sen. W. E. Chandler of Vermont suggested an alliance with Russia to oppose England in November 1895, Joseph Pulitzer's *New York World* declaimed: "Russia represents the worst despotism that civiliza-

91. See Stephen R. Rock, *Why Peace Breaks Out: Great Power Rapprochement in Historical Perspective* (Chapel Hill: University of North Carolina Press, 1989), 49–56.

92. Andrew Carnegie, "Democracy in England," *North American Review* 142 (January 1886), 74, 79.

93. *Public Opinion*, 21 June 1887, 234.

94. Alfred T. Mahan, "Possibilities of an Anglo-American Reunion," *North American Review* 159 (November 1894), 552.

tion has permitted to survive, except possibly that of Turkey. England represents Anglo-Saxon liberty and progress only in less degree than does our own government. We have much in common with the English. We have nothing whatever in common with Russia. Charity prompts the suggestion that the New Hampshire [*sic*] Senator is insane."[95] Ideologically, Pulitzer was a Jeffersonian, a battler against "plutocrats" in American society.[96] His anglophilia shows that by expanding the franchise and weakening the Crown, Britain had convinced many (though by no means all) Americans that it was a nation nearly as free as their own.

The older Federalist-Whig respect for British law was retained as well. Thomas F. Bayard, America's first ambassador to Great Britain,[97] considered that English law was more important than nominal Latin American republicanism. In 1893 Bayard wrote to Walter Gresham, then secretary of state, that the major problem in South America was not British monarchism but the very political instability the British also abhorred: "The English view of law, and of international administration, is nearer to our own than those of any other nation, and is to be regretted that a class or a party in the United States are so addicted to irresponsible abuse of everything British, and to seeking every occasion to testify hostility to Great Britain, because it does much to color the public view in both countries and prevent confidential interchanges of intentions or proposed action."[98] Antimonarchism remained powerful in the United States in the 1890s, but in many people's minds Britain had earned a special dispensation as a "crowned republic."[99]

How Liberal Was Great Britain?

Those Americans who claimed Britain was becoming more liberal were correct. The 1867 Reform Act expanded the franchise by 88 percent. Urban workers were the main group added to the rolls, and Parliamentary seats were distributed more fairly. Significantly, the next year the cabinet became directly responsible to the electorate when Benjamin Disraeli resigned as premier immediately after his party lost

95. *Public Opinion*, 21 November 1895, 648–49.

96. Piers Brendon, *The Life and Death of the Press Barons* (London: Secker & Warburg, 1982), 96.

97. Before Bayard the chief U.S. diplomat in Britain had been only of the rank of minister.

98. Charles Callan Tansill, *The Foreign Policy of Thomas F. Bayard* (New York: Fordham University Press, 1940), 660–61.

99. An important question is why the reforms of 1867 and 1884–85 impressed anglophobes more than had those of 1832. A definitive answer is not possible here, but it is likely that the objection many had had to monarchy stemmed from the belief that it necessarily entailed political hierarchy. Britain's wide suffrage and weakened Crown now persuaded these that a monarchy could be a liberal state after all.

an election—i.e., without waiting for Parliament to convene.[100] The 1884 reform act expanded the electorate by another 67 percent, the main beneficiaries being agricultural laborers and miners. The following year, the Redistribution Act established the principle of single-member constituencies (although exceptions were still allowed).[101] As many as 40 percent of adult males remained disenfranchised, however, mainly due to strict residency requirements.[102] As in the United States, women still could not vote. Moreover, the House of Lords retained veto power over legislation passed by the Commons. Still, with a cabinet and legislature freely elected, Britain earns a high liberal rating.

How Did the British Perceive the United States?

The political configuration had changed significantly since the 1860s, as Liberals split and socialism began to rise. In 1884 the Liberal Party divided over Gladstone's proposal for home rule in Ireland. Liberal Unionists (those opposing home rule) coalesced with the Conservatives, then led by the Marquess of Salisbury, to form a party dedicated to defending property, business, and social stability. While protective of aristocratic interests, the Conservatives were liberal enough to attract middle-class "villa Conservatives" newly concerned at the rise of the trade unions and menaces to private property from the left.[103]

The Liberals were left with strong reformist elements, led by "faddists" whose causes included disestablishment of the church, temperance laws, and world peace. Gladstone remained the major force in the Liberal Party until the 1890s and kept the focus on an individualistically conceived politics of morality. Their program included home rule for Ireland, minimal government, and democracy. Under the influence of philosopher T. H. Green, a new "idealist" liberal thought had arisen that argued a role for the state in fostering conditions under which individuals could prosper. Big- and small-government Liberals could still agree enough on a platform of political and religious liberty, elimination of privilege, and social reform to win the 1892 election.[104]

Less liberal was the nascent labor movement, led by working-class Radicals disaffected from their old middle-class vanguard. Granted the

100. Robert Livingston Schuyler and Corinne Comstock Weston, *British Constitutional History since 1832* (Princeton: D. Van Nostrand, 1957), 46–51; Sir David Lindsay Keir, *The Constitutional History of Modern Britain since 1485*, 8th ed. (Princeton: D. Van Nostrand, 1966), 416–17, 426.

101. Schuyler and Weston, *British Constitutional History*, 48–50.

102. John Belchem, *Class, Party and the Political System in Britain, 1867–1914* (Oxford: Basil Blackwell, 1990), 8–9.

103. Ibid., 25.

104. Ibid., 35–41.

vote by the 1867 and 1884 reform acts, working-class Britons were at first courted by Liberals (forming the Lib-Lab movement). But Gladstone's antistrike legislation convinced many that their interests differed from those of the middle class and that the franchise alone was thus not sufficient to improve their lot. The Marxian shift toward advocacy of collective ownership of the means of production was under way in the 1890s, although in the 1895 election the fledgling Independent Labour Party had done poorly. The Labour Party was to be organized in 1900.[105]

Up until the 1880s the lines were roughly the same as they had been since American independence: conservatives mistrusted the United States, Radicals idolized it, the center was admiring but ambivalent. Then political changes in both countries caused different British factions' estimations of America to shift. Conservatives began to find much to admire in the U.S. constitution. Sir Henry Maine's *Popular Government* concluded, "American experience has, I think, shown that, by wise constitutional provisions thoroughly thought out beforehand, Democracy may be tolerable." Lord Bryce's *American Commonwealth* (1888), hailed as a successor to Tocqueville's *Democracy in America*, emphasized the conservative nature of the U.S. Constitution.[106] The constitutional scholar A. V. Dicey wrote: "The plain truth is, that educated Englishmen are slowly learning that the American Republic affords the best example of a conservative Democracy; and now that England is becoming democratic, respectable Englishmen are beginning to consider whether the Constitution of the United States may not afford means by which, under new democratic forms, may be preserved the political conservatism dear and habitual to the governing classes of England."[107] As Britain changed, British conservatives' perceptions of America changed.

Liberals, meanwhile, only increased their admiration for the United States. One example is William Thomas Stead, founder of the *Review of Reviews*, an international digest that aspired to rally the English-speaking world to save civilization. Stead, a longtime democrat and anti-Tory, called upon London to "Americanise" the constitution of the British empire, and others echoed the call.[108]

---

105. Ibid., 52–61.

106. H. S. Maine, *Popular Government* (London, 1885), 110, quoted in Henry Pelling, *America and the British Left* (New York: New York University Press, 1957), 51–52.

107. Quoted in Andrew Carnegie, *Triumphant Democracy: Fifty Years' March of the Republic* (New York: Charles Scribner's Sons, 1887), 471.

108. W. T. Stead, "To All English-Speaking Folk," *Review of Reviews* (London), January 1890, 15. The Marquess of Lorne made the same suggestion nearly four years later; ibid., November 1893, 521. For information on Stead, see Brendon, *Life and Death of the Press Barons*, 72–85.

Many Radicals, too, continued to sing America's praises. A typical example is "Gracchus," a writer for *Reynolds's Newspaper*: "The Government of the Americans is a cheap and comparatively inexpensive one. Here we are eaten out of house and home by cats that catch no mice; there they have none of that sort." *Reynolds's* even advocated U.S. annexation of Canada, since "anything that adds to the power and authority of the United States among the nations of the earth is to the advantage of all mankind." Many were vexed by stories of political corruption in the United States, but, as Bryce put it, a Liberal could still admire America's social progress.[109] Joseph Chamberlain, a leading Unionist of Radical background, made clear his affinity for America in a speech in Toronto in 1887: "I should think our patriotism was warped and stunted indeed if it did not embrace the Greater Britain beyond the seas—the young and vigorous nations carrying everywhere a knowledge of the English tongue and English love of liberty and law. With these feelings, I refuse to speak or to think of the United States as a foreign nation. They are our flesh and blood."[110]

Yet, other Radicals were beginning to take a dimmer view of the United States. The writings of the American Henry George portrayed a United States where workers were no better off than in Britain. For Radicals turning to socialism the United States lost its luster and became a bourgeois democracy. The American example, they said, showed that the franchise alone was not sufficient to improve the condition of the masses. In 1886 H. M. William Clarke, a Marxian journalist, traced the change in attitude:

> A quarter of a century ago the American Republic was the guiding star of advanced English political thought. It is not so now. . . . It is not merely a question of machine politics, of political corruption, of the omnipotent party boss. . . . Over and beyond this is the great fact of the division between rich and poor, millionaires at one end, tramps at the other, a growth of monopolies unparalleled, crises producing abject poverty just as in Europe. These facts proved to men clearly that new institutions were of no use alone with the old forms of property; that a mere theoretic democracy, unaccompanied by any social changes, was a delusion and a snare.[111]

Thus, and not coincidentally, even as mainstream British perceptions of the United States improved, labor's opinion of its former promised land darkened. In turn, it was in part fear of socialism that made American-style democracy more attractive to the British middle and

109. Pelling, *America and the British Left*, 52–53.
110. J. L. Garvin, *The Life of Joseph Chamberlain* (London: Macmillan, 1933), 2:333–34.
111. Pelling, *America and the British Left*, 60–65.

upper classes, and made the United States itself appear to them a candidate for British friendship.

Actions, Interpretations, Reactions

The border between British Guiana and Venezuela had never been clear, but it was only in the late 1880s that relations between England and the South American republic became seriously roiled. In 1850 each country had agreed only to place settlers on its side of the so-called Schomburgk Line, the unofficial border. Then in 1880 Salisbury, the British foreign secretary, claimed much territory on the Venezuelan side of the Schomburgk Line, and in 1886, as prime minister, Salisbury announced that all territory on England's side of the line was no longer negotiable. Venezuela accused the British of violating the 1850 agreement and broke off diplomatic relations. The U.S. government had already taken an interest in the dispute, and between 1885 and 1895 made several attempts to mediate.[112]

In 1893 the Venezuelan government approached Grover Cleveland's administration to request another U.S. offer to arbitrate the boundary dispute. The request went nowhere until the October 1894 publication of *British Aggressions in Venezuela or the Monroe Doctrine on Trial*, by William Lindsay Scruggs, former U.S. minister to Caracas and now a Washington lobbyist for the Venezuelan government. Scruggs suggested that Europe was preparing a scramble for South America similar to the recent scramble for Africa. Other publicists took up the theme, and in December Cleveland announced in his annual message that he would renew U.S. efforts to arbitrate the dispute. The British response was polite but made clear the Salisbury government's determination to retain all land on its side of the Schomburgk Line.[113]

When Scruggs's message got through to Congress and the press, traditional anglophobia resurfaced. Cleveland had been under fire from both Republicans and his own Democrats for standing by while the British seized a Nicaraguan customs house in retaliation for the arrest of a British consul. Democratic politicians in Ohio and Texas plaintively asked Cleveland for "a little jingo" on Venezuela to help them out.[114]

In the press and in the White House, little of the new respect for Britain was in evidence. In May 1895 Richard Olney, Cleveland's new

112. Marshall Bertram, *The Birth of Anglo-American Friendship: The Prime Facet of the Venezuelan Boundary Dispute* (Lanham, Md.: University Press of America, 1992), 4–5.

113. Ernest R. May, *Imperial Democracy: The Emergence of America as a Great Power* (Chicago: Imprint, 1991), 36–37; Bertram, *Anglo-American Friendship*, 9–12.

114. May, *Imperial Democracy*, 33.

secretary of state, drafted a dispatch demanding that London submit the dispute to U.S. arbitration. Later christened a "twenty-inch gun" by Cleveland, Olney's vituperative note applied the Monroe Doctrine to the case, claiming that distance rendered any European control over "an American state unnatural and inexpedient." "Today," Olney insisted, "the United States is practically sovereign on this Continent, and its fiat is law upon the subjects to which it confines its interposition." Olney asked that London reply to the dispatch before the President's annual message to Congress on December 2.[115] Cleveland himself applauded the note, writing to Olney, "It's the best thing of the kind I have ever read."[116]

Preoccupied with other problems and refusing to take the American bluster seriously, Salisbury took four months to reply. Chamberlain, the colonial secretary, urged Salisbury to repudiate the relevance of the Monroe Doctrine to the Venezuelan case, and to remind Olney and Cleveland that Britain had been an American power long before the United States existed.[117]

In the meantime Congress and the American press devoted more and more attention to Venezuela. Sen. Henry Cabot Lodge of Massachusetts, a leading anglophobe, introduced a resolution that any European attempt at territorial expansion in the New World would be taken "as an act of hostility to the United States."[118] In October the *Chicago Sunday Times-Herald* printed a cartoon featuring an armed John Bull crossing into Venezuelan territory only to find an American cannon facing him reading, "No monarchical interference on American soil."[119] Cleveland was insulted at Salisbury's tardiness in replying, but on 2 December simply hinted to Congress that he had demanded arbitration and expected a British reply soon.[120]

On 6 December Salisbury's reply finally arrived in Washington. The British cabinet was willing in principle to submit to arbitration "certain large tracts of valuable territory" but rejected Olney's demand, saying Britain could not give in to the "extravagant pretensions" of a third party. He challenged the status of the Monroe Doctrine as international law, especially the version of that doctrine expounded by Olney. England, he wrote, was not seeking to impose a foreign "system" on Venezuela. The premier's patronizing tone was perhaps more objectionable to Olney and Cleveland than his arguments.[121]

115. Bertram, *Anglo-American Friendship*, 13–16, 19–28; May, *Imperial Democracy*, 38–40.
116. May, *Imperial Democracy*, 40.
117. Ibid., 43–45.
118. Bertram, *Anglo-American Friendship*, 26–29.
119. *Review of Reviews* (London), 15 November 1895, 385.
120. Bertram, *Anglo-American Friendship*, 26–29.
121. Ibid., 29–33; May, *Imperial Democracy*, 43–47.

An angry Cleveland sent a special message to Congress on 17 December which strongly asserted the legitimacy and applicability of the Monroe Doctrine and asked the legislature to take an extraordinary step. Congress should appropriate funds for a commission, to be appointed by the executive, which would study the dispute and recommend the final boundary line between Venezuela and British Guiana. When the commission's work was done, the president said, the United States would be obliged to resist "by every means in its power" any British attempt to extend jurisdiction where the commission had deemed it illegitimate. Cleveland added that he "keenly realize[d] the consequences that may follow," but he insisted that national honor required this policy. In his determination to get Britain's attention, Cleveland implicitly threatened war.[122]

Congress greeted the message with loud applause, and at first most U.S. newspapers roared approval. Congress quickly and unanimously voted $100,000 for a boundary commission. Sen. John T. Morgan of Alabama declared "the right of the United States, as the controlling nationality on this continent, and the first and most responsible Government, for the republican form and principles of human government." Sen. Henry M. Teller of Colorado echoed the call: "Great Britain will know . . . exactly what our determination is, and what it will cost her to continue the unrighteous attempt of the spoliation of this our sister Republic."[123] Sen. David Turpie of Indiana in supporting the President theorized about the nature and spread of republicanism. While a "great many republics have appeared" in Europe, "it would seem that there are only two republics in that quarter of the globe" (i.e., France and Switzerland). In the Americas, by contrast, "Very early the United States vindicated the doctrine of self-government. That sublime example has been followed until every nationality from the southern line of the Dominion to Cape Horn has now a government republican in form." It was the duty of the United States to preserve the republican character of the New World.[124]

Likewise in the press much of Cleveland's support was based on the claim that Britain was trying to spread monarchism in the Western Hemisphere. The *Chicago Chronicle* defended Cleveland's move not as international law but as a simple matter of self-defense. "Our policy," it added, "is simply to prevent any new encroachment upon the territory of any of the 'three Americas' and the adjacent islands by any monarchical country of Europe."[125] Also heard were appeals to national honor

---

122. May, *Imperial Democracy*, 41–42; Bertram, *Anglo-American Friendship*, 34–35.
123. *Congressional Record*, 54th Cong, 1st. sess., 18 December 1895, 28, pt. 1:265.
124. Ibid., 240, 263–64.
125. *Public Opinion*, 4 January 1896, 272.

and the need to rally behind the president. The *New York Sun* screamed that "an alien or a traitor" be "any American citizen, whether inside or outside of Congress, who hesitates at this conjuncture to uphold the President of the United States." The *New York Times*, reacting to worried voices from Wall Street, said, "Under the teaching of these bloodless Philistines, these patriots of the ticker, if they were heeded, American civilization would degenerate to the level of the Digger Indians, who eat dirt all their lives and appear to like it."[126]

Yet all the while, strong resistance to Anglo-American war was offered by those who had considered England a fellow liberal state. From London, Ambassador Bayard noted in a cable to Olney that the "good temper and moderate . . . tone" of the British contrasted to the "wholly unreliable character of the Venezuelan Rulers and her people."[127] In Congress, Sen. Edward O. Wolcott of Colorado noted that England had aided Venezuelan independence at the beginning of the century. Calling Venezuela one of South America's "so-called republics" in which the "rulers are despots and suffrage a farce," Wolcott hoped that the mines claimed by both that country and Britain would be managed by people "not . . . subject to the cupidity of the half-breeds of Venezuela," but "where the English common law and the certainty of its enforcement will furnish them shelter and protection."[128]

In pulpits around the country, the nation's Protestant clergy almost unanimously called for peace. Among the newspapers, Joseph Pulitzer's *New York World* was most exercised. In striking contrast to his attitude toward Spain two years later, Pulitzer mounted a vigorous peace campaign. On 21 December, the *World* declared: "There is not a hothead among all the jingoes who does not know that England is more likely to become a republic than the United States are to revert to monarchism. The entire trend of government for the past fifty years has been toward democracy. . . . Observe the working of the leaven of democracy in England." Pulitzer solicited peace missives from influential Britons, including two ex-premiers, the Prince of Wales, the duke of York, and a number of influential members of Parliament and clergymen. The *World* printed a selection on Christmas Day with the headline "PEACE AND GOOD WILL."[129]

The *Nation* poked fun at the idea that America should side with "republican" Venezuela over "monarchical" Britain. "During the reign of each military tyrant [in Venezuela] the forms of republican government are observed; elections are held; but the 'purity of the ballot' is pro-

---

126. John L. Heaton, *The Story of a Page* (New York: Harper & Bros., 1913), 113.
127. Tansill, *Bayard*, 660–61.
128. *Congressional Record*, 20 December 1895, 28, pt. 1:857, 859–60.
129. W. A. Swanberg, *Pulitzer* (New York: Charles Scribner's Sons, 1967), 199.

tected by troops, and the success of the governmental candidates is assured by the show of armed force." The *Nation* summed up:

> In a word, the American Secretary of State's references to Venezuelan republicanism and friendship and English monarchy and hostility have no more to do with the facts than with the planet Jupiter. Hundreds of Americans in the Turkish Empire, many of them from Mr. Olney's own State, pray God every day that England may take Syria or Armenia and give the natives justice, liberty, and protection to life and property. At the same moment the head of their own Government is asserting that if Great Britain should retain English law and representative government over 33,000 square miles in South America, where it now exists, the people of the United States would be compelled to arm themselves to the teeth and rush into a bloody war to undo the outrage.[130]

To be sure, other arguments for conciliation were heard. The Venezuelan–British Guianan border, it was said, was of no strategic interest to the United States; Cleveland was simply trying to placate American jingoes to help himself win a third presidential term; the Monroe Doctrine was no ground for policy; war would be devastating, especially for commerce; and Anglo-Saxons and Christians ought not to fight each other. As Ernest May writes, "In the past, Anglophobia had always seemed profitable and relatively safe. It was so no longer."[131]

In Great Britain, Conservative and some Liberal papers firmly declared that London could not give in. Said the *Standard*: "There can be but one answer. We decline to humiliate ourselves, and we refuse to accept the decision of Washington in matters altogether outside its jurisdiction."[132] Yet, there were almost no calls for war. The entire British nation seems to have been repulsed by the very idea. Missives for peace poured into the British foreign office from "various arbitration societies, Quaker meetings, Unitarian, Baptist, Methodist, Presbyterian, and other nonconformist churches, public rallies and assemblies."[133] Many termed a hypothetical Anglo-American conflict a "civil war"; Americans were referred to as cousins, not foreigners.

Where conservative Britons had feared the American mob in the 1840s and 1860s, they now trusted the wisdom of the American people to overrule their intemperate leaders. The *Daily Telegraph* calmly stated: "We are perfectly satisfied to rely upon the straightforward, high-bred simplicity of Lord Salisbury's diplomacy and the good sense, widespread honesty, intelligence, and kindliness of the American people."

130. *Nation*, 2 January 1896, 5.
131. May, *Imperial Democracy*, 58.
132. Bertram, *Anglo-American Friendship*, 44.
133. May, *Imperial Democracy*, 49.

The *Standard* agreed: "We feel confident that a vast majority of the Americans will soon be profoundly sorry for what Mr. Cleveland has done. He has travestied and damaged a principle that they hold dear, and has made the Republic which we have all honored on account of its supposed attachment to peace and non-intervention, figure in the eyes of Europe as a gratuitously aggressive and reckless champion of war." The empowerment of the people, that is, democracy, was now something which made the United States more rather than less trustworthy. The influential historian Goldwin Smith commented from Toronto: "I am firmly convinced that since the abolition of slavery there prevails among them no desire for territorial aggrandizement."[134]

The British press was, moreover, fully aware of the antimonarchical arguments being used against its government in the United States, and it worked to render them moot. W. T. Stead's *Review of Reviews* was obsessed with Anglo-American harmony and scolded Americans for continuing to "make a fetish of the word Republic":

> It is curious how persistent is the superstition that the United States are more democratic than the United Kingdom. The Monroe doctrine, for instance, brings out quite unexpectedly the survival of the archaic notion that Britain, because monarchical, is a less democratic country than the United States. The real fact, of course, is that we both are popularly governed countries. . . .
>
> All the difficulty arises from the prejudice against the monarchy—a prejudice that is as old as George III, and ought to have been buried with him.[135]

The *Times* remarked that the American position "will not be strengthened by MR. OLNEY's claim to moral superiority on the ground that self-government is only enjoyed by Republics."[136]

Parliament was out of session from September 1895 until February 1896. But 354 members sent a petition requesting arbitration to Cleveland and the Congress. The Liberal opposition leader in the Commons, William Vernon Harcourt, made it clear in January that he would make Venezuela a major issue in the upcoming session. Harcourt had been among the most vigorous supporters of the Union in the U.S. Civil War thirty years earlier (see Chapter 4), and he now urged the cabinet to submit to unlimited arbitration.[137]

Pacific English sentiments evidently affected American perceptions. In January the *Philadelphia Press* asserted, "Nothing in the succession for a

134. *New York Times*, 19, 21, and 25 December 1895.
135. *Review of Reviews* (London), 12 and 14 December 1895, pp. 484–85.
136. *Times* (London), 18 December 1895.
137. A. G. Gardiner, *The Life of Sir William Harcourt* (London: Constable, 1923), 2:396–97; May, *Imperial Democracy*, 49.

month past of discussion, declaration and feeling, personal and public, private and National, has so moved the American Nation as a whole as the sudden revelation which has been made of English horror of war with this country."[138] War fever in the United States was short-lived in 1895–96.

On 2 January, the president named a boundary commission of distinguished jurists. The next day brought a shock from a third party: Emperor William II of Germany sent a telegram to S. J. Paul Kruger, president of the Boer Republic in southern Africa, congratulating him for repelling a British raid "without appealing to the help of friendly powers," i.e., Germany. The infamous Kruger telegram inflamed British opinion against Germany and reinforced friendly feelings toward the United States. As H. C. Allen writes, "when 'Yankee Doodle' was cheered and 'Die Wacht am Rhein' hissed in London, it demonstrated clearly how utterly different was popular feeling towards the two countries."[139]

Still, the crucial decision lay with the British cabinet. Chamberlain was determined to keep the peace, telling a Birmingham audience: "War between the two nations would be an absurdity as well as a crime. . . . The two nations are allied more closely in sentiment and in interest than any other nations on the face of the earth. . . . I should look forward with pleasure to the possibility of the Stars and Stripes and the Union Jack floating together in defence of a common cause sanctioned by humanity and justice."[140] This was not merely public rhetoric. In December and January Chamberlain privately urged Salisbury to approve a joint Anglo-American intervention in the Turkish-Armenian crisis: "I think that such an appeal to the American people to join us in a work of charity & humanity would promote a great revolution of feeling. Here is the proper destiny of the two Nations—not to cut each others throats but to bring irresistible force to bear in defence of the weak & oppressed."[141] Salisbury, however, skeptical of moralistic foreign policy and of the United States in general, rejected the plan. He threatened to resign if the cabinet desired unlimited arbitration in the Venezuelan affair.

Nonetheless, on 11 January the cabinet voted to accept the U.S. commission's jurisdiction. Ernest May notes that, in general, "Chamberlain's views ruled the cabinet."[142] The queen's message to Parliament on 11 February welcomed American cooperation in solving the dispute with Venezuela. Over the next nine months Britain and the United

---

138. *Public Opinion*, 23 January 1896, 107. See also H. C. Allen, *Great Britain and the United States: A History of Anglo-American Relations (1783–1952)* (London: Odhams, 1954), 539.

139. Allen, *Britain and the United States*, 538.

140. Ibid., 539.

141. May, *Imperial Democracy*, 53–54.

142. Ibid., 45.

States negotiated (sans Venezuela) an agreement under which arbitration would take place. The boundary commission turned over its final report to the tribunal, which comprised two Britons, two Americans, and a Russian. The tribunal did not hand down its decision until August 1899; like Venezuela itself, it went all but unnoticed by the British and American publics.[143]

In the meantime, public opinion in both nations demanded a permanent Anglo-American arbitration treaty. The treaty was signed in January 1897 but was defeated in the Senate in May by three votes.[144] Still, never again were the United Kingdom and the United States to come close to war with one another.

Americans were as always divided over the liberal status of Britain, but after the British reforms of 1867 and 1884–85 the notion that Britain was a fellow liberal state had gained broader elite support. American elites held to their pro-British stances through the Venezuelan crisis, interpreting British actions as benign and urging a pacific resolution. There were still antimonarchists who took a hostile line, including Cleveland and Olney, but clearly war with Britain would have been highly unpopular.

British elites were more pro-American than in any previous case. Conservatives, Liberals, and many Radicals were dismayed at Cleveland's truculence, but they trusted the United States and pushed for a conciliatory policy, expressing horror at the idea of Anglo-American war. (Other Radicals had by now turned against the United States.) Salisbury was overruled by his cabinet, led by Chamberlain, into appeasing the Americans; but had the cabinet decided otherwise, it would have had great difficulty going to war over the objections of the electorate.

THE SPANISH-AMERICAN CRISIS OF 1895–98

How Did Americans Perceive Spain?

Compared to Britain, Spain was little discussed by Americans in the years before 1895. What is clear is that with the 1875 restoration of the monarchy, Spain left the category of "republic," favored by so many American liberals during the *Virginius* affair. While Britain by the 1890s had transcended its monarchism in the view of many Americans, Spain was typically seen as a nation with a continuing liberal-

143. Ibid., 60–65; Bertram, *Anglo-American Friendship*, 49–121.
144. Charles S. Campbell, *The Transformation of American Foreign Relations 1865–1900* (New York: Harper & Row, 1976), 213–19.

republican element stymied by an outdated form of government. Commenting on an exposé of widespread corruption in Madrid in 1892, the *New York Sun* wrote: "It discloses a scandalous state of affairs, and demonstrates that Madrid, under a monarchy, has been more mercilessly robbed than New York was under Tweed."[145] Months later, the *New York Tribune* asserted that the Spanish Crown had "constituted an obstacle to every kind of liberal doctrine, intellectual growth and national prosperity." Yet the *Tribune* celebrated the recent election of fifty republicans to the five-hundred-member Cortes. "Under these circumstances it is not improbable that before long we may be called upon to hail the revival in Spain of that only form of government which is in keeping with the enlightened and progressive spirit of the present age—namely, a republic."[146]

An influential American analysis of the Spanish system of government was published in 1889 by J. L. M. Curry, late U.S. minister to Madrid. Curry pointedly began his book: "The American idea of the derivation of political power from the people has not found lodgment, as an actuality, in Spanish politics, literature, or thought. The Constitution contains no declaration of rights, no abstract enunciation of fundamental truths and principles." Yet, he added, "the impartial governmental student of the science of politics can see much to encourage."[147] Most officials were "from the people" rather than the aristocracy, and Spain since 1874 had been a constitutional monarchy. Spain's biggest problem was its powerful Conservative party, whose political axioms were "perilously close to the old doctrine of the divine right of kings." Conservatives vehemently resisted the notion of universal manhood suffrage and condoned the inordinate political and social power clerics had in the countryside. Spain did have a Liberal party that favored reform, particularly regarding individual rights and an independent judiciary.[148] Most encouraging to Curry was the continuing viability of the Republican party, "with whom I must confess my sympathy." Besides favoring the end of the monarchy, the Republicans pushed for universal male suffrage, complete separation of church and state, and partial autonomy for the colonies.[149] Curry tepidly concluded, "With all the undoubted drawbacks the drift in Spain is not strong, not consistent, but hopefully towards constitutional principles, promoting the general good while conserving individual rights."[150]

145. *New York Sun*, 10 December 1892, in *Public Opinion*, 17 December 1892, 248.
146. *New York Tribune*, 25 March 1893, in *Public Opinion*, 1 April 1893, 616.
147. J. L. M. Curry, *Constitutional Government in Spain: A Sketch* (New York: Harper & Brothers, 1889), 100–101.
148. Ibid., 102ff.
149. Ibid., 114–25.
150. Ibid., 132.

To sum up: Americans were much less aware of Spain than of Britain in 1898; those journalistic and scholarly elites who knew about Spain tended to see it primarily as a monarchy and thus backward; those elites also noted encouraging signs of Spanish liberalism and republicanism; but there was less liberal hope for reform in Spain than for reform in England.

How Liberal Was Spain?

Aside from Cuba, internally Spain was a much calmer country in 1898 than in 1873. American skepticism notwithstanding, the restored monarchy had succeeded in stabilizing the country, as its architect Antonio Cánovas del Castillo had planned. Inspired in part by the English example, the 1876 constitution established a constitutional monarchy. The Crown was responsible to no one, but its decrees had to be countersigned by a responsible minister. The Cortes, summoned, prorogued, and dissolved by the monarch, was bicameral, with a Senate elected by various entities and a Congress elected by the populace. Slavery was abolished in Cuba in 1886. Under a Liberal government trial by jury and freedoms of the press and assembly were established, and universal male suffrage was restored in 1890.

Still, the foundations of this stability prevent Spain from earning more than a semiliberal rating. Despite its formally widened franchise and the existence of open opposition to government, Spain's government was on a fixed rotation: when the Conservative government of Cánovas fell, the monarch asked the Liberal Práxedes Mateo Sagasta to form a government, and vice versa. The new premier would then schedule elections and appoint local officials, or caciques, who would make certain that the election results were the desired ones.[151] José Varela Ortega argues that Spain was a "two-party-system parliamentary monarchy. It was not a democracy. . . . Spain was in fact a liberal country in which fundamental rights were granted by a constitution." Stability was the common goal, and indeed, in contrast to the 1860s and 1870s, "Military coups seemed to be a thing of the past."[152] But the fixed elections meant that actual public leverage over government was very limited. Furthermore, during the Cuban rebellion that began in 1895, the Spanish government began violating civil liberties. In early 1898 newspapers were shut down and public gatherings to discuss policy toward the United States were forbidden.[153]

151. Clarke, *Modern Spain*, 402–39; Joseph McCabe, *Spain in Revolt: 1814–1931* (London: John Lane the Bodley Head, 1931), 186–97; Martin A. S. Hume, *Modern Spain, 1788–1898* (New York: G. P. Putnam's Sons, 1903), 553.

152. José Varela Ortega, "Aftermath of Splendid Disaster: Spanish Politics before and after the Spanish American War of 1898," *Journal of Contemporary History* 15 (1980): 317.

153. *Times* (London), January-April 1898, passim.

How Did Spaniards Perceive the United States?

Carlism and republicanism remained on the far right and left, respectively, and anarchist elements were present as well, but these were all marginal in the 1890s. Power lay in the center, with the Liberal-Conservatives of Cánovas and the Liberals of Sagasta. Cánovas had successfully co-opted most conservatives in the 1870s into accepting the constitutional monarchy. Yet, his party opposed the universal male suffrage and religious toleration gained in 1869. Cánovas was essentially a pragmatic conservative, believing that the preservation of traditional Spanish society required some minimal accommodations with the spirit of the times.

The Liberals likewise were a coalition. Sagasta, their leader, was committed above all to the maintenance of the monarchy and prevention of the spasms that had racked Spain in preceding decades. To that end he duly would accept and relinquish the prime-ministership as the corrupt electoral system allowed. Because he did not favor competitive elections, he does not qualify as a full liberal by the criteria of this book. But when in office Sagasta did achieve various reforms: universal male suffrage, trial by jury, freedom of worship, and liberal press laws. Sagasta made clear his commitment to a "monarchy surrounded by democratic institutions and, for this reason, . . . a popular monarchy."[154]

The Liberal reforms won over Emilio Castelar's wing of moderate Republicans, now called "possibilists." After the turmoil of the 1868–74 period, the possibilists gradually scaled back their program to universal male suffrage.[155] Once that goal was achieved in 1890, Castelar was reconciled to the monarchy and became Spain's chief apologist to the outside world. The former President of 1873 could now write: "Spain constitutes, notwithstanding the survival after her revolutions of an historical monarchy and an official church, the most democratic state possible in a monarchical form,—if by democracy we understand the exercise of individual rights; of a jury system which places the administration of justice in the hands of the people; and of universal suffrage. . . . We may indeed feel well content with the work of the past forty years."[156]

After the defection of Castelar to the Liberals, the other wings of Republicanism were marginalized or in exile.[157] Between the defection of

154. A. Ramos Oliveira, *Politics, Economics and Men of Modern Spain 1808–1946*, trans. Teener Hall (London: Victor Gollancz, 1946), 92.

155. Ibid., 125; David Hannay, *Don Emilio Castelar* (New York: Frederick Warne, n.d.), 229.

156. Quoted in Elizabeth Wormeley Latimer, *Spain in the Nineteenth Century* (Chicago: A. C. McClurg, 1897), 389.

157. Ramos Oliveria, *Men of Modern Spain*, 125–26.

Castelar and the extremism of its remaining wings, Republicanism seemed impotent in the Spain of the 1890s.[158] As we shall see, however, the mainstream Conservatives and Liberals feared an overthrow of the Bourbon monarchy by both Carlists and radical Republicans. This fear was partly responsible for Madrid's refusal to grant Cuba independence, and thus for the war of 1898.

Information on how different factions in Spain perceived the United States in the years before 1898 is sketchy, as the decline of Republicanism meant Spaniards paid less attention to the North American republic. James W. Cortada writes that the lower classes admired the United States while the upper classes were hostile. Barcelona was the center of Republicanism and of trade with the United States as well, and its labor leaders and politicians tended to hold America in special esteem.[159] But when most Spaniards thought of the United States at all, they thought of it as the greatest threat to Spanish sovereignty over Cuba and a possible threatening example of a successful republic. One Liberal leader, Segismundo Moret y Prendergast, wrote in 1895 that Americans should abandon the wish to republicanize Cuba and let Spain handle Cuban reform in its own way: "As far as we can see, republican government has nowhere been an improvement, neither in France, nor in the United States, nor in any of the South American States."[160]

Significantly, even Republicans could be hostile to the United States. While many sympathized with Cuban rebels, and all factions managed to unite in 1897 in favor of autonomy for Cuba,[161] many in the end sided against Cuban independence (perhaps hoping to gain the favor of the army) and thus against America. For most, any lingering republican affinity for the United States seems to have been trumped by a very real threat to national integrity.[162]

Actions, Interpretations, Reactions

In February 1895, José Martí, leader of the revolutionary Cuban junta, ordered a new rebellion. From Madrid Cánovas sent a moderate general, Arsenio Martínez de Campos, to quell the insurrection, but the general soon realized that doing so would require measures more severe than he was willing to undertake. Martínez de Campos's replace-

158. Carr, *Spain 1808–1975*, 347–66.
159. Cortada, *Two Nations over Time*, 144–45.
160. Moret writing in *España Moderna* (Madrid), quoted in *Literary Digest*, 3 August 1895, 412–13.
161. May, *Imperial Democracy*, 105.
162. Cortada, *Two Nations over Time*, 144–45; John L. Offner, *An Unwanted War: The Diplomacy of the United States and Spain over Cuba, 1895–1898* (Chapel Hill: University of North Carolina Press, 1992), 11.

ment in February 1896, Gen. Valeriano Weyler y Nicolau, had no such moral qualms.[163]

Meanwhile, after Martí's death, the junta adopted a constitution and formed a government. As in the 1868–78 period, Americans began debating whether Washington ought to recognize the belligerence and even independence of Cuba. The press was reporting heinous acts by the Spanish. Weyler's brutality began affecting U.S. perceptions of Spain, perceptions which were already much more negative than in 1873 because Spain was again a monarchy. In February both houses resolved that Cleveland should recognize Cuba as a belligerent. Arguments in favor stressed that the resolution would pressure the Spanish government into protecting the twenty to thirty million dollars of U.S. investments in Cuba. More prevalent were references to Spanish despotism and the empathy Americans felt with the Cuban struggle for liberty. Opponents of recognition protested that Congress had insufficient information to decide. Passage of the nonbinding resolution led Cleveland and Olney vigorously to pursue U.S. claims against the Spanish over the coming months. The U.S. administration worked with Madrid on various compromises that would allow Cuban autonomy, but to no avail.[164]

In Cuba, Weyler brutally fought the rebellion with 200,000 troops and a civilian reconcentration program. Tens of thousands of rural residents were forced into fortified towns lacking housing, food, sanitation, and medical care. (By the time the Spanish-American War began in 1898, approximately 200,000 Cubans had died in Weyler's concentration camps; at the time, American estimates were 400,000.)[165] In June 1897 William McKinley, the new U.S. president, received an official report of the atrocities and the effects of the war on American investments. McKinley supervised a diplomatic note protesting "in the name of the American people and . . . common humanity" the "uncivilized and inhumane" war.[166]

At the same time, Liberals in Spain were denouncing Weyler's brutality. After they withdrew support for the government's Cuban policy in May, Cánovas resigned from the premiership. Sagasta, the Liberal leader, now had the opportunity to form a government; but when he proposed Cuban autonomy, the queen regent rejected the idea and reappointed Cánovas prime minister. On 24 June Sagasta issued a "Manifesto to the Nation" declaring that "all the efforts in the world [were] insufficient to maintain peace in Cuba by the bayonet alone."

163. Offner, *Unwanted War*, 1–13; May, *Imperial Democracy*, 94–100.
164. Offner, *Unwanted War*, 17–36; May, *Imperial Democracy*, 84–90. It was of course up to the President to recognize Cuban belligerency.
165. Offner, *Unwanted War*, 11–13; May, *Imperial Democracy*, 101.
166. Offner, *Unwanted War*, 44–48.

Meanwhile Cánovas worked on a reply to McKinley's demand, blaming the rebels, and implicitly their supporters in the United States, for the pathetic conditions in Cuba. Then on 28 June, in the midst of the agitation, an anarchist assassinated Cánovas.[167]

McKinley had instructed his new minister to Madrid, Stewart Woodford, to threaten that unless Spain took concrete steps to end the Cuban war by 1 November, America would follow the Congressional resolution and recognize Cuban belligerency. But significantly, when Sagasta formed a new government on 6 October, Woodford and McKinley relented. The Liberals replaced Weyler in Cuba with Ramón Blanco y Erenas, who was committed to Cuban autonomy; ordered that the concentration camps be broken up; and announced that as of 1 January 1898, Cuba would be self-governing under Spanish sovereignty. In November *El Imparcial* of Madrid printed an exposé of Weyler's atrocities.[168]

Sagasta's reforms were rewarded in the United States by a near-cessation of anti-Spanish petitions and memorials to Congress. Many in the press were unconvinced by Spanish liberalism: in the *North American Review* of November, a prominent writer doubted Sagasta's administration would make any difference in Cuba, since an oligarchy still controlled Spain. Yet, McKinley made it clear he would give Sagasta the benefit of the doubt. In his December annual message to Congress, the president portrayed the regime of the Liberals Sagasta and Blanco as radically different from that of the Conservatives Cánovas and Weyler. While Weyler had practiced "cruel rapine and extermination that . . . shocked the universal sentiment of humanity," Blanco offered relief and self-government. Spain under its new Liberal government should be given "a reasonable chance to realize her expectations and to prove the asserted efficacy of the new order of things to which she stands irrevocably committed."[169] Not only were Spanish Liberals more committed to reform and autonomy in Cuba, but McKinley also recognized their liberalism and allowed it to change his policy.

McKinley's own party backed his new line on Spain, but Democrats doubted Spanish sincerity. In Madrid, the cabinet welcomed McKinley's address. A subsequent note from the U.S. president struck the same tone of understanding. Seeking to exploit this new liberal goodwill, Moret and the queen regent pressured Woodford to convince McKinley to expel the Cuban junta. Woodford firmly declined, saying that in a democracy such as America the president could not do such things. Moreover, "the United States [could] not interfere to keep a peo-

---

167. Ibid., 47–50; May, *Imperial Democracy*, 104–11.
168. Offner, *Unwanted War*, 65–72; May, *Imperial Democracy*, 124–27.
169. May, *Imperial Democracy*, 133–34; Offner, *Unwanted War*, 77–86.

ple under monarchical rule, who [were] seeking to establish a republic." Meanwhile, the cabinet approached the European powers to ask for backing against the United States.[170]

The reaction to the new Liberal line from Madrid was not nearly so favorable in Cuba itself. While some were amenable to Blanco's offer of autonomy, both rebels and reactionaries spurned the proposal. For the rebels, the Liberals' plan was too little too late. The leader of the rebels declared that "he would die fighting for independence rather than accept autonomy." From the other side, on 12 January 1898 Spanish army officers led a massive anti-autonomy riot in Havana. Rioters attacked three pro-autonomy newspapers, shouting "Viva España, Viva Weyler, Abajo Blanco!" Moret and Blanco interpreted the riots as a signal that a Carlist-led revolt was starting.[171]

Although the riots were not noticeably anti-American, U.S. newspapers, led by William Randolph Hearst's *New York Journal*, made much of them. Congressional interest was revived, as a resolution passed the Senate asking the president to explain what he was doing to protect American property and lives in Cuba. Following urgings from the U.S. consul general in Havana and from the *Washington Times*, McKinley sent the U.S.S. *Maine*, now in Key West, to Havana harbor to pay a "courtesy call." The move was universally praised in the United States, and officially regarded by the Sagasta government as a show of solidarity with its attempt to implement autonomy.[172]

As American observers continued to report horrible conditions in Cuba, and Spanish diplomats continued to court the European powers, two shocks to Spanish-American relations quickly followed. First, a letter from the Spanish minister to Washington, Enrique Dupuy de Lôme, to a prominent Spanish Liberal in Havana, ridiculed McKinley as "weak" and a "would-be politician" who pandered to jingoes. The letter also portrayed Blanco's program of Cuban autonomy as a ploy to fool Americans while Spain reconquered the island. After the Cuban junta leaked the letter, Americans demanded the dismissal of Dupuy and intervention in Cuba. Ominously, three separate resolutions appeared in Congress calling on the President anew to recognize the Cuban rebels as belligerents.[173]

Dupuy was recalled to Spain, ending the incident, but on 15 February came a much worse shock: the *Maine* exploded while docked in Havana harbor, killing 264 sailors and two officers. The immediate reaction in the United States to the tragedy was circumspect. Most

170. Offner, *Unwanted War*, 86–92; May, *Imperial Democracy*, 160–66.
171. Offner, *Unwanted War*, 92–94; May, *Imperial Democracy*, 135.
172. Offner, *Unwanted War*, 94–100.
173. May, *Imperial Democracy*, 137–39; Offner, *Unwanted War*, 116–24.

presumed the explosion to be an accident, even if they held the Spanish indirectly responsible for not solving their Cuban problem. Businessmen, clergy, and even some jingoes called for reason to prevail over hysteria.[174] The *Nation* argued that one reason many Americans wanted war was an erroneous belief that Spain was a backward monarchy: "We misunderstand Spain. . . . We look upon her first as a monarchy. Our knowledge of the monarchical governments of Europe as they exist to-day is extremely vague, and of Spain the vaguest of all." Spain was a nation with many progressive republicans, the magazine stressed.[175]

But the general public's reaction to the *Maine* explosion was much darker. Soon many clergy were preaching on behalf of righteous war over the selfish pacifistic interests of business, and mass meetings and newspaper editorials cried for revenge against alleged Spanish treachery. Anti-interventionist opinion began fading as the weeks passed. The Cincinnati *Enquirer* said that even if the *Maine* explosion were accidental, "we have abundant cause for interference to stop the cruel war on the island of Cuba and guarantee that island a rich place among the republics of the western world."[176] The conservative Sen. Redfield Proctor of Vermont returned from a visit to Cuba and on 17 March delivered a speech in the Senate detailing the atrocious conditions there and advocating U.S. intervention as the only solution. Because he had previously opposed intervention, Proctor's speech palpably affected public opinion. As the *Literary Digest* put it, "With very few exceptions, the most conservative of newspapers now express the opinion that Senator Proctor's careful statement of conditions in Cuba . . . makes intervention the plain duty of the United States on the simple ground of humanity."[177] William Jennings Bryan, the Populist leader later famous for pacifism, announced: "Humanity demands that we shall act. . . . The sufferings of [Cuba's] people cannot be ignored unless we, as a Nation, have become so engrossed in money-making as to be indifferent to distress."[178]

Four days after Proctor's speech, the U.S. investigation of the *Maine* explosion was released. The Americans concluded that the explosion came from outside the ship, probably from a mine. By contrast, a Spanish investigation held that the explosion came from within the vessel. McKinley was now working diligently to find alternatives to war, including purchasing Cuba from Spain, allowing Spain to retain nominal sovereignty but having the United States administer the island's af-

174. May, *Imperial Democracy*, 139–41.
175. *Nation*, 3 March 1898, 157.
176. *Public Opinion*, 17 March 1898, 325.
177. Offner, *Unwanted War*, 98, 122–42; May, *Imperial Democracy*, 137–47.
178. Offner, *Unwanted War*, 153.

fairs, and simply demanding a huge indemnity from Spain for the *Maine* disaster. By the end of March, Congressional Republicans so feared that Democrats would use the Cuban issue against them that they began to contemplate pre-empting McKinley by pushing for intervention.[179]

The president and his diplomats worked to find a compromise by suggesting the purchase of Cuba. The queen regent considered the proposal, but the cabinet rejected it. At the end of March McKinley proposed an armistice, during which time Spain would end the reconcentration program; if there were no peace agreement by 1 October, the United States would act as final arbiter between Spain and Cuba. Spain had forty-eight hours to respond. The Spanish press was in no mood to grant America any say over Cuba. *El Heraldo de Madríd* called for the government to stand firm against American humiliation. Politics demanded that Sagasta circle the wagons. He responded that Spain would grant an armistice only if the new Cuban parliament requested one, and said nothing about the American arbitration offer.[180]

The Spanish press lauded Sagasta's firmness. An armistice would be "outside intervention," said *El Correo de Madríd*, damaging "Spain's national honor and affect[ing] the integrity of the nation." *El Heraldo* said, "To abandon Cuba in the midst of a rebellion offended the nation's dignity; to give it to the Yankees . . . would be even more humiliating." McKinley readied a message for Congress. Then, with all bilateral diplomacy exhausted, the European powers and the pope intervened.[181]

In early April, the Spanish cabinet made known through diplomatic channels that it would grant an armistice if Pope Leo XIII requested it. At the same time, the six European powers politely requested that McKinley give Spain more time. McKinley welcomed this démarche, hoping it would buy him time with Congress.[182] It failed. When the president announced he would delay submitting his Cuban message until 11 April, angry Congressmen accused him of cowardice. As had happened all through the crisis, many war advocates based their arguments on the fact that Spain was a monarchy. Sen. Richard Kenney of Delaware blamed "the Spanish Crown" for denying Cubans their liberty and added a reference to the Inquisition to make the point clear.[183] In contrast to 1873, peace advocates could not counter that Spain was a sister republic.

179. May, *Imperial Democracy*, 139–54; Offner, *Unwanted War*, 136–47.
180. Offner, *Unwanted War*, 143–56; May, *Imperial Democracy*, 138–39.
181. Offner, *Unwanted War*, 156–59.
182. May, *Imperial Democracy*, 154–57.
183. *Congressional Record*, 55th Cong., 2d sess., 5 April 1898, 31, pt. 4:3547–48;

On 9 April the Spanish cabinet acceded to the pope's request to suspend hostilities in Cuba, hoping finally to gain firm European backing and to induce McKinley to back down. Many in the Spanish opposition, from Carlists to Republicans, denounced the decision, while moderates approved.[184]

The Spanish and the European diplomats had high hopes for a peaceful settlement. Yet McKinley and his cabinet received word from the Cuban junta that it would accept the armistice only if the United States recognized Cuban independence first. The president decided to deliver his original Cuban message to Congress but added a request for a delay based on the Spanish desire for an armistice. Meetings with Republican Congressional leaders, however, convinced him that no delay would be forthcoming. His own party feared it would be thrashed at the next election if it delayed war any further. On 11 April a reluctant McKinley asked Congress to approve use of the U.S. military to enforce peace in Cuba.[185]

The Spanish cabinet and press were uniformly defiant. Articles accused the United States of duplicity and claimed that Spanish naval might far outstripped American. *El Correo Español*, a Carlist newspaper, called for revolution if the queen regent capitulated.[186] In the United States, conservative Republicans approved of McKinley's speech, while Democrats and liberal Republicans were disappointed that he did not ask for a war declaration. House debate was restricted, and a resolution easily passed giving the president what he wanted, including nonrecognition of Cuban independence. In the Senate, debate lasted four days. Speeches were thick with references to the backward Spanish monarchy. Sen. Frank J. Cannon of Utah used religious language: "when the war will have ended the United States will be able, I trust, to write a story of the deed in this one sentence: 'The hand of God moved this country to destroy in Cuba the divine right of kings and established there the diviner right of the people.'" Sen. Clarence D. Clark of Wyoming said, "We stand for freedom of peoples and for republican government, for free institutions and national honor."[187] The Senate approved recognition of the Cuban Republic.

The press was now nearly hysterical to rid Cuba of despotic monarchism. Hearst's *New York Journal* declared: "No considerations of loyalty to the national government can compel acquiescence in a policy which seeks to betray Cuban freedom into the clutches of Spanish monarchy."[188] In contrast to his pacific stance toward Britain in 1895,

184. Offner, *Unwanted War*, 172–76.
185. Ibid., 177–84; May, *Imperial Democracy*, 156–57.
186. Offner, *Unwanted War*, 185–86.
187. *Congressional Record*, 16 April 1898, 31, pt. 4:3953, 3968.
188. *Public Opinion*, 17 March 1898, 325; 31 March 1898, 392; 21 April 1898, 483; *Literary Digest*, 9 April 1898, 485; 30 April 1898, 516.

Joseph Pulitzer had his *New York World* screaming for war, in part because Spain was a despotism: "War waged on behalf of freedom, of self-government, of law and order, of humanity, to end oppression, misrule, plunder and savagery, is a holy war in itself." The Cuban struggle was as righteous as that of the American rebels in 1776.[189]

The House and Senate reconciled their resolutions in conference, defining Cuba as independent but not recognizing the Cuban Republic. Unable to fight public opinion any longer, on 21 April the president signed the resolutions. With no response from Spain, the next day McKinley ordered a naval blockade of Cuba, and Congress passed a joint resolution retroactively declaring 21 April the start of the war. In Spain, the public rallied behind Sagasta as he took the country into one of the greatest disasters in its history.[190]

In contrast to 1873, Spain in the 1890s had few friends in the United States. In the years leading up to the crisis over Cuba, Americans typically saw Spain as a backward monarchy with some stifled liberal elements. Spain's brutality in Cuba, which was itself a part of metropolitan Spain, worsened those perceptions. Most Americans responded to Spanish gestures with suspicion; the only respite came in the first months after Sagasta, the Liberal leader, formed a new government. In the end, McKinley was in effect constrained by public and elite opinion into declaring war.

In Spain, the Liberals do not fully qualify as objective liberals, since they did not favor competitive elections. Their perceptions of the United States are interesting, however, in that they were as negative as those of the conservatives. The Spanish government was internally constrained from peace with the United States, but because of the threat of revolution rather than electoral defeat.

The late nineteenth century shows that domestic political divisions very often were reflected in attitudes toward particular foreign states. Threat assessment and policy preferences were often tied, especially in the United States and Great Britain, to domestic vision, and thus institutional identity played a powerful role. Liberal institutions allowed these perceptions to shape policy during crises. In Spain and Chile, however, institutional identity was evidently trumped for many liberals by something else. What that something else was, and why it mattered, will be discussed next.

189. Offner, *Unwanted War*, 153; Heaton, *The Story of a Page*, 162.
190. Offner, *Unwanted War*, 190–93.

PART III

Liberalism Matters

[6]

Liberalism at Work

I argued in Part I that political liberalism pushes states that practice it toward peace with some countries and toward war with others. Liberalism does its work through the ideology liberals hold and the governmental institutions they set up. In Part II, I presented ten case studies to compare the interactions the United States had between 1794 and 1898 with liberal, semiliberal, and illiberal states. In this chapter I engage in a structured, focused comparison of the cases to see if two crucial expectations of my argument are borne out. First, I anticipate that liberals in state A will perceive state B to be liberal and therefore benign if B's domestic political institutions match those that A's liberals want (and may have) in their own state; and that those same liberals in A will perceive B to be illiberal and therefore suspicious if B's institutions match the opposite set of institutions. Second, I expect to find governments of objectively liberal states domestically constrained from war if a strong liberal elite demands peace, and the same governments constrained from peace if a strong liberal elite wants war.

Table 1 classifies the cases according to the mix of regime types.

In general, as one moves from left to right in the table, the amount of *mutual* restraint by governments during the crises decreases. The liberal-liberal dyads tend to exhibit a high degree of restraint even when governments are predisposed toward hostility. In the Oregon crisis (1845–46), the British cabinet was conciliatory throughout, offering to submit to third-party arbitration several times. The U.S. administration was publicly belligerent but privately offered compromise, and in the end it accepted a compromise. In the Civil War, the British cabinet did send an ultimatum during the *Trent* affair, but after the fall of 1862 it rejected proposals to recognize the Confederacy. Lincoln's cabinet also was highly restrained toward the British. In the Venezuelan affair, the U.S. government made highly belligerent speeches, but its concrete act was merely to appoint a commission to study the boundary question. The British cabinet was conciliatory despite Salisbury's gruffness. Only the Chilean affair shows a lack of restraint. The U.S.

Table 1 Crises According to Dyad Type

Liberal/liberal	Liberal/semiliberal	Liberal/illiberal
U.S./G.B. 1845–46	U.S./G.B. 1794–96	U.S./Fr. 1796–98[a]
U.S./G.B. 1861–63	U.S./G.B. 1803–12[a]	U.S./Mex. 1845–46[a]
U.S./Chile 1891–92	U.S./Spain 1896–98[a]	U.S./Spain 1873
U.S./G.B. 1895–96		

[a]Crisis ended in war.

secretary of state managed to prevent the president from submitting an ultimatum for several weeks, but in the end the president prevailed; the Chilean government was hostile toward the United States until its capitulation.

The liberal-semiliberal pairs featured some restraint on at least one side (note that two of these dyads fought wars). During the Jay Treaty crisis, the Washington administration was highly conciliatory; the British cabinet was much less so, enacting the Orders in Council and virtually dictating a harsh treaty. The story was similar in the crisis leading up to the War of 1812. The Jefferson and Madison administrations punished the French simultaneously with the British and left London a way out of the crisis until the end. The British cabinet was less restrained, continuing its abuses until June 1812, too late to prevent war. Events leading up to the Spanish-American War showed some restraint on both sides, as Washington and Madrid discussed various compromises regarding Cuba. Neither side could accommodate the other enough to prevent war, however.

Two of the liberal-illiberal dyads show some U.S. restraint but almost no restraint on the illiberal side. In the events leading up to the Quasi-War, the U.S. administration tried conciliation, but the French Directory was consistently abusive. The crisis with Mexico in the 1840s featured a U.S. president at first restrained, offering to purchase California, but then arguably provoking an incident to trigger war; and an extremely hostile Mexican government unwilling to receive the U.S. envoy. The third dyad is unique. The U.S. government was conciliatory despite its ultimatum to Spain, and the Spanish president was accommodating as well.

That restraint during crises tends to be stronger when both states are liberal is evidence in favor of liberal peace. But what specifically accounts for the variation in the table? For answers we look to our two sets of hypotheses, which concern (1) the sources of the perceptions elites in each state had of the other and (2) the sources of the degree of restraint on each side.

Hypothesis on Sources of Liberal Perceptions

Our three hypotheses purporting to explain why liberals classify a given foreign state as liberal or illiberal are:

1.a. *Liberal ideology: Liberals will perceive a foreign state as liberal if it matches their criteria for liberalism within their own state; conversely, they will perceive a foreign state as illiberal if it violates those criteria.*

1.b. *Balance of threat: Liberals will perceive a foreign state as liberal if that state poses no threat to them, or may help or is helping them oppose a state or states that threaten their own state; they will perceive a foreign state as illiberal if it poses a threat to them. The more powerful, the closer, and the more hostile a foreign state is, the more threatening it is.*

1.c. *Parochial interest: Liberals will perceive a foreign state as liberal if their immediate material well-being depends on good relations with that state, and as illiberal if their immediate material well-being would be served by hostile relations with that state.*

Early Cases (1794–1812)

In the *Anglo-American* crisis of 1794–96, Federalists (Hamiltonians) and Republicans (Jeffersonians) in the United States clearly disagreed vehemently over the liberal status of England. In fact, in a sense that disagreement constituted the main difference between the two proto-parties. In Britain, elites who sought parliamentary reform and disenfranchised Radicals both perceived the U.S. government as legitimate. (Conservatives, including the cabinet, do not qualify as liberal.) In short:

U.S. perceptions of G.B. (1794–96)		G.B. perceptions of the U.S.	
Federalists	Republicans	Reformers	Radicals
Liberal	Illiberal	Liberal	Liberal

In the *Franco-American* crisis leading up to the Quasi-War, Federalists and Republicans disagreed over the status of France as vehemently as over that of England, only the positions were reversed. In France under the Directory it is difficult to identify any liberals, so we leave French perceptions of the United States out:

U.S. perceptions of France (1796–98)		France
Federalists	Republicans	
Illiberal	Liberal	(N/A)

[187]

In 1803–12, the breakdown was much the same in England and America as in their earlier crisis. A few American Republicans now had switched their sympathies in the European war from France to Britain:

U.S. perceptions of G.B. (1803–12)		G.B. perceptions of the U.S.	
Federalists	Republicans	Reformers	Radicals
Liberal	Illiberal*	Liberal	Liberal

*A few Republicans classified Britain as liberal.

In the *United States*, the liberal ideology hypothesis provides a plausible explanation for many or even most liberals, for there are strong correlations between the institutions a given liberal faction favored for its own country and its perception of the foreign state. The American Federalists wanted a strong central government run by the educated and propertied. Fearful that too much democracy could endanger true liberty, they were at pains to limit popular sovereignty in the United States. John Adams, Alexander Hamilton, and their followers had admired England for its political institutions well before 1794. At the same time Adams mistrusted the French Revolution from the start, while Hamilton turned against it when Louis XVI was deposed in 1792. Federalist partiality toward England over France in the wars of 1793–1814 can be seen as a direct product of their belief that democracy had ruined France and hierarchy was saving England.

The Republicans, heirs of the Antifederalists, by contrast believed that unmerited privilege and hierarchy were the greatest threats to individual freedom in their own country. They thus considered republicanism—elected rather than hereditary government—constitutive of the liberal state. Ecstatic at the 1789 revolution in France, they defended the revolutionaries in Paris after the regicide and aggression against England in early 1793, and even after the XYZ Affair in 1797. Their views of England were the same as those of Jefferson in 1776: it was a despotism and a corrupting influence on American society. An interesting if minor split occurred among Republicans when Napoleon Bonaparte seized power in Paris. A few Republicans shifted their sympathies to the British; the majority, including Jefferson, still trusted Napoleon, a "republican emperor," more than monarchical Britain.

Balance-of-threat theory does not provide a compelling explanation for these perceptions. Between 1790 and 1812 it is not self-evident whether France or Great Britain was objectively the greater threat to the United States. America was a weak state in its first few decades, with a population, economy, and military and naval strength far inferior to either European power. England's navy and control of Canada made it more able to hurt the United States quickly. Yet, France had the more powerful army. Not surprisingly, then, Americans disagreed over which nation was more dangerous. In fact, it appears that their assessments of the two belligerents' relative power may have been driven by liberal ideology, rather than vice versa. Advocates of confrontation or accommodation toward England or France argued that questions of power favored their argument—for example, Republicans in 1794–96 and 1811–12 asserted that England was too busy fighting France to defy America, and that the United States could easily grab Canada if it did come to war. If rationalization was taking place, it may have concerned power assessments.

The parochial interest hypothesis has some support. In the 1790–1820 period Federalists were stronger in northern coastal cities, where merchants relied heavily on trade with England. Meanwhile, in 1795 private Americans owed an estimated £5 million to the British; half of that amount was held by Virginians, whose state was the center of anglophobic Jeffersonianism. Economic interest thus appears a plausible cause. Still, there were Federalists in the South and Republicans in the North arguing against their respective regions' economic interests. More damaging to the parochial interest theory is the fact that even when offered article 6 of the Jay Treaty, allowing the federal government to assume private debts owed the British, Republicans vehemently opposed the treaty. The debtors, predominantly Virginians, did not want the national government to amass power precisely because they adamantly opposed the British model of government. By the early 1800s, moreover, Southern cotton planters were becoming dependent on exports to Britain, but Southerners tended to favor confrontation of the British. Many Republicans, then, were willing to violate their immediate economic interests in favor of an ideologically shaped notion of interest.

Liberals in *Great Britain* also provide strong support for the liberal ideology hypothesis. In the 1790s the conciliators were men such as Charles James Fox, Richard Brinsley Sheridan, and the Marquess of Lansdowne, men who also pushed for liberal reforms in Britain itself (and who also sympathized with the French Revolution). The Radicals' love for the United States, meanwhile, is clearly linked to their program for Britain; their movement was in fact precipitated by the American Revolution. In 1803–12 some of the strongest advocates for repeal of the Orders in Council that were punishing the American merchant marine were those who advocated parliamentary reform. Significantly, during the brief government of Fox in 1806, Anglo-American relations improved markedly.

That British conservatives during this time both loathed the American political system and favored confrontational policies fits in with the basic argument of this book. But since those Conservatives should probably not be labeled liberal, we ignore them.

The 1840s: U.S./G.B. and U.S./Mexico

American Whigs labeled England a legitimate state during the Oregon crisis of 1845–46. Most Democrats followed the Jacksonian line of condemning Britain as a despotism, although a few more elitist Democrats agreed with the Whigs. In Britain, the Liberals (primarily Whigs) and Radicals both favored accommodation based on the claim that the United States had a model political system:

U.S. perceptions of G.B. (1845–46)		G.B. perceptions of the U.S.	
Whigs	Democrats	Liberals	Radicals
Liberal	Illiberal*	Liberal	Liberal

*Some Democrats classified G.B. as liberal

In the Mexican-American crisis of 1845–46, Americans' perceptions of Mexico paralleled those of Great Britain: Whigs and elitist Democrats insisted that Mexico was a republic, while Jacksonians were at pains to show that its recent coups d'état rendered it a dictatorship or proto-monarchy. In Mexico, liberals were of two minds about the United States. Moderates favored accommodation, while purists considered their northern neighbor a despotism and were highly bellicose:

U.S. perceptions of Mexico (1845–46)		Mexican perceptions of the U.S.	
Whigs	Democrats	Moderates	Purists
Liberal	Illiberal*	Liberal	Illiberal

*Some Democrats classified Mexico as liberal.

Institutional identity plausibly explains Americans' perceptions of England and, indirectly, of Mexico. Jacksonian Democrats, including Polk, wanted an egalitarian, agrarian, laissez-faire United States with a weak central government. They considered the British example and influence, which for them was tied up in the institution of monarchy, as the greatest foreign threat to their country.

Two decades earlier the Jeffersonians had rejoiced at the spread of republicanism in Latin America and expected a Western Hemisphere of peace and prosperity to stand against the Holy Alliance of monarchical Europe. The Monroe Doctrine was an instantiation of this antimonarchism. Chronic instability, particularly in Mexico, effaced this vision for many, so that by 1845 Jacksonians saw Mexico as a virtual cipher for British influence. Thus during these simultaneous crises, Jacksonians charged that England was trying to spread monarchical institutions in North America via Oregon and Mexico. That they were belligerent in both crises is no accident.

The Whig vision for America, meanwhile, was closer to that of the Federalists (who had faded away by 1820). The Whig Party was formed by men, including former Jeffersonians such as Henry Clay, who wanted a strong central government, state-directed development, and protection for industry. Whigs envisaged a government by the enlightened, and they openly admired Britain for its balanced institutions and ordered liberty. They countered the Jacksonians during these crises by arguing that the United States ought not to worry about British monarchical influence in Oregon or Mexico. Certain less populist Democrats, including Martin Van Buren, John C. Calhoun, and Thomas Hart Benton, tended more toward the Whig view of England and thus of Mexico.

Liberals in Great Britain also provide support for the liberal ideology hypothesis. The middle classes, enfranchised in 1832, and the working-class Chartists had for decades seen the United States as a model of popular, rational government. Elites who wanted Britain to become more like the United States made excuses for American belligerence during the Oregon crisis and pleaded with the Americans to demonstrate that democracy was a pacific form of government.

In Mexico, the perceptions some liberals held of the United States can be explained by the liberal ideology hypothesis. In the 1820s and early 1830s Mexican liberals had admired the United States as a model for their own country. (Conservatives had by contrast admired and favored better relations with Britain.) So-called *moderados* maintained this admiration up to the time of the war, even favoring the cession of huge tracts of territory and hoping for American tutelage. In the late 1830s, however, others—labeled *puros*—turned against the United States even though neither their own liberal vision nor U.S. institutions had changed. The balance-of-threat theory provides the best explanation of the purists' change of heart.

Balance-of-threat realism again has difficulty accounting for the variety of perceptions held by actors, especially in the United States and Britain. In material terms, the greatest potential threat to American security in 1845–46 was Britain. Although the U.S. population was nearly even with the British, England still enjoyed vast naval and military superiority. Yet, Canada was more vulnerable than ever, and a rebellion there beginning in 1837 suggested that many British subjects would join the American side in the event of war. As in the previous crises, those already inclined to hate England argued that America would win the war, and those already inclined to admire England said war would be devastating. Nor does realism provide much help with the simultaneous Mexican crisis. Those liberals who labeled Mexico illiberal tended to be the same ones who labeled Britain illiberal. They believed Britain was trying to force a monarchy on Mexico and interpreted every Mexican action in that light. Meanwhile, American liberals who were not worried about England tended to argue that Mexico was still a liberal state and therefore ought not to be fought.

Balance-of-threat theory has a similar problem explaining British perceptions of America. The United States clearly threatened to seize parts of Canada, and indeed Americans had for several years been aiding Canadian rebels across the border. Yet, liberals who had previously perceived the United States to have a legitimate system of government saw no danger to British interests. Radicals even urged their government to cede Canada to the United States so as to let republican institutions have wider scope. Elitist liberals such as Palmerston, who believed that American-style democracy was actually a threat to individual liberty, did feel threatened by the United States. It is unlikely that either the Radicals or Palmerston's men were analyzing British security free of ideological presuppositions.

The Conservative government, however, does provide support for balance-of-threat theory, in that the policies of Peel and Aberdeen varied with power factors. In the summer of 1844 Britain and France apparently agreed to guarantee Mexican and Texan independence from the United States, in effect balancing against Washington. By October Mexican uncooperativeness had killed the agreement, and Aberdeen was left trying to contain U.S. ambitions without French help. It was apparently power politics that led Aberdeen partially to appease the United States and to propagandize in favor of "liberal" America.[1] Aberdeen and Peel, who held no particular affinity for U.S. institutions,[2] evidently were responding to realist imperatives.

It is in Mexico that balance-of-threat theory finds its greatest support. The *puros* who turned against the United States in the late 1830s were reacting to the secession of Texas, which they (correctly) saw as an overwhelming threat to Mexico's sovereign territory and a precursor to U.S. acquisition of California.

Parochial-interest theory tells a credible story about the perceptions of some elites. In the United States, for example, Daniel Webster, one of

---

1. Kenneth Bourne, *Britain and the Balance of Power in North America, 1815–1908* (London: Longmans, 1967), 124.

2. As I explained in Chapter 4, Peel was a great reformer who has been compared to Andrew Jackson; but he was neither republican nor democrat.

Britain's strongest supporters, had served as legal council for Baring Brothers, a London banking house that had invested huge amounts in the United States. U.S. manufacturers' best customer was Britain.[3] It is also difficult to disentangle the ideological basis of the anglophilia of Calhoun's southern Democrats from cotton planters' interest in remaining at peace with the world's biggest textile manufacturer. Some of the American affinity for Britain is overdetermined.

In the case of Western Democrats, though, conceptions of interest were heavily shaped by liberal ideology. Ironically, British liberals argued vigorously that parochial interest lay behind American anglophobia: repeal the Corn Laws that kept U.S. grain out of Britain, they said, and the Oregon crisis would end. But these British liberals made the same mistake that today's economic determinists do. Western Democrats continued to demand all of Oregon after the Corn Laws were repealed.

The abolitionist Whigs probably fall outside any of the three explanations tested here. Normally anglophilic, they were fully as belligerent on Oregon as the Jacksonians, and they discovered despotic attributes in Britain to buttress their case. As discussed below, however, they vehemently opposed the Mexican War. It was their desire to halt the spread of slavery that led to their positions on the two questions. John Quincy Adams was an expansionist only over areas that would definitely be free soil; Oregon qualified, and Texas did not. As Adams stated before the crisis: "My own disposition with regard to all questions in negotiation with Great Britain . . . is essentially pacific. I am especially averse to everything irritating in form or offensive in language, and against everything of war tendency, *excepting the Boundary question,* upon which we should be inflexible."[4] Thus a domestic politics explanation, particular to the times, best accounts for the perceptions of the American abolitionists. Their enemies, the proslavery Southerners, are not so easily explained. Calhoun and his bloc wanted war with neither England nor Mexico.

Parochial interest provides a plausible answer for the perceptions of many British elites. The landed interests tended to be conservative; and as demonstrated by their opposition to repeal of the Corn Laws, they saw the United States as a potential agricultural rival. The manufacturing and banking interests were friendlier toward America, an important

3. U.S. merchandise exports to and imports from the United Kingdom both totaled slightly over $45 million in 1845; America's second biggest trading partner was France, which received $12.3 million in manufactures from the United States and sold $21 million worth to Americans in the same year. U.S. Bureau of Statistics, *Statistical Tables Exhibiting the Commerce of the United States with European Countries from 1790 to 1890* (Washington: Government Printing Office, 1893), xxvi, xliv.

4. Samuel Flagg Bemis, *John Quincy Adams and the Union* (New York: Alfred A. Knopf, 1956), 458–59.

supplier and customer. It is difficult to disentangle interest from ideology in this case, and so for now we may conclude that British perceptions were overdetermined.

A theory of parochial interest is of little help in understanding either American or Mexican perceptions. Economic ties between the United States and Mexico were minimal, and so it is doubtful that either war or peace advocates were driven by desire for personal wealth.[5]

The Civil War, 1861–63

Britain and the United States came close to war three times during the War between the States. Americans' perceptions of England for much of the war fell along partisan lines. Following their party's tradition, Democrats typically labeled Britain a hierarchical monarchy. Following the Federalist and Whig traditions, Republicans continued to label Britain legitimate or "constitutional." By 1863, however, Republicans had begun to agree with Democrats that Britain had an illegitimate government after all. In Britain, meanwhile, Liberals and Radicals early on were divided as to whether the Union was more liberal, and more deserving of sympathy, than the Confederacy. In the fall and winter of 1862, however, more and more began proclaiming that the Union was fighting to free the slaves:

U.S. perceptions of G.B.		G.B. perceptions of the U.S.	
Republicans	Democrats	Liberals	Radicals
Liberal→Illiberal	Illiberal	Mixed→Liberal	Mixed→Liberal

Balance-of-threat theory might account at least for Republican perceptions. As in earlier cases, the state that could bring the most power to bear quickly in North America was Great Britain, and in concert with the other European powers Britain could seal Southern independence. In 1860 Britain had 357,000 men under arms, produced 19.9 percent of world manufacturing output (compared to 7.2 percent for the entire United States), and possessed what was by far the world's most powerful navy.[6] The Union would have an incentive to balance with England against the Confederacy (just as the Confederacy tried to do against the Union). Realism could also account for the way Republi-

---

5. In 1843 Santa Anna had cut off virtually all U.S.-Mexican trade. Some did argue that punitive war was the best way to restore the trade, but many argued the opposite. Justin H. Smith, *The War with Mexico* (New York: Macmillan, 1919), 1:72–73, 122.

6. Paul Kennedy, *The Rise and Fall of the Great Powers* (New York: Random House, 1987), 149, 154.

cans later recategorized Britain as a despotism. Gestures from London, particularly the government's allowing ironclad vessels to be delivered to the Confederacy, were so hostile and threatening that the Republicans were compelled to come around to the traditional Democratic view of England.

Yet, realism has trouble explaining why Democrats were hostile to England throughout the war, to the point of advocating policies that would have led to Anglo-American war. The Republican Henry Raymond of the *New York Times* charged the Democrat James Gordon Bennett of the *Herald* of wanting war with England so as to help the South gain independence.[7] Since Bennett did support Lincoln and the war effort (even the Emancipation Proclamation), however, Raymond's charge appears scurrilous, more a product of newspaper rivalry and wartime passion than of evidence. In fact Bennett had always hated England and hoped for a U.S.-inspired revolution there. It was also the case that most Republicans had always admired Britain, whether for its constitutionalism and ordered liberty or its antislavery leadership. Thus liberal ideology provides a plausible explanation of both Democratic and Republican perceptions of Britain at least until 1863.

Parochial interest, by contrast, is of little help. As in the 1840s, Democrats tended to represent rural interests who benefited from wheat exports to England. Republicans tended to represent urban interests who sought protection from British manufactures.

In Britain, liberals' perceptions provide perhaps the most dramatic support for the ideological hypothesis in this book. British liberals had long been staunchly antislavery, and thus ideology would seem to predict sympathy for the Union from the start of the war. But in fact Lincoln himself had emphatically declared that the Union was not fighting to end slavery. Since many border states in the Union allowed slavery, the war could be construed to be one part of America fighting for independence from another—two democracies at war. With liberal ideology giving little guidance during the first year of the war, realism and economic interest give more plausible bases for uncharitable British perceptions of the Union. Realism would say (and realists said at the time) that Britain had an interest in supporting Southern independence as a way to keep the United States permanently divided and weakened. As the Earl of Clarendon said in April 1862, "I hate the Confederates almost as much as the Federals but I hope for success and the consequent prolongation of the war because it is only the complete exhaustion of both parties that will prevent their uniting against us."[8] With the Union fighting for its

7. *New York Times*, 20 December 1861, 4.
8. Brian Jenkins, *Britain and the War for the Union* (Montreal: McGill-Queen's University Press, 1980), 2:63.

life, British victory was more likely than ever. Economic interest would clearly suggest favoring the South, both because the Northern blockade was keeping precious Southern cotton from England and because the Morrill Tariff lowered British exports to the Union.

But more and more Britons began perceiving the Union as liberal in the fall of 1862. What accounts for the shift? Several parochial-interest hypotheses have been offered by historians over the years. Some assert that Britain was more reliant on Northern wheat than on Southern cotton. The "King Wheat" hypothesis is effectively turned away by Frank Lawrence Owsley, who argues that there is no evidence that British statesmen worried about a loss of American wheat. Owsley avers instead that British manufacturers profited too much from the Civil War to allow intervention. The cotton famine itself raised prices of finished goods, provided incentives to develop Indian sources of cotton, and resuscitated woolen and linen manufacturers; British munitions makers and shipbuilders also did well by the war.[9] Owsley's argument would imply that those interests that were profiteering would propagandize against intervention and thereby portray the Union as liberal. The hypothesis would then have two problems. First, Owsley provides no evidence that those interests lay behind the pro-Union agitation following the Emancipation Proclamation. Second, he cannot account for the *shift* in perceptions in the fall and winter of 1862–63. It is also questionable whether these profits would have more sway than the cotton famine itself, or the continuation of the Morrill Tariff, which was attacked even by friends of the Union. Thus, parochial interest cannot account for the shift in British perceptions.

What about realism? Norman Graebner argues that the cabinet backed away from intervention because the South never established to Palmerston's satisfaction that it could win, and thus the North was never driven to the point where it would accept European intervention without a fight.[10] Graebner's argument suggests that British perceptions of Union liberalism fluctuated with Union success on the battlefield. In fact, however, the Union did not begin to look decisively more militarily powerful in the fall of 1862. Lee did retreat from Maryland after the Battle of Antietam in September, but Antietam was technically a stalemate, and still to come were Confederate victories at Fredericksburg in December and Chancellorsville in May 1863. The decisive Battle of Gettysburg was not to come until July 1863. Perceptions

9. Frank Lawrence Owsley, *King Cotton Diplomacy: Foreign Relations of the Confederate States of America*, 2d ed. (Chicago: University of Chicago Press, 1951), 542–58.

10. Norman A. Graebner, "Northern Diplomacy and European Realism," in Thomas G. Paterson, ed., *Major Problems in American Foreign Policy*, 2d ed. (Lexington: D. C. Heath, 1984), 1:307–22.

of the Union as liberal remained staunchly pro-Union through these later events.

Liberal ideology provides the best explanation. Early in the war many British liberals felt betrayed by a Union that declared itself neutral on the question of slavery. For most British liberals, the seminal event then became Lincoln's preliminary Emancipation Proclamation in September 1862. When Lincoln declared that the slaves would soon be freed in the rebellious states, the meaning of the Civil War changed in British eyes from self-determination for the South to emancipation for the slaves. Liberals and Radicals said this, and both acted for the rest of the war as though they believed it. American power and economic ties were now refracted through this ideological lens.[11]

The United States and Spain, 1873

Americans were of two minds about Spain during the *Virginius* crisis, and the division apparently did not fall along partisan lines. The remarkable fact is the variation in U.S. perceptions of Spain. Before early 1873 most Americans counted Spain as a backward monarchy, the last European power to practice slavery. In February the perception shifted and large numbers of American elites muted their demands that Spain emancipate the slaves in Cuba. In Spain, meanwhile, liberals, most of whom were Republicans, disagreed over the status of the United States:

U.S. perceptions of Spain		Spanish perceptions of the U.S.
Republicans	Democrats	Republicans
Illiberal→Mixed	Illiberal→Mixed	Mixed

Balance-of-threat theory suggests that one look to power, propinquity, and purpose to explain the February 1873 shift in American perceptions. Yet, there was no obvious threat that should lead Americans to balance with (or against) Spain. U.S. military strength was still dwarfed by the five European powers,[12] and Britain with its navy and Canadian possessions was still potentially the most dangerous to U.S. security. Yet, Britain was not behaving in an especially hostile manner;

11. Some scholars have argued that France was constrained from intervention for the same reason. French liberals wanted France (then ruled by Napoleon III) to become politically more like the United States and sympathized with cause of abolition. See Serge Gavonsky, *The French Liberal Opposition and the American Civil War* (New York: Humanities, 1968). Interestingly, Frank Owsley agrees with this interpretation. Owsley, *King Cotton Diplomacy*, 543–44.

12. In 1880 military personnel figures were as follows: United Kingdom, 248,000; France, 544,000; Russia, 909,000; Germany, 430,000; Austria, 273,000; and the United States, 36,000. Paul Kennedy, *Rise and Fall*, 154.

in 1872, in fact, London had paid $15.5 million to Washington in compensation for the *Alabama* incident of the Civil War. Spain itself was no threat. Richard Bradford reports that the Spanish at the time ranked fifth among the world's navies, while the American was not even in the top ten. The U.S. Army numbered 35,000 men, larger than before the Civil War but small by European standards.[13] The United States had also recently slid into a deep economic recession. But America was again politically unified while Spain was in the throes of insurrection not only in Cuba but on the Iberian peninsula itself. Spain, having lost virtually all but the last jewel of its New World empire, had not been a threat to U.S. territory for fifty years.

Parochial interests do tell a credible story for many anti-Spanish Americans. Although bilateral economic ties were slight,[14] many Americans had bought bonds from the unrecognized Cuban Republic and thus were interested in successful Cuban independence. This interest could easily have led them to whip up indignation against Spain.

The timing of the perceptual shift in Spain's favor, however, makes the causal role of liberal ideology difficult to refute. A marked change in elite statements and official U.S. policy toward Spain took place in February 1873, as Americans (including the Grant administration) suddenly stopped pushing Spain to abolish slavery in Cuba. The source of the change was clearly the establishment of the First Spanish Republic. American liberals had always said republicanism mattered to them, and their actions and statements after February show their sincerity. The power of this change is seen in the crisis itself, as Fish, Sumner, and others were determined not to bring about the restoration of monarchy even as they strove to resolve the crisis with U.S. honor intact. These men continued to base policy preferences on a supposed international struggle between republicanism and monarchism.

Liberal ideology is a much poorer predictor of perceptions in Spain, however. Consistent with their liberal predispositions, Castelar and a group of Republican deputies opposed war. Yet, after the *Virginius* crisis many other liberals evidently were eager for war. In February Republicans had thanked the U.S. minister for his help in establishing the new government; during *Virginius,* the minister's life was in danger from angry Spaniards, and the Republican press was uniformly hostile. Economic ties and the form of government in the United States had remained constant. It is balance-of-threat theory that provides the most plausible explanation for anti-American liberals' perceptions.

13. Richard Bradford, *The "Virginius" Affair* (Boulder: Colorado Associated University Press, 1980), 68–69.

14. U.S. exports to Spain in fiscal year 1872–73 totaled $10 million; in comparison, exports to the United Kingdom totaled $312.3 million. U.S. Bureau of Statistics, *Statistical Tables,* 402, 404–5, 444.

Cuba was part of metropolitan Spain; the U.S. government's refusal to stop filibustering expeditions to Cuba was so obviously a hostile series of gestures because it touched Spanish sovereignty over Spanish territory. Pushed to the wall, many Spanish liberals turned against America.

The United States and Chile, 1891–92

During the *Baltimore* crisis some American elites labeled Chile a sister republic, and forgave it its diplomatic insults; others classified it as a nation of savages. While some Chilean liberals, such as the ousted Balmaceda, had perceived a liberal United States, virtually all Chilean elites during the crisis were anti-American:

U.S. perceptions of Chile		Chilean perceptions of the U.S.
Republicans	Democrats	
Mixed	Mixed	Illiberal

By Stephen Walt's criteria, there were no obvious threats to U.S. security in 1891–92 that would lead America to balance with or against Chile. America had gained in population and industrial, military, and naval strength since the 1870s, to the point that it was arguably a great power.[15] As before, Britain was the greatest potential threat, but the British had shown little if any hostile intent toward America.[16] There

15. As of 1890:

	Pop. (millions)	Iron prdn. (million tons)	Military personnel	Warship tonnage
Russia	116.8	0.95	677,000	180,000
U.S.	62.6	9.3	96,000	240,000
Germany	49.2	4.1	504,000	190,000
Austria	42.6	0.97	346,000	66,000
Japan	39.9	0.02	84,000	41,000
France	38.3	1.9	542,000	319,000
Britain	37.4	8.0	420,000	679,000
Italy	30.0	0.01	284,000	242,000

Source: Data from Paul Kennedy, *The Rise and Fall of the Great Powers* (New York: Random House, 1987), 199–203.

16. The late 1880s had brought serious fishing and sealing disputes with Canada, whose foreign policy was still under the control of London. In 1888, moreover, the British minister to Washington, Sir Lionel Sackville-West, privately endorsed Grover Cleveland for reelection over Benjamin Harrison; the endorsement was leaked to the press, and the ensuing public outrage led to Sackville-West's recall to London. See Charles S. Campbell, *The Transformation of American Foreign Relations 1865–1900* (New York: Harper & Row, 1976), chap. 7. It is difficult to see these actions as threats to U.S. security.

were no *Realpolitik* imperatives emanating from Europe. Tiny Chile itself was no threat, even though the Chilean Navy had humiliated its U.S. counterpart in the War of the Pacific more than a decade earlier. In 1879 Blaine had tried to intervene to help Peru and Bolivia against Chile; Chile essentially sent the Americans home. By 1891, however, the U.S. Navy far surpassed the Chilean.

Economic ties between the two nations were slender,[17] but relations with Chile did touch on the parochial interests of some Americans. Most strikingly, the U.S. Navy had wanted to answer its humiliation of 1879. During the 1880s, under the influence of Alfred Thayer Mahan, Benjamin F. Tracy, the navy secretary, had built up U.S. naval offensive capabilities to make America a great power.[18] Tracy and many others yearned for a demonstration of American power against Chile in particular.[19] There were also potential economic benefits to defeating the new Chilean regime. The Congressionalists were committed to restoring traditional British control over Chile's nitrate industry, control that Balmaceda had hoped to end. A successful war against the Congressionalists could open Chile to U.S. capital.

Despite these strong parochial interests, many American liberals, including Blaine, gave Chile the benefit of the doubt. Liberal ideology provides an explanation. Now as throughout the nineteenth century, American liberals were consciously biased in favor of fellow republics. Blaine, who had for more than a decade been the hemisphere's leading advocate of republican solidarity, fought to keep Harrison from delivering an ultimatum to Chile.

What of the Chilean hostile perceptions of the United States? As Andrew Carnegie cabled Harrison at the time, "Why Americans are so unpopular in any sister republic needs inquiry."[20] Ideology offers a plausible answer in light of the Chilean civil war. The Balmacedists preferred a strong presidency, while the Congressionalists (who governed Chile at the time of the *Baltimore* crisis) wanted a more parliamentary model of government. Since the United States epitomized presidential govern-

17. As John Trumbull told Blaine, "the difficulty was that the United States produced almost everything Chile produced, with the exception of nitrates." Joyce S. Goldberg, *The "Baltimore" Affair* (Lincoln: University of Nebraska Press, 1986), 96. Trumbull was evidently unfamiliar with the concept of comparative advantage.

18. The U.S. South Atlantic Squadron had five ships, 1,081 men, thirty-eight main battery guns, and thirty-nine secondary guns; the Pacific Squadron had five ships, 1,339 men, forty-four main battery guns, and sixty-six secondary guns. Goldberg, *"Baltimore,"* 118–19.

19. William F. Sater, *Chile and the United States: Empires in Conflict* (Athens: University of Georgia Press, 1990), 45–48; Goldberg, *"Baltimore,"* 115–23.

20. Harry J. Sievers, *Benjamin Harrison: Hoosier President* (New York: Bobbs-Merrill, 1968), 193 n. 37.

ment and Britain parliamentary, Balmacedists would naturally favor good relations with the United States, while Congressionalists would prefer to tilt toward England.[21]

Yet, Balmaceda may also have seen the United States as a potential ally in his attempt to break the British hold over the Chilean nitrate industry. The Congressionalists' ties to the British may have contributed to their anti-Americanism.

The best answer is probably supplied by balance-of-threat theory. In fact, Chileans had many reasons before for mistrusting Americans. From unwanted U.S. interference in the War of the Pacific (1879–84) to U.S. favoritism toward Balmacedists in the Chilean civil war, Congressionalists perceived an aggressive America. Like Mexican *puros* of 1845 and Spanish Republicans of 1873, these Chilean liberals were forced by power politics to recategorize the United States from friend to enemy.

The United States and Great Britain, 1895–96

As in all previous Anglo-American crises, the antimonarchical tradition was alive and well in the United States. Yet, more and more elite Americans now perceived Britain as their fellow liberal state, on the side of peace and civilization. Meanwhile, the British were as always divided over America, but the divide had moved since the 1860s. Now many Radicals had turned away from the U.S. model,[22] while Liberals embraced it more enthusiastically than ever, and even some Conservatives sang the praises of American-style democracy. While Chamberlain proposed a joint Anglo-American intervention in Armenia, the conservative British press that had once berated the American "mob" now revealed a new trust of the American public's rationality.

U.S. perceptions of G.B.		G.B. perceptions of the U.S.		
Republicans	Democrats	Conservatives	Liberals	Radicals
Mixed	Mixed	Mixed	Liberal	Mixed

American anglophobes were following the century-old loathing for monarchy and aristocracy begun by Jefferson and Paine. What needs explaining in this case is the fact that by the 1890s many Americans

21. Blaine was pleased with Balmaceda's affinity for U.S.-style government. Henry Clay Evans, Jr., *Chile and Its Relations with the United States* (1927; reprint, New York: Johnson Reprint, 1971), 136–37. Compare the liberal-conservative divide in Mexico in the 1820s and corresponding attitudes toward the United States and England.

22. Information on British socialist opinion of the United States during the crisis is difficult to come by. In any event, despite the alarm they inspired in liberals and conservatives, the socialists were not yet very influential in foreign policy.

had granted Britain a special dispensation as a "crowned republic." Balance-of-threat theory would predict that a new menace was driving Americans to embrace England. The United States was not the only rising power in the world. Germany, Japan, and Italy had all increased enormously in naval strength between 1880 and 1890. The question is, was any power or combination displaying hostile intentions toward the United States? The 1880s had seen European powers, England included, divide most of Africa among themselves and claim Pacific colonies as well. No state was taking an unusual interest in the Western Hemisphere, however. As we have seen, various Americans were worried about various other great powers prior to 1895, but it is difficult to attribute such worries to power, proximity, and intentions alone. American liberals had no *Realpolitik* reason to balance with Britain.

Economic ties were strong between the two nations. In the 1890–94 period, half of all U.S. exports went to the United Kingdom; in 1895, the value of these exports was $387 million.[23] British investors held huge amounts in U.S. securities; the figure in 1899 was roughly $2.5 billion.[24] Cleveland's December message led these investors to unload securities, causing a scare on Wall Street.[25] It is possible that many U.S. businessmen suddenly "discovered" British liberalism when stock and bond prices began to fall. But as previous cases demonstrate, Americans had always depended heavily on British trade and investment, and as always it was not only Wall Street or chambers of commerce that called for peace.

Many liberals evidently conceived of their interests in ideological terms.[26] In the years since the last Anglo-American crises in the early 1860s, Britain had become more popularly governed. Chapter 5 demonstrated that Americans had noticed the reforms of 1867 and 1884–85, by which the British franchise was expanded to include much of the working class and cabinets were made more directly responsible to the electorate. Well before the crisis, many Americans had predicted in print

23. H. C. Allen, *Great Britain and the United States* (London: Odhams, 1954), 62; U.S. Department of Treasury, *The Foreign Commerce and Navigation of the United States for the Year Ending June 30, 1895* (Washington: Government Printing Office, 1896), pt. 1, 2:980–81.

24. Louis Hacker, *England and America, the Ties that Bind* (Oxford: Clarendon, 1948), 21.

25. Ernest R. May, *Imperial Democracy: The Emergence of America as a Great Power* (Chicago: Imprint, 1991), 57–58.

26. Stephen Rock recently argues that, at least on the British side, culture (or ethnicity) is more responsible than ideology for Anglo-American affinity. Rock, "Anglo-American Relations, 1845–1930: Did Shared Liberal Values and Democratic Institutions Keep the Peace?" in Miriam Fendius Elman, ed., *Paths to Peace: Is Democracy the Answer?* (Cambridge: MIT Press, 1997). For evidence Rock relies almost wholly on contemporary statements about Anglo-Saxonism. He says little about the societal changes in the two countries.

that England would be a less aggressive power now that it was a democracy.

But why did many British conservatives become more friendly toward the United States? Economic ties between the countries were strong, but they had always been so. Balance-of-threat theory points us toward the fact that the United States was a rising power with a growing navy. The United States was still capable of seizing Canada.[27] American diplomatic behavior toward Britain did not suggest particularly friendly intentions, as evidenced by the Canadian fishery and seal disputes and the Sackville-West incident of the late 1880s. And of course the Olney note and Cleveland's speech, and the U.S. public's enthusiasm at receiving them, should have indicated that at least a strong current of hostility existed toward England.

Yet Britain faced other foreign threats. Russia and Germany were likewise rising, ambitious powers making hostile gestures to Britain. Russia challenged its border with Afghanistan in 1885, raising the specter of danger to Britain's Indian possessions. Germany challenged Britain by claiming Southwest Africa and acquiring Samoa and New Guinea, colonies too close to Australia and New Zealand for comfort. In addition, French and British interests clashed in northern Africa and Indochina.[28] Thus isolated, Britain indeed had reason to try to balance with one or more powers against others.

But balance-of-threat theory alone cannot say why the British trusted the United States more than these other powers. Germany was challenging England in Africa; Russia, in Asia; France, in Africa and Indochina; the United States, in South America. A clue is seen in the fact that in England the Olney note elicited indignation while the Kruger telegram provoked hysteria. Stephen Rock explains that the British in the 1890s were ideologically predisposed to favor the United States over Germany. "Englishmen, who could agree on practically nothing else, were in fact almost unanimous in their distaste for the German political system, its ideology, and its methods."[29] Evidence supporting

27. John A. S. Grenville and George Berkeley Young point out that although the U.S. Navy was no match for the British, the British Army feared that its U.S. counterpart would easily seize Canada. Grenville and Young, *Politics, Strategy, and American Diplomacy: Studies in Foreign Policy, 1873–1917* (New Haven: Yale University Press, 1966), 171–73. The authors attribute British capitulation to the United States to London's isolation in Europe. For the same interpretation, see Christopher Layne, "Kant or Cant: The Myth of the Democratic Peace," in Michael E. Brown, Sean M. Lynn-Jones, and Steven E. Miller, eds., *Debating the Democratic Peace* (Cambridge: MIT Press, 1996), 176–80.

28. G. P. Gooch and J. H. B. Masterman, *A Century of British Foreign Policy* (London: G. Allen & Unwin, 1918), 33–37.

29. Stephen Rock, *Why Peace Breaks Out: Great Power Rapprochement in Historical Perspective* (Chapel Hill: University of North Carolina Press, 1989), 86–87. In light of Rock's more recent work (see note 26 above), it should be noted here that in 1898 Chamberlain

Rock's contention is seen in British writings about Germany and America in the early 1890s. When the British public welcomed William II, the new Emperor of Germany, on his visit to Britain in 1891, W. T. Stead worriedly noted that William "believes that he reigns by right Divine." Moreover, Stead noted, "The mercurial mobility of the Kaiser's convictions renders it impossible for any one to feel any confidence in the stability of his policy."[30]

It was liberalization within Britain itself that led conservatives to their pro-American bias. When the expansion of the franchise in 1884 did not better the lot of the workers, many Radicals had turned away from the American model and toward socialism. The writings of conservative Britons in the 1880s show that to the upper classes worried about this turn, America began to look more attractive as a model of reasonable democracy. The middle and upper classes saw socialism as the greatest threat to their liberty, and saw the United States as an ally against socialism. H. C. Allen argues that geopolitics combined with changes within Britain itself to foster kinder attitudes toward America: "Thus in all the tensions of the period, and particularly in the Venezuelan dispute, the most important influence for amity and peace was the new English democracy."[31] Britons could no longer claim to be troubled by American slavery. Now when they looked about the world for friends, their own liberalization made the United States the most obvious choice.

The United States and Spain, 1896–98

In the United States, the contrast with 1873 could not be starker. Most Americans now perceived Spain as a medieval monarchy, not as a fellow liberal state. Significantly, the one exception came during the first few months of the Liberal Sagasta government in October 1897, when most Americans granted Spain a short reprieve from criticism. For their

---

did propose a defensive alliance with Germany, and began speaking publicly of "a new Triple Alliance between the Teutonic race and the two great branches of the Anglo-Saxon race." Berlin rebuffed London; but the fact that Chamberlain wanted the alliance does show that race, and not merely liberalism, was part of the filter he used to read the world. Still, it is not clear that his racial take on the balance of power was shared by all. Not only was the British public less friendly to Germany than he; in addition, when in 1901 Chamberlain proposed an Anglo-German-Japanese alliance, Salisbury himself noted that British public opinion would probably not support such an alliance. René Albrecht-Carrié, *A Diplomatic History of Europe since the Congress of Vienna*, rev. ed. (New York: Harper & Row, 1973), 226–31.

30. W. T. Stead, "William II, Emperor of Germany," *Review of Reviews* (London), August 1891, 127, 132.

31. Allen, *Britain and the United States*, 525.

part, all Spaniards—reactionaries, Conservatives, Liberals, and Republicans—seem to have regarded America as a greedy country out to fulfill its long-held plan to snatch Cuba away:

U.S. perceptions of Spain	Spanish perceptions of the U.S.
Illiberal*	Illiberal

*Except for Republicans for a brief period after the Liberal government took office in Spain in October 1897.

Was the judgment of most Americans that Spain was illiberal a product of the need to justify the wish to go to war? Balance-of-threat theory directs us to look for an objective Spanish menace. The United States, however, was certainly in no danger from Spain. The simple power ratio between the two navies favored America: Spanish figures said the U.S. Navy displaced 116,445 tons, while the Spanish Navy displaced only 56,644 tons. In addition, although the Spanish Army in Cuba outnumbered the whole U.S. Army by 150,000 to 25,000, the Spanish had already been severely weakened by their struggles with rebels and disease in Cuba.[32] The U.S. population and economy far outstripped those of Spain.[33] The hostility Spain was displaying was defensive, a demand that the United States dissolve the Cuban junta and let Spain settle its own problems.[34]

As for parochial interest: American economic ties with the Iberian peninsula were minimal, but Americans owned thousands of dollars of property in Cuba that was endangered by the insurrection. Commercial and banking interests, however, were divided on the question of war. Ernest May demonstrates that in cities such as New York, Chicago, Cleveland, and Omaha financiers and industrialists opposed

32. David F. Trask, *The War with Spain in 1898* (New York: Macmillan, 1981), 63; Graham A. Cosmas, *An Army for Empire: The United States Army in the Spanish-American War* (Columbia: University of Missouri Press, 1971), 5, 76–77. Interestingly, power perceptions were not so clear at the time. In January 1898, Theodore Roosevelt, then assistant secretary to the navy, believed the two nations' Atlantic fleets to be equal; the sinking of the *Maine* convinced him the America's was inferior, and he knew Spain was also negotiating to buy two British-built cruisers. John L. Offner, *An Unwanted War: The Diplomacy of the United States and Spain over Cuba, 1895–1898* (Chapel Hill: University of North Carolina Press, 1992), 128–30.

33. Spain's population in 1900 was 18.5 million. Colin McEvedy and Richard Jones, *Atlas of World Population* (New York: Facts on File, 1978), 101.

34. Traditional realist writers have generally regarded the Spanish-American War as a violation of realist practice by the United States. George Kennan attributes the war to (imprudent) economic and humanitarian impulses. Norman A. Graebner calls 1898 a turning point at which America abandoned seeking its own national interest in favor of "ideological" policy to further American "political, social, and religious beliefs." See Robert L. Beisner, *From the Old Diplomacy to the New, 1865–1900* (New York: Thomas Y. Crowell, 1975), 15.

war as a disruption of commerce.[35] But Walter LaFeber notes that while many commercial interests were antiwar, others, especially in the South and Middle West, favored war as a way to boost production of steel and other commodities.[36] It is probable that prowar interests encouraged the portrayal of Spain as a medieval despotism so as to induce war fever. At least in Eastern cities such as New York, however, the vehement anti-Spanish polemics cannot be attributed to manipulation by businessmen, because businessmen there were mostly pacific.[37]

On the other hand, as with Chile in 1892 the U.S. military had a parochial interest in an easy war. Indeed, Russell A. Alger, the secretary for war, and Theodore Roosevelt, the assistant navy secretary, were leading war advocates who labeled the Spaniards barbarians. On the other hand, John D. Long, the navy secretary, told reporters after the *Maine* explosion there was no need for war.[38] Here, too, parochial interests were divided.

Liberal ideology provides a strong explanation of the perceptions of those actors without parochial interests. As in 1873, Cuba was struggling for its independence, Spain was ruthlessly suppressing that struggle, and American lives were lost. In 1873, however, Spain was a republic bravely facing a world of hostile monarchies. In 1898 Spain was a monarchy, and unlike Britain an undemocratic one. With the restoration of the Bourbons in 1875, Spain slipped back into the category of monarchy, and thus back underneath the cloud of suspicion so many Americans pictured hanging above all nonrepublics. In the 1880s and 1890s American publicists and editors recognized certain liberal reforms and elements in Spain, and explicitly hoped for the reestablishment of a republic. Madrid's conduct toward its own people in Cuba, however, darkened those perceptions. The American partiality toward liberalism showed in the period from October 1897 through January 1898, the first three months of Sagasta's new Liberal govern-

---

35. May, *Imperial Democracy*, 139–40.

36. Walter LaFeber, *The New Empire: An Interpretation of American Expansion, 1860–1898* (Ithaca: Cornell University Press, 1967), 385.

37. Louis A. Pérez, Jr., argues that many influential citizens, including McKinley, wanted to incorporate Cuba into an American empire; the Spanish-American War was a U.S. intervention to prevent Cuba from securing true independence. Pérez further argues, however, that McKinley wanted to acquire Cuba peacefully and was forced by Congress into war. Even if Pérez is correct about McKinley's object, then, McKinley and his advisors cannot be held responsible for portrayals of Spain as a despotism. Pérez, *Cuba between Two Empires 1878–1902* (Pittsburgh: University of Pittsburgh Press, 1973), esp. 139–93.

38. Offner, *Unwanted War*, 123, 128.

ment, as Republican calls for intervention quieted. But on the whole, Spain had not reformed itself enough to satisfy Americans the way the Britain had done.

What of Spanish liberals' perceptions of the United States? If Sagasta and his party did regard the United States as a fellow liberal state, they did not leave any evidence of it. Ideology offers a possible reason: the Liberal Party (which according to our criteria was not fully liberal) was staunchly monarchist and may naturally have opposed the United States as a republican model. But the fact that the remaining Spanish Republicans were also anti-American suggests that hostile American gestures and statements about Cuba, dating from the 1850s, are most likely responsible for Spanish perceptions (see the *Virginius* affair, above). Clearly the United States, with its obsession over Cuba, its proximity, and its rising naval power, was the country most dangerous to Spain. As in other cases, here balance-of-threat theory offers a credible account of liberals' perceptions that the United States was illiberal. In a world without the Cuban question, Spanish Republicans and Liberals may have been conciliatory toward the United States. In the event, however, the interest in maintaining Spanish territorial integrity outweighed any interest in cultivating good relations with a state whose liberalism they may have admired.

Table 2 summarizes the plausibility of each hypothesis in each case. Since each country yields its own values for the dependent variable (perceptions), each case study actually comprises two cases. Thus there are nineteen rather than ten cases (France in 1796–98, as already explained, is not part of this first test).

The most important question is this: Is institutional identity really motivating at least some actors to label foreign states liberal, and is liberal ideology thus shaping their notions of self-interest, as I argue? In two cases (16 and 20) and for many actors in two more (10 and 11), as already explained, the answer is no, because realism provides the best explanation. In all other cases, however, ideology plausibly accounts for perceptions. That is, we can predict how a subject will perceive the foreign state based on his or her vision for his or her own state. We can divide these remaining cases into two groups: those in which ideology clearly accounts for perceptions, and those in which ideology plausibly does so but realism and/or parochial interest does as well. The first group can be further divided into two:

The first subgroup consists of cases where the temporal sequence is tight. Where the time between an alleged cause and its effect is very short, i.e., where changes in perceptions closely follow institutional changes, it is difficult to deny the causal role of ideology. During the

Table 2 Hypotheses on Causes of Perceptions: Results

	Case	Liberal ideology	Realism	Parochial interest
Jay Treaty	1 U.S.	x		x[b]
	2 G.B.	x		x
Quasi-War	3 U.S.	x		x
	4 (Fr.	–	–	–)
War of 1812	5 U.S.	x		x
	6 G.B.	x		x
Oregon	7 U.S.	x		x[b]
	8 G.B.	x	x	x
Mexico	9 U.S.	x		
	10 Mex.	x	x	
Civil War	11 U.S.	x	a	a
	12 G.B.	x		
Virginius	13 U.S.	x		
	14 Sp.	x	x	
Baltimore	15 U.S.	x		x
	16 Chile		x	
Venezuela	17 U.S.	x		x
	18 G.B.	x	x	x
Sp-Am War	19 U.S.	x		
	20 Sp.		x	

[a]In the *Trent* crisis.
[b]Ideology clearly wins for some key groups (see Table 3)

Civil War British Liberals and Radicals relabeled the Union as more liberal than the Confederacy after Lincoln issued the preliminary Emancipation Proclamation in the fall of 1862 (case 12). Americans declared Spain a sister republic upon the abdication of King Amadeo in February 1873 (case 13). In a weaker example, Americans granted the Spanish government a brief respite from criticism when a Liberal government took office in October 1897 (case 19).

In the second subgroup, ideology clearly shaped self-interest. In three cases, parochial interest and ideology (or, more precisely, ideologically shaped interest)[39] pointed in opposite directions, and ideology triumphed. In 1795–96 American debtors to the British in Virginia and elsewhere refused to support the Jay Treaty even though it provided for assumption of their debts by the federal government (case 1). In 1845–46 Congressmen representing western U.S. farmers refused to

39. Here I reiterate that the ideological hypothesis does not deny that self-interest matters; it merely denies that actors always conceive of their interests in fundamentally parochial terms. Rather, they believe they have an interest in a particular set of governmental institutions. See my discussion in Chapter 1.

support compromise over Oregon even when the British government lowered tariffs that had kept American grain out of England (case 7). (In these two cases, as Table 2 notes, parochial interest plausibly accounts for the perceptions of *other* actors.) Third, in case 12 British liberals backed the Union after the fall of 1862 even though intervention to help the Confederacy would have helped the British economy. These cases, summarized in Table 3, demonstrate that ideas can and do shape notions of self-interest and that these ideas affect the foreign policies of liberal states.

In a second group of cases, more than one hypothesis is plausible. In most cases, realism and/or parochial interest offers a credible explanation as well as ideology. We have a strong reason, however, for favoring ideology: it explains a striking aspect of the cases that the others cannot. This study has shown a *strong correlation between the political institutions liberals favor in foreign states and those they favor in their own*. For example, those liberals who want no monarchy or aristocracy in their own country dislike foreign countries with monarchies and aristocracies. Institutional identity, as explained in Chapter 2, predicts this correlation, that is, tells us why it is a causal relationship. This predictive power is important because a theory that predicts novel, unexpected findings is, ceteris paribus, superior to those that do not.[40] And realism and parochial interest have difficulty accounting for this finding.

Realism, for example, must say that the correlation is either accidental or spurious. Accidental correlation seems unlikely, since the relationship is so strong. Spurious correlation would mean that a third variable, power, drives both perceptions and institutional identity. For example, realism might assert that it was actually rising U.S. power in the 1890s that led Britons to perceive the United States as a liberal power; it would then have to assert that rising U.S. power also led them

Table 3 Where Ideology Clearly Caused Perceptions

Cause and effect tightly linked	Immediate material interest superseded by ideological interest
G.B. perceptions of Union, Fall 1862	Private U.S. debtors, 1795–96
U.S. perceptions of Spain, Winter 1873	U.S. wheat farmers, Spring 1846
U.S. perceptions of Spain, Fall 1897	G.B. workers, middle class, Fall 1862

40. In Imre Lakatos's terms, a theory that predicts and corroborates new empirical findings is *progressive*. Lakatos, "Falsification and the Methodology of Scientific Research Programmes," in Imre Lakatos and Alan Musgrave, eds., *Criticism and the Growth of Knowledge* (Cambridge: Cambridge University Press, 1970), 91–180, esp. 118.

to favor U.S.-style liberalism within Britain itself. Similarly, parochial interest might suggest that actors in state A who are economically dependent on state B will want A to have the same institutions as B. For example, if John Bright's investments in America led him to perceive America as a liberal state, they would then also have led him to want an American-style democracy in Britain.[41]

Such hypotheses are intriguing but far-fetched. At the very least, proponents would have to describe a link between cause and effect—i.e., explain why actors should want their country to organize itself politically like the country they fear or trade with the most. Such is not to say that no actors would let external factors determine what they want their own country's internal regime to look like. But it seems highly unlikely that all do so. Contra realism, it is more likely that the elites in question assessed threats through an ideological lens. Contra parochial interest, it is more likely that people such as Bright, who was an indefatigable campaigner for political reform in Britain, invested in liberal states because they liked their form of government. For key elites, from Jefferson and Hamilton to Clay and Polk to Fish and Blaine, from Brougham to Palmerston to Chamberlain, from Paredes to Castelar, institutional identity subsumes balance-of-threat and parochial interest.

But do these perceptions actually affect foreign policy and crisis outcomes? Next we turn to the hypotheses on liberal institutions.

Hypotheses on Liberal Institutions

The liberal-institutional hypothesis is:

2.a. *During crises, the stronger liberal institutions are within a state, the more constrained its decision makers will be to follow policies advocated by its liberal elites.*

A realist counterhypothesis is:

2.b. *Decision makers will not be constrained to follow liberal elites in making foreign policy.*

---

41. Relatedly, Bruce Russett and Elizabeth Hanson found that variation in the foreign policy attitudes of U.S. businessmen in the 1970s correlated much more strongly with domestic ideology (e.g., laissez-faire vs. welfare state) than with economic interest. Bruce M. Russett and Elizabeth C. Hanson, *Ideology and Interest: The Foreign Policy Beliefs of American Businessmen* (San Francisco: W. H. Freeman, 1975), chap. 4.

These opposed hypotheses defy definitive testing. Since we cannot read the minds of decision makers—particularly deceased ones—we can never know for certain what truly drove and constrained decision making. Strong evidence exists, however, that liberal institutions influenced decision makers in most of the cases examined here. In some cases the constraint was *actual*: the executive branch wanted to pursue cooperation (or confrontation) with a foreign state but was evidently prevented from doing so by the legislature, elite agitation, or public opinion. In other cases, the constraint was *potential*: decision makers were already predisposed to follow liberal ideology; but had they not been so, they would have had to wage a propaganda battle with determined liberal elites in the legislature, press, etc.

In the *United States*, throughout the period studied the key liberal institutions—free discussion and regular competitive elections—were strongly in place. Therefore we would expect American governments in every case to face strong institutional constraints on war and peace decisions. In 1794–96, George Washington and Alexander Hamilton faced vehement opposition to the Jay Treaty from pro-French Republicans. Only through careful legislative maneuvering and a scare campaign were the Federalists able to pass and implement the treaty. In 1796–98, it is clear that the Federalists were constrained by the Republicans to send three envoys to Paris. There is no doubt that the High Federalists wanted war following the XYZ Affair, and that Adams considered it as well. These men settled for the Quasi-War because they knew Republicans in Congress would block a war declaration.

In 1803–12 Jeffersonians were constrained by Federalist opposition from policies that overtly favored France over Britain. The various economic sanctions against England were imposed against France as well, and it took nearly a decade for the Republicans to declare war against Britain.

In 1845–46, James K. Polk faced a Congressional coalition of anglophilic Whigs and southern Democrats who opposed war over Oregon. Polk was evidently not ready to compromise with Britain in the spring of 1846, but his cabinet, knowing how unpopular war would be, persuaded him to let Congress decide. The same coalition opposed war with Mexico, but was less able to constrain Polk from hostilities. The peace party was weakened by the Matamoros incident—the fact that "American blood [was] shed on American soil" by Mexican soldiers—even though many suspected that Polk had deliberately provoked the incident. Polk also took pains to emphasize in his war message that Mexico was no longer a republic. The Mexican case shows that in the end liberal institutions do not constrain leaders in every case.

[211]

In the *Trent* affair of 1861 Abraham Lincoln probably needed no domestic constraints to submit to England. Had he remained intransigent about handing over the Southern envoys to London, however, Seward, Sumner, and others would doubtless have constrained him.[42] In 1873 President Grant relied on Hamilton Fish to make foreign policy, and Fish clearly treated Spain gingerly for fear that he might precipitate the overthrow of the Spanish Republic. But it is also apparent that Congress would have challenged a presidential call for war against Spain. In 1891–92 Benjamin Harrison was constrained for a time from acting against Chile by Blaine, his secretary of state, who was the leading advocate of republican solidarity in the Western Hemisphere. Yet, even after Harrison overruled Blaine, resistance in Congress and the press to war with a sister republic was strong. In the event, Chile backed down before Congress could act, but there was no strong war party in Congress.

In 1895–96, a strong current of pro-British liberalism welled up that helped move public opinion away from belligerence. That Cleveland's warlike noises toward England gave birth merely to a proposal for a U.S. panel to arbitrate the Anglo-Venezuelan dispute suggests that the president knew he would have had a difficult time declaring war. The United States in 1898 shows how governments in liberal states can be domestically "constrained" to go to war. McKinley was clearly forced by Congressional and public opinion to use force to end Spanish rule in Cuba. McKinley wanted a more accommodating policy, but other elites and the public would not allow it.

In *Britain* during the 1794–1812 period, the government was only semiliberal: the press was not wholly free and elections were not wholly fair. We would thus expect only moderate domestic constraints on war decisions. In 1794–96, reformers agitated in Parliament for leniency toward America but were thwarted by their own lack of leverage and access to information. In 1808 and 1811–12, reformers again pressed the government to stop alienating the Americans through harsh maritime policies. In June 1812 they finally had their way, as the cabinet agreed to stop abusing the U.S. merchant marine; but it came too late, as the U.S. Congress had already declared war.

By 1845–46 Parliament had been reformed to make elections fairer, and civil liberties were greater. We would therefore expect more government responsiveness to liberal pressure. As it happened, for reasons of their own Peel and Aberdeen were determined not to have war with the

---

42. Lincoln's consuming desire to restore the Union may itself have been a product, as he said, of a belief that if the Union failed, liberal democracy in the world was doomed. In that case his realist calculations in 1861 were instrumental to a liberal end. Investigating such a proposition is beyond the scope of this study.

United States over Oregon, and so the substantial liberal pressure for peace was superfluous. In 1861 there was some Radical pressure not to make war over the *Trent* affair, but prior to the Emancipation Proclamation the pressure was not great enough to constrain the Palmerston government from delivering an ultimatum. In the fall of 1862, however, Palmerston himself admitted that intervention in the Civil War would be extremely unpopular now that the Union had made abolition its cause. By 1863 the Confederacy was so unpopular that Russell bent English law and stopped delivery of ironclad ships to the South. In 1895–96 Salisbury yielded to the cabinet, which favored giving in to the Americans on Venezuela. The dominant force here was Joseph Chamberlain, a liberal who admired U.S. institutions. Even without Chamberlain's influence in the cabinet, war would have been prohibitively unpopular.

In *France*, the Directory had jettisoned liberal institutions by 1798. Whatever pro-American sentiment remained in France was impotent.

In *Mexico* the political system was close to chaotic in 1845–46. Herrera was constrained, but by the threat of military insurrection rather than by liberal institutions. Paredes claimed to be bound by the 1836 Constitution, but he in fact declared war unilaterally.

In *Spain*, during the *Virginius* crisis in 1873, there was open opposition in the Cortes to war with the United States, Spain's sister republic. Castelar himself also sought peace, and so this constraint was superfluous. By 1898, under the restored monarchy, discussion was relatively free but elections were rigged; we would expect little constraint on the Sagasta government's decision making. As it happened, Sagasta and the queen regent were constrained toward belligerence out of fear of revolution.

In *Chile* the state was liberal; but because of the recent civil war the pro-American Balmacedists were shut out of power. As recounted above, what information is extant shows that Chilean elites were anti-American. Montt and Pereira agreed to the American conditions apparently not because they feared domestic pro-Americans, but because they feared U.S. naval might.

The findings are summarized in Table 4. My argument expects that leaders of liberal states will be highly constrained; leaders of illiberal states, only weakly so; and leaders of semiliberal states, moderately so. Cases 1, 3, 7, 12, 18, and 19 show strong institutional constraints in liberal states. Case 6 shows moderate constraints in a semiliberal state. Cases 4 and 10 show weak constraints in illiberal states. The other cases fall into two groups. First are those cases marked "potential," where a strong elite agitated for its preferred policy but the government already favored and pursued that same policy. In such cases no constraint was necessary. Second are those cases where predictions were moderately or seriously wrong. The most serious is the case of the Chileans in 1891–92.

Although liberal institutions often constrain leaders, they do not guarantee peace. First, if elites perceive the other state as illiberal, governments may be constrained (or goaded) to declare war, as happened in both the United States and Spain in 1898. Second, there are times when the realist argument is correct, when governments overcome peace agitation. Such ultimately happened in the United States in 1812, when after years of restraint Republicans finally overwhelmed Federalists and declared war against England; and it happened again in 1846, when Polk put U.S. troops in harm's way and triggered the Matamoros incident, thereby making Congress an offer to declare war that it could not refuse. In both of these cases the government had to temper its hostility to the foreign power because of liberal opposition, but eventually the government won. The checks and balances envisaged by liberalism sometimes check the quest for peace or are unbalanced by a determined executive.

Moreover, the "potential" cells in Table 4 do not provide conclusive evidence for the liberal-institutional hypothesis, because realism can still claim that government *could have* overcome any opposition. For example, the British and American governments, realism says, could have talked their publics into war in 1896.[43] Such counterfactuals are impossible to falsify, but evidence from the other cases give credibility to my claims about "potential" cases. Liberal elites with institutional

Table 4 Hypotheses on Institutional Constraints: Results

	Case	How liberal?	Degree of constraint		Case	How liberal?	Degree of constraint
Jay Treaty	1 U.S.	liberal	strong	Civil War	11 U.S.	liberal	(potential)
	2 G.B.	semiliberal	weak		12 G.B.	liberal	strong
Quasi-War	3 U.S.	liberal	strong	*Virginius*	13 U.S.	liberal	(potential)
	4 Fr.	illiberal	weak		14 Sp.	illiberal	(potential)
War	5 U.S.	liberal	moderate	*Baltimore*	15 U.S.	liberal	(potential)
of 1812	6 G.B.	semiliberal	moderate		16 Chile	liberal	weak
Oregon	7 U.S.	liberal	strong	Venezuela	17 U.S.	liberal	(potential)
	8 G.B.	liberal	(potential)		18 G.B.	liberal	strong
Mexico	9 U.S.	liberal	moderate	Sp-Am	19 U.S	liberal	strong
	10 Mex.	illiberal	weak	War	20 Sp.	semi-liberal	strong

43. Layne, "Kant or Cant," 178–79.

identities are a determined lot. Because of their agitation, in most cases the government of a liberal state cannot bend public opinion to its will.

The effects of liberalism on the outbreak of war and the maintenance of peace are complex. American foreign relations from the 1790s through the turn of the twentieth century do show that institutional identity, liberal ideology, and domestic institutions affect international security. But they also show that at times liberalism is trumped by other factors, particularly material threats. In the final chapter I suggest the conditions under which liberalism is superseded. I also extend the analysis to two key current non-Western dyads.

[7]

Implications and Conclusions

This analysis of liberalism carries implications for policy makers and scholars. I begin by extending the analysis to two important non-Western bilateral relationships: Japan and South Korea, and India and Pakistan. I argue that the dynamics in these relationships are similar to those of the Western states analyzed in Chapters 3–6, although, particularly in the Indo-Pakistani case, harmonious relations are by no means guaranteed. I then discuss implications of my general argument for foreign policy makers in liberal states today and for students of international relations.

For liberalism as defined in this book to have no causal effect on international security, only one of two skeptical propositions need be true:

1. Liberals' perceptions of other states' liberalism or illiberalism are epiphenomenal.
2. Liberals' positions on war and peace do not constrain war decision makers.

I have presented strong evidence that in many cases both of these skeptical propositions are false. I have shown that liberals often—perhaps usually—perceive foreign states as liberal or illiberal based on a priori judgments of those states' internal institutions and practices. I have shown that decision makers in liberal states are constrained during crises to follow this ideology. These findings mean that liberalism is a force in international security. What does this proposition imply about our fin-de-siècle world? If liberalism affects war and peace, what should we expect the nature of future international relationships to be? In particular, should non-Western liberal states have internal dynamics and foreign policies similar to those of the Western states in Part II? In the next section I probe the plausibility of my argument in two important non-Western bilateral relationships: Japan and South Korea, and India and Pakistan. Recent events confirm that liberal elites in Japan and India, like their counterparts in the West, have strong institutional identities and that these identities shape threat perceptions and foreign policies. These two cases are especially difficult for a theory that predicts a pacifying effect for liberalism. Both pairs of states have deep mutual historical and cultural or religious animosities. Signs that liberalism can efface or submerge such animosities would be evidence that deep cultural differences do not inevitably lead to conflict.[1] India and Pakistan in addition both claim sovereignty over the state of Jammu and Kashmir, and both have nuclear weapons. Evidence that liberalism can overcome such material bases for conflict would further undermine materialist realism.

Two Current Cases

Japan and South Korea

A long history of animosity between these two countries would suggest that relations could be rocky in the medium term. In particular, Japanese colonization of Korea between 1905 and 1945, culminating in the wartime Japanese attempt to wipe out Korean language, culture, and religion, left a bitter legacy. As of the mid-1990s Japanese films and music albums were still banned in South Korea. The Cold War brought these nations toward peace with each other, as they found themselves both allied with the United States and threatened by the Soviet Union, China, and North Korea. The demise of the Soviet Union, the stupendous growth of the South Korean economy since the 1960s, economic reform and imminent leadership change in China, and the prospect of the unification of the two Koreas, however, have created uncertainty. A security rivalry is highly unlikely as long as U.S. troops remain in both countries, but bilateral relations could still be quite chilly.[2]

The liberalization of both nations, however, suggests that the rivalry could be a friendly one, like those of post-1945 Western Europe and North America. Japan's 1947 constitution is a highly liberal document, vesting sovereignty in the citizens rather than the emperor. The citizens elect both houses of parliament, and parliament chooses the cabinet. Freedoms of the press, speech, and religion are protected.[3] That the

1. Samuel P. Huntington, *The Clash of Civilizations and the Remaking of World Order* (New York: Simon and Schuster, 1996). Huntington argues that Korea is part of Sinic civilization and that Japan constitutes its own civilization.

2. For a comprehensive treatment of this question, see Victor D. Cha, "Alignment despite Antagonism: Japan and Korea as Quasi-Allies" (Ph.D. diss., Columbia University, 1994).

3. T. J. Pempel, "Prerequisites for Democracy: Political and Social Institutions," in Takeshi Ishida and Ellis S. Krauss, eds., *Democracy in Japan* (Pittsburgh: University of Pittsburgh Press, 1989), 19–23.

Liberal Democratic Party (LDP) held office without interruption from 1955 to 1992 casts some doubt on the leverage held by voters over governmental decision makers, but the electoral machinery has been in place the entire period and elections have been fair.

South Korea had more or less authoritarian governments from the end of the Korean War until the late 1980s, when the liberal movement became irresistible. In 1988, voters elected General Roh Tae Woo president in a free and fair election but denied his party a majority in the National Assembly then and in March 1992. The ruling party nominated Kim Young Sam, a former dissident and opposition party leader, as its candidate for the December 1992 presidential election, and Roh resigned and appointed a caretaker cabinet to ensure elections were fair. Kim won the election promising a "New Korea" reform program to consolidate democracy.[4]

The argument of this book does not let us prophesy the precise future of relations between a liberal Japan and a liberal South Korea. It does offer us some indicators as to whether continuing liberalism will incline them toward peace. Among these, elite perceptions of the other nation are extremely important. If Japanese in government, the media, universities, business, and banking view South Korea as a fellow liberal state, they will be predisposed to give Korea the benefit of the doubt in any disputes. Do Japanese liberals become more or less friendly toward Korea based on how liberal Korea is internally? Have events in Korea since 1988, especially the election of Kim in 1992, shifted Japanese opinions of Korea? There is strong evidence that they did so.

Well before the late 1980s, Japanese-Korean relations were affected by authoritarianism within South Korea. In 1973, for example, the government's kidnapping of Kim Dae Jung, a leading dissident, darkened Japanese perceptions of South Korea. As Okonogi Masao writes, "There emerged a tendency among Japanese to try to interpret Korean politics in terms of the perspective of democracy vs. dictatorship." Writing in 1985, Okonogi predicted that the future tone of relations would partly hinge on whether Korea liberalizes:

Another reason for political friction originates from the inherently different nature of two political systems in Japan and South Korea. . . . [S]ome people in Japan have come to maintain a special feeling of the authoritarian tendency in politics in South Korea since the Kim Dae Jung case. Of course this kind of feeling in Japan will disappear in relation to the political developments in South Korea. However, if the ROK government can not succeed in delivering its pledge to transfer power peacefully in 1988 according to its constitutional procedure, or if it would fail to maintain po-

4. Victor D. Cha, "Politics and Democracy under the Kim Young Sam Government," *Asian Survey* 23 (September 1993), 849–51.

litical stability before 1988, it might be unavoidable that the unfavorable feeling of some Japanese will, more or less, arise once again.[5]

More obliquely, the Korean scholar Ahn Byung-joon made a similar point: "From the Japanese point of view . . . the very nature of political and economic development in Korea engenders ambivalence and sometimes poses challenges. . . . To a large extent, major issues in Korean-Japanese relations are created by the interaction between the two different political and economic systems."[6]

The Korean election of 1988 impressed Japanese intellectuals. Kobayashi Keiji predicted shortly after Roh's victory that the Japanese people would be more inclined to reach out to Koreans. "Japanese found it distasteful to deal with South Korea when it was an authoritarian state, but now that the presidential election has signaled a turn toward democracy, the two peoples can reach out to each other," Kobayashi wrote, adding that Japanese ought to acquaint themselves with their nation's past mistreatment of Korea in order to understand contemporary Korean animosity.[7]

Kim Young Sam's election in December 1992 was greeted with optimism by liberal Japanese elites. Okonogi commented:

> The coming to office of the first civilian president in 32 years also provides Japan with a chance to improve relations with South Korea. In Japan Kim Young-sam is known as a fighter for democracy, but actually he is much more than that. . . .
>
> No doubt his stance toward Japan will take on a different bent from that taken by his military-minded predecessors. Unlike Chun and Roh, he will not be standing on principle and pressing Japan forcefully for economic aid and for apologies for its past transgressions. He is more likely to foster friendly relations and to pursue the South's real interests while soothing nationalist sentiments at home.[8]

The *Yomiuri Shimbun*, Japan's largest daily, noted that the Japanese government would now seek "future-oriented ties" with South Korea, adding that "Kim is South Korea's first civilian president, ending 32 years of rule by regimes dominated by the military and former generals."[9]

5. Okonogi Masao, "A Japanese Perspective on Korea-Japan Relations," in Chung Chi-Wee et al., eds., *Korea and Japan in World Politics* (Seoul: Korean Association of International Relations, 1985), 26, 36.

6. Ahn Byung-joon, "Political and Economic Development in Korea and Korea-Japan Relations," in Chung et al., *Korea and Japan,* 68.

7. Kobayashi Keiji, "A Muted Welcome for Roh," *Japan Quarterly* 35 (April-June 1988), 206.

8. Okonogi Masao, "Whither South Korea under Kim Young-sam?" *Japan Echo* 20 (Summer 1993), 66; reprinted from *Gaiko Forum* (February 1993), 4–9.

9. "Govt. Seeks 'Future-Oriented Ties' with ROK," *Daily Yomiuri,* 26 February 1993.

A November 1993 summit meeting between Hosokawa and Kim raised the hopes of the editors of the *Yomiuri Shimbun.* "Having the same sense of values for freedom, democracy and the market economy, the two nations are required to play a role in constructing a new order in the region," the newspaper wrote.[10] Following a March 1994 summit Kim opened a press conference by saying, "Prime Minister Hosokawa and I completely agreed that since we share the values of liberal democracy and market economics we must join forces to play a leading role in shaping the Asia-Pacific age."[11]

It is difficult to tell whether Korean liberalization has truly dampened the potential for conflict between the two nations. There have been unprecedentedly friendly gestures from both sides. During Roh's May 1990 visit to Tokyo, both Emperor Akihito and Prime Minister Kaifu Toshiki offered fuller apologies for Japanese treatment of Korea during the 1910–45 occupation than Japanese leaders had ever offered. Korea's hardships, said the emperor, "were brought about by my country," for which he felt deepest regret.[12] Japan also officially admitted to having forced Korean women into prostitution during the war (the so-called "comfort women"). While as late as February 1993 Kim stated that the Korean public was still not satisfied with Japanese apologies,[13] Korean elites were showing signs of forgiveness. In August 1993 Han Sung Joo, the foreign minister, "discounted a widely held fear in his country—that Japan may grow into a military giant—and expressed his substantial support for Japan's joining the UN Security Council as a permanent member."[14] The next month a joint statement by young legislators in the two countries pledged to form a committee to map out positive relations between the two countries.[15] And in February 1994 Gong Ro Myong, the ambassador to Japan, called for an end to the Korean ban on Japanese cultural imports.[16]

Still, these are only encouraging indicators, not proofs that liberal Korea and liberal Japan can never go to war with one another. There still lingers in each country popular animosity toward the other—more precisely, Korean resentment toward Japan and Japanese condescension toward Korea. Korean elites are moving ahead of large segments

10. *Daily Yomiuri,* 6 November 1993.
11. "President Kim Outlines His Summit Goals in Beijing and Tokyo Press Conferences," *Korea Update,* 4 April 1994, 5.
12. "It Helps to Say You're Sorry," *Economist,* 26 May 1990, 34.
13. Takuji Kawada, "Kim Says Apology Sought More than Compensation," *Daily Yomiuri,* 22 February 1993.
14. "Han Sees No Reason to Fear Japan," ibid., 28 August 1993.
15. "S. Korean, Japanese Legislators Outline New Cooperation," ibid., 4 September 1993.
16. "Japan Culture Proposal Rocks S. Korea," ibid., 4 February 1994.

of popular opinion in putting the past behind them and look to liberal principles in the future;[17] Gong's proposal, for example, shocked the Korean public and was repudiated by Han Sung Joo. Illiberal practices in Japan itself feed the animosity. Even third-generation ethnic Koreans in Japan are denied citizenship, and must be fingerprinted.[18]

This discrimination against Koreans points to a more fundamental question: Is Japan a liberal country, in the Lockean sense used in this study? In particular, are the Japanese attached to the ideas of the fundamental similarity of and liberty for all individuals? Or are they more communitarian, seeing themselves primarily as members of society rather than as individuals, and as essentially different from all other peoples?[19] This book has used institutional criteria to identify liberal states, but there may be deeper sociological factors that make such a criteria problematic in the case of Japan.

I shall not attempt to answer the question here, but there is much evidence that Japan is not a Lockean society. The Japanese had difficulty with Western categories when they were first introduced to Japan in the nineteenth century. In 1869 Fukuzawa Yukichi published *Seiyo Jijo* (Situation in the West), which included a translation of the U.S. Declaration of Independence. The Japanese word for "freedom" or "liberty," *jiyu*, however, is a pejorative term connoting selfishness, and Fukuzawa was at pains to explain that *jiyu* was not egoistic as used by Jefferson. Similarly, in translating J. S. Mill's *On Liberty*, Nakamura Masanao could not understand the distinction between state and society. He thus misunderstood Mill's worry about the tyranny of the majority, reading it as state rather than societal despotism.[20]

On the other hand, many societies Westerners now regard as liberal were once thought outside the liberal camp. Germany is the most obvious example of a liberal nation that once was seen by all, including many of its own citizens, as a non-Western, illiberal country, and indeed openly fought the liberal world. Furthermore, it is not difficult to find signs that any country, including the United States, is not Lockean all the way down. American racism, for example, has shown that the normative notion that all individuals are essentially the same has not always filtered into practical behavior. The question of Japanese liberalism merits further study.

17. I am grateful to Kim Sunhyuk for his insights on the differences between elite and mass South Korean opinions of Japan.

18. Pempel, "Prerequisites for Democracy," 25–26. An excellent source on Japanese treatment of ethnic Koreans is Lee Changsoo and George De Vos, eds., *Koreans in Japan: Ethnic Conflict and Accommodation* (Berkeley: University of California Press, 1981).

19. The same question could fairly be asked about Korea.

20. Ishida Takeshi, *Japanese Political Culture* (New Brunswick N.J.: Transaction Books, 1983), 70–71.

India and Pakistan

A much more dangerous relationship is that between these two South Asian powers. Since the 1947 partition separating them, India and Pakistan have fought three wars and come close to several more. Territorial disputes, in particular over the Indian-governed, Muslim-majority state of Jammu and Kashmir, threaten to escalate into military confrontations. Indians hold Pakistan partly responsible for the rise in Islamic fundamentalism and other separatist movements within India itself. That both states have nuclear capabilities makes the question of peace especially vital.[21]

Liberalism gained a foothold in India in the nineteenth century, as intellectuals such as Gopal Krishna Gokhale and Mahadev Govind Ranade sought to rationalize and modernize Indian society in hopes of preparing it for independence under liberal government.[22] India's first president, Jawaharlal Nehru, was a committed liberal, and for most of its years of independence from Great Britain India has had a liberal political system.[23] The constitution of 1950 guarantees freedoms of speech, expression, assembly, religion, and movement. It mandates governmental elections every five years and holds the government accountable to the legislature rather than the president.[24] Like all liberal states it has deviated from liberal practice many times. For several years following the 1962 war with China, India was under a state of emergency in which habeas corpus was limited; in 1976–77 Indira Gandhi suspended key civil rights and ruled as an authoritarian. For most years of its existence, however, India has upheld liberal political practices.[25] India is a land of staggering diversity, but it clearly has an elite that favors political liberalism both within India and elsewhere. Organs such as the *Times of India* and *India Today* are voices for liberal institutions at home and abroad.

21. For an inquiry of the effects of democratization on Indo-Pakistani relations that looks at specific crises, see Sumit Ganguly, "War and Conflict between India and Pakistan: Revisiting the Pacifying Power of Democracy," in Miriam Fendius Elman, ed., *Paths to Peace: Is Democracy the Answer?* (Cambridge: MIT Press, 1997).

22. See the essays in S. P. Aiyar, *Modernization of Traditional Society* (Delhi: Macmillan India, 1973), especially "Liberalism and the Modernization of India: An Interpretation," 26–47.

23. See Nehru, *Toward Freedom: The Autobiography of Jawaharlal Nehru* (New York: John Day Co., 1941). I thank Sumit Ganguly for pointing out this source to me, and for comments on this entire section.

24. Ganguly, "India and Pakistan"; M. V. Pylee, *Constitutional Government in India* (Bombay: Asia Publishing House, 1977), 230, 278–80, 364, 394–97.

25. India has generally practiced socialist rather than liberal or free-market economics, and some states have been and are still governed by communists. However, the emphasis in this book is on political liberalism.

Though rising from the same roots, Pakistan has less claim to being a liberal state. Its political history is turbulent, with periods of partial liberalization invariably interrupted by spasms of military authoritarianism and Islamicization. The Islamic Republic of Pakistan was born with a Constituent Assembly elected by perhaps 15 percent of the population. Following a state of emergency in 1954, a new Assembly promulgated a constitution with a president as head of government. But in October 1958 General Ayub Khan dismissed the Assembly and president and declared martial law. Ayub Khan ruled a so-called "tutelary democracy" until March 1969, when public demonstrations led him to resign. Hopes were high for democracy, but Ayub's replacement, General Agha Mohammed Yahya Khan, declared martial law and proclaimed himself president. Yahya Khan finally held elections in December 1970, but the new Constituent Assembly never met: a dispute between the Awami League of East Pakistan, which gained a majority, and the People's Party of Pakistan (PPP), which won in West Pakistan, led to civil war in the east. The Pakistani army violently suppressed Awami supporters, India invaded, and in December 1971 East Pakistan became independent Bangladesh.[26]

The rump state of Pakistan installed Zulfikar Ali Bhutto, leader of the PPP, as president. The National Assembly, elected by universal suffrage in 1972, enacted a parliamentary constitution, and Bhutto became prime minister. Bhutto promised a social democracy but also saw to it that the constitution gave the prime minister dominance over the legislature. When Bhutto rigged elections in March 1977, General Zia ul-Haq seized power, declared martial law, and arrested and eventually executed Bhutto. Zia declared himself president and then strengthened the power of that office in 1985 with the eighth amendment to the 1973 constitution, giving the president the power to dismiss the prime minister. Zia ruled until his mysterious death in an airplane crash in August 1988.[27]

At that point Ghulam Ishaq Khan, an army general and chairman of the Senate, was sworn in as acting president. Ishaq Khan called for elections in November. In a clean election the PPP, now headed by Bhutto's daughter Benazir, won a plurality of seats and was able to form a government. Prime Minister Benazir Bhutto clearly had a liberal program in mind for Pakistan. But Ishaq Khan dismissed her government in August 1990 for corruption. In the tainted elections of October 1990 the PPP lost dozens of seats, and the Islami Jamhoori Ittehad (IJI, or the Islamic Democratic Alliance), created by the army to undermine Bhutto, formed

26. Robert LaPorte, Jr., "Another Try at Democracy," in J. Henry Korson, ed., *Contemporary Problems of Pakistan* (Boulder: Westview, 1993), 171–76.

27. Ibid., 176–81.

a government under Mian Nawaz Sharif. Nawaz Sharif liberalized the economy, privatizing banks and firms that had been nationalized under Z. A. Bhutto. But he himself was dismissed for corruption by Ishaq Khan in April 1993. In a stunning decision a month later the Supreme Court declared Ishaq Khan's action unconstitutional, and Nawaz Sharif took office again.[28] More recently, Benazir Bhutto has become prime minister again, and then been ousted and replaced again by Nawaz Sharif.[29]

Have these oscillations in Pakistani politics affected relations with India? More precisely, do Indian liberals trust Pakistan more when it is governed by civilians? Or do Indian perceptions of Pakistan respond only to power politics or economic interest? And have perceptions made a difference in actual bilateral relations?

It is clear that Indian liberals talk as though they strongly prefer dealing with a liberal Pakistan. Following the defeat of Pakistan in 1971 and the accession of Z. A. Bhutto, the *Times of India* opined, "The root cause of the present crisis in Pakistan lies in the way in which over two decades of despotic and military regimes have choked the springs of democratic life in this country." Indira Gandhi, then India's premier, had already made a similar diagnosis.[30] Rhetorically, Bhutto was extremely anti-Indian at first, yet he eagerly sought to make peace with India, meeting with I. Gandhi only six months after Pakistan's humiliating 1971 defeat and loss of its eastern half. In the Simla accords, the two nations agreed to respect one another's territorial integrity, meaning Pakistan accepted Indian control of Kashmir. In August 1973 Gandhi congratulated Bhutto on enactment of the new liberal constitution: "It is my earnest hope," Gandhi wrote Bhutto, "that with a vigorous and responsive parliamentary system of government functioning in the countries of this sub-continent, the problems that we face in common will be resolved through goodwill and discussion, and that we should be able to lighten the burden of our people."[31]

Zia, after overthrowing Bhutto, attempted to keep relations with India stable. Interestingly, however, Indian liberals welcomed the end of his rule and the coming of elections in November 1988. Prime Minister Rajiv Gandhi himself publicly stated the hope that an elected civilian government in Pakistan would lead to better Indo-Pakistani relations.[32] The *Times of India* heralded Benazir Bhutto's accession to power as "not merely a change of government . . . [but] a change of regime."

28. Ibid., 181–86.
29. Ahmed Rashid, "State of Strife: Bhutto's Rival Calls for Military to Dismiss Her," *Far Eastern Economic Review,* 6 October 1994, 20.
30. "Bhutto Swears to Avenge Defeat at Hands of India" and "Enter Mr. Bhutto," *Times of India* (Bombay), 21 December 1971.
31. "PM's Message to Bhutto," ibid., 14 August 1973.
32. "PM Hails Elected Govt in Pak," ibid., 2 December 1988.

While cautious about Benazir's attitude toward India, the newspaper declared, "Even so the advent of a democratic set-up in Pakistan offers a good opportunity for the two countries to review their ties."[33] Writers for *India Today* magazine could hardly contain their enthusiasm for Benazir. "Now, as she stands poised to become the youngest leader of any democratic country, it is perhaps fitting that she should be the one to guide Pakistan on its first hesitant steps towards a new era of hope and transition," wrote one. Another noted that Benazir and Rajiv were both "educated abroad, are distinctly western in their outlook. . . . A more liberal regime in Islamabad will certainly mean better relations with India, but it would be unrealistic to expect dramatic changes overnight, cautions a diplomatic observer."[34]

Significantly, most lingering Indian skepticism about Pakistan stemmed from the perception that the military still largely controlled politics in Islamabad. In December *India Today* cautioned, "Lacking the majority to change Zia's constitution Benazir has to compromise with the army. Ruthless generals have dominated Pakistani politics and the army may not retreat to the barracks quietly."[35] One writer warned, "A little democracy—like a little learning—is a dangerous thing. . . . The presence of the big brother, the army, will be an inhibiting factor, but, even within the restrictions of an army-supervised polity, we might see powerful exuberance having its say."[36] Another noted, "Her hope may be that she will eventually consolidate enough power to work out a different equation with the military, and become the prime minister that she wants to be. This is unlikely to happen any time soon, if ever. In the meantime, India and the rest of the world will have to deal with Benazir Bhutto with the knowledge that she has Gen. Beg [chief of the army staff] breathing down her neck."[37] Indian pundits certainly wrote as if they believed Pakistan's form of government made a difference. They were simply not sure if Benazir Bhutto's election marked a decisive change.

Bearing out their hope was the fact that Indo-Pakistani relations did improve in the first part of Bhutto's administration. Prime Minister Rajiv Gandhi wrote Bhutto a personal letter saying, "The news of your assumption of office as prime minister of Pakistan has been warmly greeted and widely welcomed throughout India."[38] In December Gandhi

33. "Benazir's Pakistan," ibid., 3 December 1988.

34. Dilip Bobb, "Woman of Substance," *India Today*, 15 December 1988, 48–49; M. Rahman, "The New Challenge," ibid., 47.

35. *India Today*, 31 December 1988, 86.

36. S. Nihal Singh, "Democracy in Pakistan: Army Still Rules the Roost," *Times of India* (Bombay), 6 December 1988.

37. Dilip Mukerjee, "Benazir Will Have to Ride in Tandem with Gen. Beg," *Times of India*, 6 December 1988.

38. Salamat Ali, "A Warm Reception," *Far Eastern Economic Review*, 22 December 1988, 22.

traveled to Islamabad for the annual South Asian Association for Regional Cooperation (SAARC) meeting, the first visit by an Indian premier to Pakistan since 1960. The two government heads met several times privately, agreeing not to attack each other's nuclear facilities and to cooperate on cultural matters.[39] When the two met again in Paris for France's July 1989 bicentennial, Gandhi stated, "I feel that with Prime Minister Benazir Bhutto we have for the first time in eleven and a half years an opportunity to solve our problems. We found it very difficult to deal with the military dictatorships."[40] Gandhi again went to Islamabad to meet with Bhutto; the results of the summit were disappointing, as agreements on nuclear matters and Kashmir eluded them. The *Times of India* guardedly noted, "Even so, India favours going ahead in good faith though doubts persist in New Delhi about the fledgling democratic government's ability to deliver on its promises."[41]

Relations soon worsened, as V. P. Singh replaced Gandhi as premier and took a hawkish line on Kashmir. Bhutto was hawkish in return. Yet Ishaq Khan's dismissal of Bhutto in August 1990 was viewed with alarm in India. In an editorial titled "Back to the Brink," the *Times of India* wrote: "The events leading to the dismissal of Ms Bhutto can only confirm India's historical fears about Pakistan—viz. that it can justify its existence only insofar as it espouses religious fundamentalism and at best a 'militarised' democracy at home and promotes hostility to secular India abroad. The dramatic turn of events in Islamabad must coax New Delhi to step up its vigilance on the border and to spare not the slightest effort to safeguard communal harmony in the country."[42] With the reassertion of military authority, liberal India's trust of Pakistan receded. Still, Ishaq Khan was true to his word and held elections in October. His dismissal of Nawaz Sharif in April 1993, followed by the Supreme Court's declaration that the action was unconstitutional, perplexed Indian liberals. The resurrected Nawaz Sharif told Indian journalist Shekhar Gupta that he now planned to have the eighth amendment repealed, thus removing the president's power to dismiss the government. "India and Pakistan should fight only in the field of economy," the prime minister said. Gupta then said, "But your sincerity is taken with scepticism in India because of the feeling that Pakistan's prime minister does not have real powers, so what is the point of talking to him?" Nawaz Sharif's replied, "For that also we have to change the Constitution here."[43] Again, Indian liberals ascribed great impor-

---

39. Salamat Ali, "A Hint of Hope," ibid., 12 January 1989, 10–11.

40. Christina Lamb, *Waiting for Allah: Pakistan's Struggle for Democracy* (London: Hamish Hamilton, 1991), 269.

41. "Back from Islamabad," *Times of India* (Bombay), 18 July 1989.

42. "Back to the Brink," ibid., 7 August 1990.

43. "I'll Reform the Constitution," *India Today*, 30 June 1993, 34–35.

tance to how liberal Pakistan's internal organization was, especially its constitution.

On the whole, despite some progress in Pakistan's political system, Indo-Pakistani relations are still dangerous. The eighth amendment to the Pakistani constitution was repealed only as this book went to press.[44] The questions of Kashmir, Islamic fundamentalism, and nuclear policies remain unsettled. Benazir Bhutto and Nawaz Sharif have not only strayed rather far from liberalism within Pakistan but have also sounded more hostile toward India as well. The hostility cannot solely be attributed to pressure from Pakistan's generals. In each country, hawkishness toward the other is popular with large portions of the electorate. This book has stressed that liberal foreign policy is spearheaded by liberal elites. In both countries, those elites have had a difficult time liberalizing what are in many ways still very traditional societies. The parliamentary plurality that the Bharatiya Janata Party, a Hindu nationalist party, gained in the Indian elections of May 1996 is a reminder that not all Indian elites, much less citizens, retain a secular liberal vision for their country.

Still, it is clear that Indian liberals do believe that it matters who is in power in Pakistan and how they got there. Indian perceptions of Pakistan's trustworthiness are in large part driven by how liberal Pakistan's governmental system is. Liberalism evidently operates in this relationship, however much it must compete with other forces. Thus we should expect that further liberalization in Pakistan would lead to increased trust between the two nations. Further liberalization, however, is somewhat doubtful at the time of this writing.

In conclusion, the current cases of Japan and South Korea and of India and Pakistan illustrate why the proposition that there is a clearly delineable liberal zone of peace is problematic. Whether these states become friends depends not simply on whether their institutions match the supposedly detached scholar's liberal list, but also on whether liberals in each state perceive the other state as liberal. These perceptions respond to real constitutional events, but they always have an unpredictable quality to them. At the same time, these cases show that liberalism does operate outside the Western world from which it sprang. East and South Asian liberals talk and act as though it matters to them whether the countries with which they deal are liberal. Their relations improve, however haltingly, when they liberalize. While both these relationships, especially the Indo-Pakistani one, are still far from harmonious, evidently liberalism has at times provided them with some space for trust.

44. John F. Burns, "Pakistan Acts to Cut Power of President," *New York Times*, 2 April 1997.

That liberalism matters implies that the United States and its liberal-democratic allies should continue to enjoy pacific relations and encourage (but not enforce) liberalization around the world. Liberal states tend to believe that they have common interests, and they are therefore unusually likely to maintain cooperative relations.

It does not imply, however, that liberal policy makers can control world politics. The proposition that liberal democracies do not wage war against one another has become a truism for many. For the United States and the United Nations in the 1990s, liberal peace is taken as a law upon which foreign policy and conflict resolution may be based. The insistence that torn countries will be mended if only their people pick their own rulers is a hallmark of U.S. foreign policy.

Yet, this study shows that free and fair elections alone are no guarantor of peace. Each liberal state must contain elites who perceive the other states as liberal. If they do not, then public leverage over foreign policy could actually make war more likely.[45] Furthermore, in some countries with liberal institutions there may not be a strong enough liberal elite to move foreign (or domestic) policy in a liberal direction. In fact, illiberals may exploit free and fair elections to gain power and impose an illiberal regime. In 1992 the people of Algeria were poised to elect a fundamentalist Islamic government freely and fairly. Many in the liberal West silently breathed a sigh of relief when the Algerian military stepped in to prevent the elections. The German elections of 1933 cast a long shadow.

I have also shown how liberalism can cut both ways in a crisis. If the foreign country is already perceived as liberal, liberal ideology can give actors the time needed to come to a peaceful settlement of the dispute. If the foreign country is perceived as illiberal, however, the same ideology can cheat actors of that time. Liberals who view another country as illiberal may be overly suspicious of that country and bring on a war that does not serve their ends. In 1812 American Republicans were driven by fear of a principle of government that in hindsight looks to us relatively benign, at least as practiced in Britain at the time. No doubt many illiberal governments do pose special threats to liberal states—even paranoids, as Freud said, have enemies—but policy makers in liberal states should be aware of their ideological biases in dealing with illiberal states. Furthermore, particular varieties of liberal ideology may actually lead toward expansion and aggression. Jacksonian Americans

45. See Edward D. Mansfield and Jack Snyder, "Democratization and the Danger of War," in Michael E. Brown, Sean M. Lynn-Jones, and Steven E. Miller, eds., *Debating the Democratic Peace* (Cambridge: MIT Press, 1996), 301–34.

were convinced that individual liberty required an agrarian society, which in turn required territory that belonged to Britain and Mexico.

This book also shows that liberal ideology itself can sometimes be altered or overridden by other factors. If I am convinced that someone is my friend, then his approaching me with a gun will not alarm me; but if he points it at me and begins to pull the trigger, I will probably quickly abandon my belief that he is my friend. Policy makers who pin their hopes for peace on solidarity between liberal states should keep in mind that liberals who regard a foreign state as liberal may change their minds under dire enough circumstances. Thus for example liberal statesmen should not take the supposed guarantee of liberal peace as permission to exploit fellow liberal states with impunity, believing those states will never attack them militarily. Serious hostile gestures, particularly threats to sovereign territory, can cause liberals to perceive the gesturing state as illiberal and an enemy.

Taken together, these warnings are not sufficient to cancel out the pacifying effects of liberalism. The United States and other liberal states should continue to work for liberalization in other countries. They cannot simply assume, however, that states with the correct set of institutions will automatically launch into perpetual peace with one another.[46]

IMPLICATIONS FOR INTERNATIONAL RELATIONS THEORY

As explained at the start of this book, I have not set out to propose a purely idealist theory of liberal peace, that is, one that treats material phenomena as irrelevant. Matter exists whether we believe it or not. Rather, I have agreed with those who seek to expand the repertory of ideas that can credibly be said to affect international relations. As I argued in Chapter 1, the premise that structures and ideas can be separated in international relations has hindered our understanding of liberal peace. In international relations, as in all social activity, structures— those factors that constrain and provide opportunities for action—are nearly always constituted in part by ideas. A state is more than simply physical territory, wealth and weapons more than paper or metal. A state is territory given particular meaning by people living on and outside of it.

The real issue, then, is not whether ideas matter, but which ideas matter under what conditions. This book has demonstrated that liberal

46. For a masterful treatment of American efforts, successful and otherwise, to export liberal democracy in the twentieth century, see Tony Smith, *America's Mission: The United States and the Worldwide Struggle for Democracy in the Twentieth Century* (Princeton: Princeton University Press, 1994).

people interpret structures such as states, wealth, and weapons in distinctive ways. A liberal state is good, its weapons benign, its wealth an opportunity for mutual gain. An illiberal state is bad, its weapons malign, its wealth a potential source of corruption. The meanings liberals attach to various structures affect their actions. During crises, they are likely to work for accommodation if they regard the foreign states as liberal, but will be confrontational otherwise. For international relations theory, this means not that a state's gross domestic product, population, warship tonnage, or nuclear warheads are inconsequential, but that their consequences are mediated by subjects' presuppositions.

Still, in most cases in this study it is undeniable that liberal institutional identity was trumped for at least some actors. Some favored policies according to parochial interest, as when the U.S. Navy wanted to confront the Chilean Republic in 1891–92. And in some cases an obvious threat to security evidently caused liberals to change their perceptions of a state once thought liberal, as when many Mexican liberals reversed their attitudes toward the United States following U.S. annexation of Texas.

These findings do not mean that at some point ideas drop out and the brute data of material facts take over. Rather, the idea that institutional identity is unimportant can come to predominate. Nor is it the case that ideas about self-preservation and prosperity will always win out and may thus be considered a rational baseline. Thucydides, considered by many the father of political realism, relates a story of Melos, a city whose inhabitants valued honor over survival. Neutrals in the Peloponnesian War, the Melians knew they could not defeat Athens but preferred their own destruction to surrender. "We will not in a moment deprive of freedom a city that has been inhabited these seven hundred years," the Melian leaders told the Athenians, trusting their fate to the gods and the Spartans. A few months later the Athenians did kill all the men of Melos and sold the women and children into slavery.[47] Athens's material resources had gruesome consequences, but the outcome was very different from the surrender to which the Melians would have agreed had they held modern Western ideas of rationality to be true.

So ideas do matter in international relations. Those actors in this study who confounded the expectations of the liberal ideology theory were not free of ideas and therefore "rational." They held to a particular set of ideas that valued self-preservation or prosperity, but they either modified or did not hold at all the liberal foreign policy ideology I laid out in Chapter 2. Ideas are inescapable; it is simply a question of which ideas will dominate.

47. Thucydides, *The Peloponnesian War* 5.84–116, ed. T. E. Wick, trans. Richard Crawley (New York: Random House, 1982), 349–57.

The question then arises: Can we say in advance when liberal foreign policy ideology will be trumped by other ideas? Could we have predicted the U.S. Navy's wish to humiliate the sister republic of Chile in 1891? Even military and naval organizations can be influenced by liberal ideas. Recently Gen. George Lee Butler, head of U.S. Strategic Forces from 1991 to 1994, used a liberal decision rule in cutting U.S. nuclear targets from 10,000 to 2,500: "Butler reviewed each target one by one, tossing many out like a spring cleaner in a cluttered attic. One day, Butler eliminated about 1,000 targets in newly liberated Eastern Europe by declaring to colleagues, 'We do not target democracies,' people involved remembered."[48] The question of when militaries will pay attention to such liberal concerns merits further study.

The question of when liberals will recategorize a foreign state that has not changed its domestic institutions—and thus pose an anomaly to my theory—is easier to answer. The clearest cases of this reversal of perceptions were Mexico, Spain, and Chile. What these cases had in common was foreign belligerence: the United States, a state with the power to hurt, was acting in ways that even the most pro-American observer should construe as threatening the territorial integrity of the nation. The United States had annexed Texas, which most Mexicans considered part of their country, and Anglo-Saxons were settling and claiming California even as the slogan "manifest destiny" was first coined. The Ostend Manifesto of 1854 made clear that at least some Americans had designs on Cuba, then part of metropolitan Spain. Private American support of the rebel Junta and filibusters to help Cuba gain independence, and the U.S. government's refusal to stop this support, showed Spaniards that manifest destiny extended to the Caribbean as well as the Pacific. Blundering American attempts to prevent Chile from defeating and gaining territory from Peru and Bolivia in 1880, and U.S. aid to the Balmacedists in the 1891 civil war, were taken as jeopardizing Chilean sovereignty and security.

These gestures evidently brought on cognitive dissonance that forced Mexican, Spanish, and Chilean liberals to change their perceptions of the United States. They began with a theory that liberalism was the best form of government because inter alia it made nations more peaceful. American belligerence posed an anomaly for this theory. If the belligerence had been mild, it could have been interpreted

48. David B. Ottaway and Steve Coll, "Trying to Unplug the War Machine," *Washington Post*, 12 April 1995. Interestingly, the writers then point out, "That principle only went so far. By the time Butler retired in February 1994, he had helped hack the SIOP (single integrated operational plan) to about 2,500 targets. But the SIOP still primarily targeted Russia—now a democracy, if a very fragile one." Both Butler's action and Ottaway's and Coll's interpretations of it show again the problem perceptions pose for the democratic peace proposition. I thank Kevin Hula for drawing my attention to this article.

as harmless, a misunderstanding, or attributed to circumstances rather than American ill will.[49] But belligerence that threatens physical security is so overt that unless the entire theory that liberal states are peaceful is discarded—a wrenching psychic change indeed for liberals—the belligerent nation itself must be recategorized as illiberal. Such extreme belligerence is not a brute datum, unmediated by ideas. For it to bring about recategorization, the subjects must value the survival of their national territory (as Mexicans willing to cede Texas and California, and Spaniards willing to cede Cuba, did not).

That A's perceptions of B's regime type can be changed by B's behavior is a warning to those who argue for a "law" of liberal peace. One state regarded as liberal by elites of another state may change those elites' minds by acting illiberally. Perceptions are not weathervanes, turning with the breezes from every gesture a foreign state makes. Indeed, a core finding of this book is that subjects do not "update" perceptions with every gesture by the perceived state; perceptions of "liberalism" or "illiberalism" are stickier than students of international politics have allowed.[50] Yet, under extreme pressure they do shift. In such cases war can take place between two states that might objectively qualify as liberal.

On a happier note, gestures can evidently prod states to recategorize one another as liberal. Chapter 5 showed how American perceptions of England improved between the Civil War and the Venezuelan border crisis. Friendly British behavior during the Venezuelan crisis itself, and British support for the United States in the Spanish-American War two years later, further softened American liberals' perceptions of Britain.[51] Appeasement, it seems, sometimes works if the appeased is a liberal state.[52]

To Begin the World All Over Again?

In a sense, the argument of this book is thus one of social constructivism. It is not the full-blown constructivism that brackets domestic

49. See the brief discussion of attribution errors in Chapter 2.

50. In the language of the sociology of knowledge, actors strive to maintain "plausibility structures." On the maintenance and alteration of these structures, see Peter L. Berger and Thomas Luckmann, *The Social Construction of Reality* (New York: Doubleday, 1966), 147–63.

51. Lionel M. Gelber, *The Rise of Anglo-American Friendship: A Study in World Politics 1898–1906* (Oxford: Oxford University Press, 1938).

52. Compare British appeasement of the United States in the late nineteenth century with appeasement of Germany in the 1930s, in Paul Kennedy, "Appeasement in British Foreign Policy, 1865–1939," in Kennedy, *Strategy and Diplomacy 1870–1945* (London: Allen & Unwin, 1983). See also Stephen R. Rock, "When Appeasement Worked: British Conciliation of the United States, 1895–1905," typescript, Vassar College, September 1989.

regime type and argues that friendly interactions among states can construct a pacific international system. Clearly, regime type matters: liberal states' very identities inhibit them from friendly interactions with states they perceive as illiberal. But I do imply that human beings can alter reality through ideas and practices that open up certain avenues for action and close off certain others. The social construction takes place both within states and among actors across state boundaries. Interactions among states can transform identities and interests; but domestic and transnational interactions do so as well, and these identities and interests affect the way foreign states and the international system are perceived and responded to.[53]

This social construction does not mean human beings can control their world. The most energetic promoter of the first "liberal peace," that between the United States and France in the 1790s, displayed characteristic Enlightenment hubris when he wrote, "We have it in our power to begin the world all over again."[54] Thomas Paine was convinced that in freeing themselves from the shackles of ignorance and coercion, men would finally reach the natural goods of peace and prosperity. He was overreaching. The argument of this book implies that we do indeed have the power to alter the world by holding certain ends, by believing that others hold these ends, and by setting up political institutions that make it likely that these ends will be pursued.[55] But it does not imply that we can thereby determine our fate.

In fact, the very insistence that we can have universal peace by setting up the right institutions or by inculcating the right norms—what might be called dogmatic rationalism—can lead to self-defeating behavior. As Michael Howard points out, at the very time when liberalism's hubris was highest it was clearing the way for savagery and war such as Europe had perhaps never seen before.[56] Paine, Jefferson, Condorcet, and

53. Thus my argument is distinct from that of Alexander Wendt, whose social construction is explicitly systemic, i.e., takes place among rather than within states. Of course, Wendt does not deny that social construction within the state may affect international relations. And as just mentioned, this book acknowledges that, as Wendt argues, interactions among states can transform perceptions and hence identities. See Wendt, "Anarchy Is What States Make of It: The Social Construction of Power Politics," *International Organization* 46 (Spring 1992), 391–425; "Collective Identity Formation and the International State," *American Political Science Review* 88 (June 1994), 384–96.

54. Thomas Paine, "Common Sense" (1776), quoted in Michael H. Hunt, *Ideology in U.S. Foreign Policy* (New Haven: Yale University Press, 1987), 19.

55. For an argument that international relations theory should recognize the transformational aspect of social structure, see David Dessler, "What's at Stake in the Agent-Structure Debate?" *International Organization* 43 (Summer 1989), 441–73.

56. Michael Howard, *War and the Liberal Conscience* (New Brunswick, N.J.: Rutgers University Press, 1978). I am grateful to Harvey Mansfield for suggesting I pursue the following Hegelian critique of Kant.

even Kant blessed the French Revolution in all its destructiveness because they shared the liberal impulse to replace what is inherited with what is rational. In their zeal they lost their liberalism and created mortal enemies at home and abroad. The drive for perpetual peace brought on what seemed at the time to be perpetual war.

Of course, liberalism has rarely degenerated into such horrors. More typically, it has pacified domestic and international politics to an extent. Yet, liberals do perceive illiberal states as deformed and irrational. Kant himself spoke of the right of republics to go to war to bring about the rule of law in despotic states. Something like this happened as Americans contemplated going to war against Mexico in 1845–46 and Spain in 1896–98. Arguably, North and South in the United States went through the same process in deciding for war in 1861.

Although many liberals are optimistic that liberalism has won the millennia-old struggle of ideas,[57] it is not at all clear that history is at an end. Liberalism has often failed in the past to fulfill the very material expectations it raises, as in Weimar Germany. In a world of finite resources there is no guarantee that it will not do so again. There also are areas of the world that explicitly reject liberalism as decadent, materialistic, and impious, most notably many countries dominated by Islam. Liberalism stirs up new dissatisfactions, such as alienation from community and loss of meaning, even as it eliminates old ones. The rise of communitarian critiques of liberalism from left and right show the weakness of liberalism within its own citadels.[58]

Even so, in the 1970s and 1980s liberal institutions spread to new places. What if liberalism continues to expand and mature throughout the world? What if all the world were to comprise liberal democracies? According to the argument of this book, we would not then have perpetual peace. Hegel's treatment of identity formation provides the explanation. Hegel wrote that Kant's plan for a league of republics could not usher in perpetual peace, because of the very process of negation by which republics define themselves: "Perpetual peace is often advocated as an ideal towards which humanity should strive. With that end in view, Kant proposed a league of monarchs to adjust differences between states, and the Holy Alliance was meant to be a league of much the same kind. But the state is an individual, and individuality essentially implies negation. Hence even if a number of states make them-

57. Francis Fukuyama, *The End of History and the Last Man* (New York: Free Press, 1992).

58. Michael J. Sandel, *Liberalism and the Limits of Justice* (New York: Cambridge University Press, 1982); Alasdair MacIntyre, *After Virtue*, 2d ed. (Notre Dame: University of Notre Dame Press, 1984). For an insightful liberal interpretation of the global spread of liberalism, see Václav Havel, "Forgetting We Are Not God," *First Things* 51 (March 1995), 47–50.

selves into a family, this group as an individual must engender an opposite and create an enemy."[59] That is, just as individuals and groups within the state define themselves in terms of what they are not, a group of states must have an "other" against which to define itself. If the pacific union were to appear, it would only be because another, opposite "thing" had been identified. Take away the other—the existence of illiberalism—and liberals would not be able to define themselves or identify one another.[60]

This book has shown that liberals always invoke the existence of illiberal enemies when justifying liberal peace. Jeffersonians, Jacksonians, and British Radicals talked and wrote of aristocrats and monarchs; Federalists and Whigs, of the untutored, despotic mob. During the Civil War, many British were uncertain whether the Union was truly liberal until it exhibited qualities that distinguished it from the Confederacy, and in fact saw little reason not to go to war over the *Trent* affair. Liberals need illiberals in order to identify one another. Hegel is correct: the liberal impetus toward peace has a twin, the impetus toward war, and the twins are symbiotic.

That liberalism matters in international security and that liberalism is spreading may give us hope, but this should not make us optimists. Even if liberalism does mature in previously illiberal areas of the world, it will not be an unadulterated force for peace. Today's materialists slight the importance of liberal ideas, but realists seem to be correct when they hold that wars and rumors of war are always with us. Our task, then, is familiar but difficult: we must seek peace both vigorously and humbly, realizing that human autonomy, liberal or otherwise, is no final solution. In a world where we need enemies in order to know who our friends are, perpetual peace must remain, like Plato's Republic, "a model laid up in heaven."[61]

59. G. W. F. Hegel, *The Philosophy of Right*, trans. T. M. Knox (New York: Oxford University Press, 1967), 295.

60. Fukuyama, *End of History*, interprets Hegel as a prophet of perpetual peace, and James Lee Ray concurs; see Ray, *Democracy and International Conflict: An Evaluation of the Democratic Peace Proposition* (Columbia: University of South Carolina Press, 1995). For a discussion of this tension in Hegel's international thought, see Torbjörn L. Knutsen, *A History of International Relations Theory* (Manchester: Manchester University Press, 1992), 147–50.

61. Plato, *The Republic*, trans. G. M. A. Grube (Indianapolis: Hackett, 1974), 592b.

Index

Index

crisis of 1796–98 (Franco-American),
81–88; France begins seizing U.S. merchant ships, 83–84; Adams sends three
envoys to Paris, 84; XYZ Affair, 84;
Adams drafts war message, 85; Jeffersonians continue to support France,
86; Adams resorts to quasi-war,
86; Franco-American economic ties,
87; hypothesis test results, 187–90,
207–14

crisis of 1803–12 (Anglo-American),
88–97; British Orders in Council hurt
U.S. merchant marine, 90; Americans
divided over response, 91; U.S. imposes total economic embargo (1807),
91; Fox's government tries conciliation,
91; British liberals pressure government to rescind Orders in Council,
92–93; U.S. Republicans begin calling
for war, 93; Anglo-American economic
ties, 94; U.S. declares war, 94; hypothesis test results, 188–90, 207–14

crisis of 1845–46 (Anglo-American),
99–113; Polk claims all of Oregon, 105;
British defy Polk but quietly work for
peace, 106; British debate repeal of
Corn Laws, 107; U.S. Democrats intransigent, 108; Democrats and Whigs
disagree over Oregon policy, 109;
British conservatives and reformers
disagree over policy toward U.S., 112;
resolution, 113; hypothesis test results,
190–94, 207–12

crisis of 1845–46 (Mexican-American), 39,
113–24; United States annexes Texas
and Mexico breaks relations, 119–20;
Polk sends troops to Texas, 120; Spanish conspire with conservatives to establish monarchy in Mexico, 120–21;
Jacksonians fear monarchism in Mexico, 121, 124; Democrats and Whigs
disagree over policy toward Mexico,
122; Paredes declares war, 122; United
States declares war, 124; correlation between U.S. perceptions of Mexico and
of Britain, 124; hypothesis test results,
190–94, 207–10, 211–14

crisis of 1861–63 (Anglo-American),
124–38; importance of anti-slavery to
British, 128–30, 134; Union disappoints
British, 130; British declare neutrality
in U.S. Civil War, 130; *Trent* crisis,
131–33; France proposes Anglo-French
intervention, 133; Emancipation
Proclamation helps prevent British intervention, 134–36; Laird rams crisis,

136–37; hypothesis test results, 194–97,
207–10, 212–14

crisis of 1873 (Spanish-American),
140–49; founding of Spanish republic
alters Americans' perceptions of
Spain, 141, 144; Ten Years' War in
Cuba (1868–78), 141, 143; *Virginius* is
captured, 144; U.S. concern to preserve Spanish Republic, 144, 147; U.S.
and Spanish public debate over *Virginius* affair, 145–46; resolution, 148;
hypothesis test results, 197–99, 207–10,
212–14

crisis of 1891–92 (Chilean-American),
149–58; Chilean Revolution of 1891,
151; *Baltimore* incident, 153; U.S. reaction, 154; Harrison's belligerence, 154,
156; Blaine's efforts at conciliation, 154;
Matta's belligerence, 155; U.S. Congress and public reluctant to make war
on fellow republic, 156; resolution, 157;
hypothesis test results, 199–201,
207–10, 212–14

crisis of 1895–96 (Anglo-American),
158–70; Venezuela asks for U.S. help,
163; U.S. threatens Britain (Olney
note), 163; Britain's response to Olney,
164; Cleveland's angry response, 165;
U.S. debate on policy toward Britain,
165; most British deplore war with the
United States, 167; Cleveland appoints
a boundary commission, 169; resolution, 169; hypothesis test results, 201–4,
207–10, 212–14

crisis of 1895–98 (Spanish-American), 39,
170–81; Cuban rebellion begins anew,
174; Americans deplore Spanish conduct in Cuba, 175; Liberals form government and U.S. perceptions of Spain
improve, 176; Cubans reject Madrid's
offer of autonomy, 177; explosion of
U.S.S. *Maine*, 177; McKinley works for
compromise, 179; Cuban rebels reject
armistice, 180; war, 181; hypothesis test
results, 204–10, 212–14

Crittenden, John J., 123
Croker, John Wilson, 94
Cuba. *See* crisis of 1895–98 (Spanish-
American)
Curry, J. L. M., 171
Cushing, Caleb, 147

Dana, R. H., Jr., 147
Davis, Jefferson, 134
DeConde, Alexander, 83–87, 130
democracies, illiberal, 17

Index

Gladstone, William E., 128, 134, 137, 160–61
Godkin, E. L., 141, 148
Gokhale, Gopal Krishna, 224
Goldberg, Joyce, 154–56, 200
Goldstein, Judith, 17, 19–20, 33
Gong Ro Myong, 221, 223
Gowa, Joanne, 9
Graebner, Norman A., 196, 205
Graham, Sir James, 108
Graham, Thomas W., 45
Grant, Ulysses S., 140–41, 143–45, 147–49, 198, 212
Great Britain, 18, 46, 82, 84–85, 87, 98, 121, 139, 148, 150, 155, 157, 172, 180; how liberal (1794–96), 41, 74–75; perceptions of the United States (1794–96), 41, 75–76, 187–90; perceptions of the United States (1803–12), 89–90, 188–90; how liberal (1845–46), 102–3; perceptions of the United States (1845–46), 103–5, 190–94; how liberal (1861–63), 127; perceptions of the United States (1861–63), 127–30, 194–97; how liberal (1895–96), 159–60; perceptions of the United States (1895–96), 160–63, 201–4; liberalization in, 98, 101–3, 127. *See also* Conservatives (British); crisis of 1794–96; crisis of 1803–12; crisis of 1845–46; crisis of 1861–63; crisis of 1895–96; Liberals (British); Radicals (British); Whigs (British)
Greeley, Horace, 126–27, 133, 141
Green, T. H., 160
Grenville, Lord. *See* Buckingham
Gresham, Walter, 159
Gupta, Shekhar, 231
Gutiérrez de Estrada, José María, 118

Habsburg, House of, 27
Hagan, Joe D., 43, 61
Haiti, 145
Hale, Charles A., 117–18
Halifax, Lord, 63
Hall, John A., 33
Hamilton, Alexander, 31, 69–73, 76, 78–79, 84, 88, 96, 99, 188, 210–11, 231
Han Sung Joo, 221, 223
Hannegan, Edward, 108
Hanson, Elizabeth C., 19, 210
Harcort, William Vernon, 168
Harrison, Benjamin, 150, 153–58, 200, 212
Hartz, Louis, 40–41, 69–70, 101
Hashmi, Sohail, 23
Havel, Václav, 234
Hearst, William Randolph, 177, 180

Hegel, G. W. F., 25–26, 233–35
Hendrickson, David C., 89
Hennessy, C. A. M., 142–43, 146
Hermann, Margaret G., 14, 23
Herrera, José Joaquín de, 115–17, 119–22, 213
Hietala, Thomas, 100
Hinckley, Barbara, 45
Hobbes, Thomas, 35
Hobson, John A., 53
Hoffmann, Stanley, 26
Holsti, Ole R., 43, 48
Holy Alliance, 28
Horsman, Reginald, 89–94
Hosokawa Morihiro, 221
Houston, Sam, 123
Howard, Michael, 30, 233
Howe, Daniel Walker, 100–101, 111
Hume, David, 35, 89
Huntington, Samuel P., 7, 217
Hutchinson, John, 26
Huth, Paul K., 8
hypotheses: concerning domestic institutions; 58–59, 61, 210–15; concerning perceptions, 57–58, 59–61, 187–210

ideas as explanations, 17–20, 234
identity: formation of, 25, 37; institutional, 24, 27–29, 31, 43, 46, 50, 57, 63, 207, 235
ideology: defined, 19; role in producing liberal peace, 19–20, 37–41
illiberal states, 12, 19, 29, 37–39, 46; liberals' perceptions of, 5, 38–39, 228; necessary to liberal identity, 22–29, 234–35. *See also* negation
India, 62, 231–32; how liberal (1947–), 224. *See also* Indo-Pakistani relations
Indo-Pakistani relations, 217, 222–27; Pakistani liberalization alters Indian perceptions of Pakistan, 227; relations improved by Pakistani liberalization, 229
interests as explanations, 54. *See also* ideas as explanations
Isabel II, Queen of Spain, 141
Islamic Democratic Alliance (IJI), 226
Italy, 82, 142, 202
Iturbide, Agustín de, 114

Jackson, Andrew, 100, 104–5, 114
Jacksonians. *See* Democrats (U.S.)
Jacobins, 31, 67, 72, 82
Jacobs, Lawrence R., 47
James, Patrick, 45
James, Scott C., 109

Index

Index

CORNELL STUDIES IN SECURITY AFFAIRS

A series edited by

Robert J. Art
Robert Jervis
Stephen M. Walt